Déjà Vu

American Political Problems in Historical Perspective

JAROL B. MANHEIM
Virginia Polytechnic Institute and State University

Déjà Vu

American Political Problems in Historical Perspective

St. Martin's Press • New York

For Amy
Who Makes It All Worthwhile

Library of Congress Catalog Card Number: 75-29943

Manufactured in the United States of America
09876
FEDCB
For information, write: St. Martin's Press, Inc.,
175 Fifth Avenue, New York, N.Y. 10010

Preface

There is in any given age a common historical myopia that tends to exaggerate the importance and the uniqueness of contemporary events. At present this tendency seems to be especially pronounced as expanding technology and mass communication accelerate the rate of *apparent* social change. Because our personal experiences give to the present a degree of reality that history books can never impart to the past, we tend to assume that violence, corruption, urban decay, social injustice, and a host of other ills have reached new heights during our own era, and we perceive the gravity of these problems and the political future of the United States in this context. This loss of historical perspective on contemporary political issues entails potentially serious consequences: the misperception of what is happening in contemporary American society and the misdirection of public policy for dealing with the nation's problems.

It is my hope in these pages to respond to this loss of perspective through the technique of historical juxtaposition, by setting before the reader not only a current analysis of contemporary issues, but some indication of the historical roots of those issues as well. However, the emphasis here is less on specific events or periods in American history than it is on the underlying political culture of the United States. And the thrust of my argument is not that history repeats itself but, rather, that certain problems, however their manifestations may change, tend to remain central to our political life because of powerful cultural continuities.

I should like to express my gratitude to all those who have assisted in the preparation of this book. To my good friend Ned Lebow, whose contributions were many and indispensible; to my editor Barry Rossinoff, whose faith in the project never wavered; to Gilbert Jardine, whose energy and ideas were instrumental in getting the project underway; to Carol Berkin, Theodore P. Kovaleff, Jeffrey Pressman, and Michael Smith for their early encouragement and suggestions; to Daryl R. Fair, Peter Schwab, and Max J. Skidmore, whose comments on drafts of the manuscript were of great value; to Melanie Wallace, whose bibliographic research and other assistance were important contributions; and to Anita Morse, whose editorial judgment added much to the final manuscript, I can only say thank you. To my wife Amy, to whom this book is dedicated, I can say much more.

The writing of *Déjà Vu* has been an enjoyable, enlightening, and worthwhile experience. I very much hope the reading of it may prove the same.

Contents

Déjà Vu

American Political Problems in Historical Perspective

1

On the Importance of Historical Perspective: An Introduction

It was the best of times, it was the worst of times, it was the age of wisdom, it was the age of foolishness, it was the epoch of belief, it was the epoch of incredulity, it was the season of Light, it was the season of Darkness, it was the spring of hope, it was the winter of despair, we had everything before us, we had nothing before us, we were all going direct to Heaven, we were all going direct the other way—in short, the period was so far like the present period, that some of its noisiest authorities insisted on its being received, for good or for evil, in the superlative degree of comparison only.

Charles Dickens, *A Tale of Two Cities*

It would seem to be a fundamental trait of human nature—particularly, one is tempted to add, in times such as our own—to become literally overwhelmed by the present, to focus, not on the enduring process of human society, but merely on its middle product. We tend, in other words, to be rather nearsighted when it comes to ranking historical periods in terms of their relative significance, to see our own era, as Dickens's contemporaries saw theirs, as one to be treated only in superlatives. We tend to overestimate the efficacy of social or political changes that we might institute or observe and to overlook the continuities between our own times and others. These tendencies are not surprising in any generation, and they are certainly not so today. For we, as citizens of a highly technocentric society, are, from the moment of birth, forcibly integrated into an extensive communications matrix the principal function of which is to make us not only oriented to, but effective within, the all-consuming present. As a result, we tend collectively, for all our accumulated wisdom and culture, to isolate ourselves on a small island in time.

There are, of course, advantages to this drawing in of perspective. These advantages are of the most practical nature, for in a complex society contemporaneity (often euphemized as "relevance") offers a necessary basis for understanding political and social life. Those who can comprehend the present on its own terms are able to be more proficient participants in the ongoing sociopolitical process. But there is a danger here as well, a danger that our understanding may be limited and our judgment of contemporary experience distorted for lack of a standard of comparison or a longer-term perspective. For human society is, after all, little more than the collected experiences of past generations adapted to present circumstances, and much of our contemporary experience either flows directly from the events of earlier periods or so resembles earlier events that the past can well prove instructive. Indeed, in many cases the relationship between past and present is so close or the resemblance in events so striking that it would seem that one simply could not fully comprehend either the most salient elements or the real significance of the present except in the context of the past. It is to be the argument of this book, then, that a grasp of the historical process *as it applies to contemporary problems* is vital to attaining that standard of judgment that will help us not only to understand or to cope with the present but also to appreciate it in the largest sense.

In selecting a title like *Déjà Vu,* which refers to that unexplained feeling that one sometimes experiences of having been somewhere or done something before, I am by no means trying to suggest either that nothing ever changes or that history repeats itself. On the contrary, I take both assertions to be demonstrably false. What I am suggesting, however, is, first, that the present draws in great measure upon the legacy of the past and, second, that there exists through time a sufficient number of substantive continuities in the American historical experience (as in that of other nations) to permit the past to serve as a useful guide to the present.

In the first instance, it should be clear that any of a variety of alternative pasts would have resulted in a present that differed from what we actually experience in a number of respects. In some ways this is, of course, simply a statement of the obvious. Had England successfully put down the American Revolution, had the South held out in the Civil War, had George Washington held power for life or Franklin Roosevelt for only two terms, or had any of a number of other events transpired differently, political life as we know it today would have been changed to a greater or a lesser extent. In some ways we might be better off, in some ways worse off; but whichever was the case, things would be somehow different. And, though it is perhaps less obvious, other elements in our common historical experience might—had they, too, been different—have similarly altered subsequent events. Had we, for example, developed over time a different style of leadership selection, an alternative pattern of economic organization, or some other criteria for social stratification within American society, again the present would have been other than it is. For these and other pervasive but often subtle patterns of preference and behavior bear as much or more upon contemporary political life as do the more dramatic and more easily identified finite events of American history. In this very direct sense, then, what Americans as a people are today is a function of what Americans as a people have been for more than two hundred years, and the collective experiences of the present are simply extensions of the collective experiences of the past.

The second assertion, that one may detect significant *substantive* continuities in the American experience, though an extension of the first point, may be less apparent. For to suggest that there exists through time a more or less recognizable chain of events, a connective logic that ties each era to the next, is to stop short of suggesting that the types of events that occur or the styles of political action that are reflected in those events will remain more or less constant with the passage of time. That is, in arguing that one event leads to the next, one does not necessarily argue that there will exist noticeable similarities between those events or even that the first event predetermines the second, but only that a logical progression is apparent. Indeed, any one occurrence does *not necessarily* predetermine or structure the next; it merely creates (or precludes) a unique set of policy options that the political actors of the time may exercise. And it is the choices of those political actors, be they leaders or common citizens, that will determine the flow of events.

Yet if these political actors bear some resemblance to one another through time—if, that is, those who make the political decisions of one era have much in common with those who make such decisions in another—it then becomes reasonable to expect that there will be similarities in the kinds of decisions that they make and that there will, as a consequence, be a great deal of continuity between the events of one era and those of the next. If these individuals, and through them the society as a whole, maintain common perceptions, common ideologies, common concerns, and a host of other shared characteristics through time, if they subscribe to what social scientists would term a "political culture," a set of widely held ideas about the nature and goals of their political system that endures through generations, one would have every reason to expect that this commonality would lead men of different eras to respond to situations or events according to certain common tendencies. As a result, one might expect to note a logical progression not only of events but of events that are more or less internally consistent with one another. One might, in other words, expect history to emerge less as a random process than as a systematic one. It is both the premise of *Déjà Vu* and its purpose to illustrate that this continuity does exist in the American experience over the last hundred or so years and that its existence has implications not only for the present but also for the future.

With this in mind, we shall review the historical development of several political problems that face the United States today, seeking in each instance to suggest the contribution of historical perspective to an understanding not only of the configuration of the issue itself but of the potential value or efficacy of proposed solutions as well. In chapter 2, for example, we shall investigate the violence that periodically manifests itself in American domestic politics. Beginning with a consideration of several relatively recent acts of political violence, we shall trace the history of labor violence, racial conflict, assassination, vigilantism, and state violence from the years immediately following the Civil War until the present. In so doing, we shall discover a number of recurrent themes, not only in the patterns of violence but also in its causes, that we shall place in the context of recent sociopolitical theories. We shall conclude, in effect, that violence is endemic to the American political culture and that our tendency to see it largely as a modern-day phenomenon reflects a misperception of the historical experience.

Of equally long-standing and perhaps even greater importance than political violence has been a second factor in American politics and a second source of political problems today, urbanization. For it has been the city that has served as the focal point of political life in the United States from the outset, and it has been the concentration of economic wealth and power in the nation's cities and the massive population movements to which that concentration has given rise that have contributed most to the development of the current urban dilemma. In chapter 3, therefore, we shall explore the rise of American urban centers, focusing on social and political threats to the quality of urban life. In particular, we shall examine the impact of and reaction to large-scale influxes of immigrants, the development of urban technologies, the rise and fall of urban political machines and the reform movements that opposed them, and the impact of suburbanization on the well-being of the cities. We shall argue that the cities represent in microcosm the larger social dilemma facing the nation today, that of an increasingly polarized society.

If violence is a persistent feature, and urbanization a driving force, of American political life, however, another problem that has concerned us in recent years, that of political corruption at the highest levels of government, is more intermittent in character. Thus, in chapter 4, we shall discuss the three best-known incidences of presidential misbehavior, the numerous scandals of the Grant era, the Teapot Dome and other scandals of the Harding years, and the Watergate and related scandals of the Nixon administration, and we shall find several remarkable similarities in the ways in which the various scandals developed, in the role of the president in each, and in the relationship between each wave of scandal and the temper of the times in which it occurred. Here we shall argue that the expectations that the American people have of their leaders will combine with the styles of action that the leaders themselves adopt to determine the likelihood of executive malfeasance.

In chapters 5 and 6, we shall turn our attention to the various political movements that occasionally capture the interest of the American public, particularly those focusing on women's rights and consumer protection. While these two political movements differ in their appeals, their styles, and the types of goals that they seek, they may be said to have much in common with one another (and with other political movements as well) for they draw upon much the same constituencies, display similar cycles of prominence and obscurity, reflect similar dissatisfactions, and occasion similar responses from the political system. We shall, in fact, argue in these chapters that most political movements are symbiotic, that they arise at the same periods of history and from the same fundamental causes, that each benefits directly from the growth and development of the others, and that all fade in importance as the dissatisfactions that gave them rise are dissipated. Political movements are thus seen, much as political corruption was, as creatures of the times and of the underlying political culture.

No nation in the modern world, of course, exists in splendid isolation, and the United States, for all its occasional pretense to the contrary, is no exception. Thus, our analysis of the American historical experience and its implications for the present could not be complete without a consideration of two very closely related questions. First, how does the political culture of the United States project itself into world affairs? And second, how do world affairs influence or interact with the American political culture? In chapter 7, we shall approach each of these questions in turn, and we shall find much the same continuity through time that we have noted on the domestic scene. Looking first at the expansionist and humanitarian instincts that have fueled most of the nation's overseas ventures and second at the long history of repression that has recurred whenever international difficulties or uncertainties have produced domestic feelings of insecurity, we shall find a dualism of ethnocentrism and xenophobia that, along with counterpart tendencies in domestic affairs, has its roots deep in American tradition.

Finally, in chapter 8, we shall close our analysis by drawing together the various themes we shall have developed in our earlier discussions—and by suggesting once again the importance of the historical perspective in helping us appreciate our present circumstance. In the process, we shall suggest several key elements of the American political culture that are reflected in and that contribute to the continuity of events.

One final word is in order before we commence, a word about what this book is and is not. *Déjà Vu* is neither a comprehensive history of the United States nor a comprehensive description of the American people. It is neither a commentary on the grand flow of human history nor a definitive treatise on the nature and functions of political culture. It is, instead, a project far less presumptuous, but, one might hope, a project of some value nevertheless. For *Déjà Vu* represents an attempt to bring together historical political analysis and contemporary political analysis, to wed past and present, and in the process to help the reader develop both an appreciation of the complexity of the political problems that face the United States today and a sense of history. All too often, it seems, historians and political scientists compartmentalize themselves, each either overlooking or rejecting the value of the other's theories, techniques, and findings. Yet both deal, in effect, with the same questions and, in time, even with the same evidence. Both contribute to an understanding of American political life. Thus, it can only be through a union of the two perspectives, the historical and the contemporary, that the most meaningful analysis can be performed and that we can learn how best to comprehend the issues before us. The marriage is more than one of convenience, and the lesson is an important one.

2

Political Violence: An American Legacy

Nature conspired to make violence common in America. A frontier, a totally foreign and largely uncivilized aboriginal people, the early development of brutalizing slavery of a different race from a distant continent, pioneers moving beyond the reach of established institutions, the interaction of a wide range of cultural, racial, ethnic, and social backgrounds in a new melting pot, an early and devastating civil war, a tradition of guns, an immense population growth both native and immigrant, vast industrialization and urbanization, high mobility and rootlessness, and sweeping technological development—all these and more contributed to change and instability beyond that experienced by any other people at any time in history.

Ramsey Clark[1]

We are frequently told, and it is indeed easy enough to believe, that we live in violent times. One need only pick up the morning newspaper to be confronted with evidence of the seemingly unrestrained use of force in modern American life. Urban riots, crime in the streets, assassination, police brutality—the litany is a familiar one and, by constant repetition, virtually overwhelms our consciousness. We cower behind doors with multiple locks; we restrict our local travel to certain "safe" areas, however we may choose to define them; we publicly doubt the potential longevity of our elected officials. In short, we suffer from a pervasive fear and expectation that violence may strike any one of us at any time.

But do we *really* live in such violent times, or do our expectations of violence exceed the actual threat? Is ours *really* such a uniquely violent period in American history, or is it, in fact, more or less typical? Do we, in other words, perceive contemporary political violence to be so pervasive because in fact it is, or is our perception distorted by the fact that we ourselves are actually experiencing these events rather than merely reading about them in some history book?

These are important questions; they bear not only on the quality of life in the United States today but also on the potential for survival of the American social and political system into the future. At the same time, these are complex questions; they defy understanding and resolution by simple analysis and expedient policy. When a whole society seems bent on self-destruction, no single present-day cause can suffice as an explanation, no single present-day cure as a solution. On the contrary, only through a consideration of the historical development of collective tendencies toward violence, and only through a careful assessment of the continuities apparent in that development, can we hope to gain a perspective on the nature and extent of contemporary political violence. Only by an examination of the historical experience can we hope to attain clarity of view and validity of judgment in the present. For despite appearances, violence in contemporary American politics is not in the largest sense random, nor even, from a historical perspective, unexpected. It is instead yet another manifestation of a recurrent tendency that results from a number of contributing causes and that has, over the years, become ingrained in the American psyche.

In the present chapter, we shall explore the history of American political violence and seek out both its continuities and its causes. Beginning with a consideration of several relatively recent instances of violence, and continuing with an analysis of the historical record that helps put these latter-day examples in context, we shall examine in turn labor violence, racial violence, assassination, and proestablishment violence; and we shall find that each tends to arise from certain kinds of social, economic, or psychological pressures—which themselves endure or recur in the

American political culture through time. We shall argue, in effect, that political violence is less a problem in itself than it is a symptom of several more fundamental difficulties that confront American society today much as they have in the past. The implication of this assessment, of course, is that efforts to deal with the violence itself rather than with its sources stand a good chance of coming to naught.

Violence in Our Time

Let us begin our analysis with some examples of recent political violence in the United States, and more particularly with an examination of four episodes from the 1960s and 1970s, all of which can best be understood only in the context of historical perspective. The episodes are the violent demonstrations of support for the Vietnam War by New York construction workers in 1970, the Watts Riot of 1965 which decimated a large section of Los Angeles, the assassination of civil rights leader Dr. Martin Luther King, Jr., and the police response to antiwar demonstrations at the Democratic National Convention in Chicago in 1968. Each of these events was stimulated by forces that had been at work in American society for more than a century, forces that, as events continue to demonstrate, are still with us today. Together, they suggest a panoply of social and political unrest that, as we shall see, is very much a creature of American tradition.

LABOR VIOLENCE: HARDHATS ON WALL STREET

The Vietnam War spawned innumerable demonstrations of support and remonstrance during its long and bloody history, but none of these matched in duration, breadth, or intensity the public outcry that followed the unexpected invasion of Cambodia by American forces in the spring of 1970—at a time when most Americans believed that, in one way or another, that unpopular and controversial war was finally drawing to a close. In one such protest, at Kent State University in Ohio, events culminated in the apparently undirected but fatal shooting of four bystanders by National Guardsmen who had been sent to the scene to quell a disturbance. Instantly, though with the notable exception of then-President Richard Nixon, who referred to the victims as "bums," many Americans went into a period of bitter mourning, and increasingly angry demonstrations resulted. The level of rhetoric mounted, and the potential for violence, already so amply demonstrated, rose to new heights. It was in this superheated atmosphere that a number of antiwar rallies were scheduled for the early weeks of May in New York's Wall Street section, and it is out of those rallies that our first example of contemporary political violence emerged.

The trouble began on Wednesday, May 6, when some medical students from the Whitehall Medical Center held an impromptu meeting in an area of lower Manhattan known as Battery Park. During this meeting, one ill-advised participant ripped down an American flag that had been placed at a nearby construction site by a group of steelworkers. Incensed at this affront to their patriotism, the steelworkers, who were less than sympathetic to the antiwar demonstrators to begin with, poured out of the construction site and bloodied a number of heads. The medical students dispersed with considerable haste.

The steelworkers, however, continued to discuss the incident among themselves and with other construction workers in the area, and eventually they came to the conclusion that something ought to be done about all those protestors. A peace demonstration scheduled for the Wall Street area for Friday, May 8, seemed to offer a ready opportunity. Shortly after noon on that day, a band of about two hundred construction workers marched up Broad Street from their various job sites, penetrated police lines with minimal resistance, and began to assault demonstrators on the steps of the Federal Hall Building. Many demonstrators were kicked, mauled, or beaten while the police looked on, unable or unwilling to subdue the helmeted attackers. And when injured demonstrators were removed to nearby Trinity Church, the church itself became the object of the assault.

At this point the hardhats, now numbering about five hundred, turned up Broadway and laid siege to City Hall. Enraged by the fact that Mayor John Lindsay, although absent at the time, had ordered the City Hall flag flown at half-mast to honor the victims at Kent State, and not incidentally angered by the mayor's longer-term role in helping blacks get jobs in the construction trades, the mob forced the acting mayor to raise the flag to full staff, then, pausing only to sing "The Star Spangled Banner," continued its rampage, this time charging though nearby Pace College and beating anyone in its path. Finally, having made their point, the hardhats drifted back to their construction sites.

Over the next several days, the construction workers returned to the streets in a number of less violent demonstrations of their support for the administration and its foreign and domestic policies. These expressions of support culminated on May 20, when an estimated 100,000 persons turned out for a labor-organized rally in behalf of President Nixon, who expressed his own gratitude the following week in a personal meeting with Peter I. Brennan, president of the Building and Construction Trades Council of Greater New York, and other union leaders.[2] Brennan was later named secretary of labor in the second Nixon administration.

RACIAL VIOLENCE: THE WATTS RIOT OF 1965

Of longer duration and still greater intensity than this labor-based display of patriotism is our second example of modern American political violence, the 1965 race riot in the section of Los Angeles known as Watts. The Watts Riot of 1965, which lasted from August 11 to August 17 and which marked a high point in urban insurrection, was actually triggered by the arrest of a young black man by white police officers on a sultry summer evening, but its sources can be traced back at least half a century. As early as 1916, a small black community had begun to develop in an area known as Mud Town, now the Watts section of Los Angeles, and that community expanded rapidly in the years after World War I as wave after wave of black migrants left the South for California and the industrialized urban centers of the North. By the end of World War II, it is estimated that some 2,000 black migrants were arriving in Los Angeles each month, with the vast majority settling in Watts.[3] As the area swelled with these migrants, many of the middle-class blacks fled, leaving in their wake a population of which less than one adult in three had a high school education and one in eight was illiterate. Housing was a problem as well. In 1965 when the outbreak occurred, fully 87 percent of the housing in Watts predated World War II, and, although most of that housing was in the form of one- and two-story stucco houses rather than the now familiar tenements of the East, most units were seriously overcrowded. This combination of social deprivation, lack of an adequate economic base, and the continuing influx of migrants undoubtedly contributed much more than any single event to the Watts explosion.[4]

Still, it was a single event that finally touched off the violence. The precipitating incident began innocently enough at 7:45 on Wednesday evening, August 11, when two white policemen gave chase to an erratic and apparently intoxicated driver, twenty-one-year-old Marquette Frye. After a six-block pursuit, the officers caught up with Frye near the front of his home and arrested him. At this point, as Frye's mother came out of the house and started to scold her son, he reportedly began to struggle with the arresting officers. The commotion attracted a good deal of attention, and a crowd began to form. Sensing danger, the officer holding the suspect drew his gun. Then, under cover provided by an officer from a back-up unit who held the crowd at bay with a shotgun, Frye was taken off to jail.

In the meantime, a rumor had spread that the police had used clubs on Frye. Numbers of angry blacks poured into the area, and the crowd, swelled to perhaps 1,500, began to hurl rocks and bottles at stores and passing cars in an eight-block area. When about 100 helmeted police, most of them white, entered the area with nightsticks at the ready, the rioters broke up into smaller groups and roved through the streets damaging or setting fire to a number of vehicles, including two fire trucks.

By Thursday morning the violence had subsided, but it recurred that evening in an increasingly organized fashion—and with the added impact of a new weapon, the Molotov cocktail. Whites were pulled from their cars and beaten, streets were barricaded, stores were looted, and firemen responding to the numerous calls and false alarms were driven off by gunfire. The riot area expanded that evening and all day Friday until it reached about 150 blocks.[5] "Burn, Baby, Burn" and "Get Whitey" became the rallying cries of a new force in urban America.

It is estimated that as many as 10,000 blacks may have participated in the Watts Riot at its peak. When it was over, 34 persons lay dead, 1,032 were injured. Arrests totalled 3,952, and property damage exceeded $40 million. Some 200 buildings were destroyed by fire and 400 more damaged, though, interestingly enough, no residences were purposely put to the torch, and damage to public buildings was minimal. The Watts Riot ended with an area of 46.5 square miles under martial law and with the entire population of Los Angeles in a state of shock and fear. Yet, as it turned out, Watts was only the harbinger of things to come, for in the years 1965 to 1968 fully 150 major riots took place in American cities, and for a time it appeared as if urban revolution along racial lines was a very real possibility.[6]

POLITICAL ASSASSINATION: THE MURDER OF MARTIN LUTHER KING, JR.

Our third incident of political violence, the assassination of Martin Luther King, Jr., appears to have been a much more individual act than those we have considered above, but its political impact cannot adequately be gauged by the simplicity of the deed, and the political significance of King's death cannot be understated.

It is unlikely that when Martin Luther King, Jr., left Harvard University in 1954 to become pastor for an upper-income Baptist congregation in Montgomery, Alabama, he expected to find himself three years later in the forefront of a powerful, nationwide civil rights movement. In fact, he thought he might eventually find a career in college teaching. But in December 1955 King was elected president of the Montgomery Improvement Association, an organization formed to carry out a local boycott in protest of segregation, and in 1957 he assumed leadership of the newly formed Southern Christian Leadership Conference. In that capacity, he became the leading voice of nonviolent protest in the burgeoning civil rights movement. Yet by 1964, when he was awarded the Nobel Peace Prize for his efforts to promote harmonious racial progress in the United States, King was engaged in a struggle to retain both his moral and his philosophical leadership in the movement, and in 1968 he found himself and his nonviolent tactics rapidly losing influence, particularly in the urban centers of the North. Indeed, the reflexive wave of violence that followed his death that year bears ironic testimony to the declining acceptance of his chosen course.

April 4, 1968, found King in Memphis, Tennessee, lending his support to a strike of black garbage collectors. As he paused on the balcony of his motel room before leaving to deliver a speech to a strikers' rally, he was felled by a fatal bullet fired from a nearby rooming house. Though his assailant succeeded in fleeing the scene of the crime under what are, at best, suspicious circumstances, a petty criminal named James Earl Ray was subsequently identified as the assassin and was ultimately arrested in London some two months later. Questions regarding a possible conspiracy that might have been responsible for financing Ray's activities prior to the assassination and aiding in his escape remain unanswered.

As word of the assassination spread, blacks in cities across the nation took to the streets to vent their grief and anger, and in the rioting that followed 46 people—including 41 blacks—were killed, 2,600 were injured, and property damage reached an estimated $45 million. A total of 21,270 arrests were made, and literally tens of thousands of army troops and National Guardsmen were called out to assist local police forces in quelling the disturbances.[7]

Yet the assassination of Martin Luther King, Jr., did not stand as an isolated act of political murder. It followed closely a chain of outrages, including the shooting of civil rights leader Medgar Evers in Jackson, Mississippi, in June 1963; the assassination of President John F. Kennedy in Dallas in November of that year; and the fatal assault on Black Muslim leader Malcolm X in New York in February 1965. It was itself followed in short order by the fatal shooting of Senator and presidential candidate Robert F. Kennedy in Los Angeles in June 1968; the attempt on the life of Alabama Governor and presidential candidate George C. Wallace in Laurel, Maryland, four years later; and the murder of Dr. King's mother, Mrs. Alberta King, in Atlanta in June 1974. As much as any individual death might be mourned by the American people, the collective impact of this lengthy series of deaths must bear a greater impact still.[8]

THE RESPONSE TO VIOLENCE: THE CHICAGO "POLICE RIOT" OF 1968

Finally, let us consider an example of a rather different kind of political violence, that which has at least the tacit approval of the state or the social establishment. It has often been said that violence begets violence, that the only way to meet force is with force. Sometimes, however, the violence of the response may be out of all proportion to the stimulus, or at least the perception of the stimulus may be somewhat exaggerated. One or the other was apparently the case in Chicago in August 1968, when, as the members of the Democratic party gathered to select their presidential candidate for the coming election, there raged in the streets surrounding their convention hall what amounted to a war between thousands of vociferous protestors against the Vietnam War on the one hand, and the city's police force on the other. Piecing the story together afterward, an investigatory arm of the National Commission on the Causes and Prevention of Violence termed the incident a "police riot."

The call had been sounded early for the expanding forces of the antiwar movement to confront the incumbent president, Lyndon B. Johnson, and his party as they prepared for the electoral campaign of 1968. The disingenuous, yet modestly successful, presidential candidacy of Senator Eugene J. McCarthy and the violently abbreviated efforts of Robert F. Kennedy had not only buoyed hopes of successfully forcing a disengagement in Vietnam but had had the additional effect of giving a much-needed aura of legitimacy to what many had perceived, to that time, as a ragtag army of hippies and radicals bent upon destruction and demoralization. Yet Chicago had greeted the promised arrival of hordes of demonstrators with something less than eager anticipation, and by the time the first large contingents of protestors began to reach the city on Sunday, August 18, feelings were running as high as expectations.

For a week, tensions mounted as demonstrators engaged in legal wrangling with the recalcitrant city administration over park and parade permits; as activists trained in karate, judo, and washoi (a technique used by Japanese student demonstrators for retreating from a riot situation without injury); and as police observed these activities fully aware of Mayor Richard J. Daley's order during the recent disturbances following the King assassination to "shoot to kill arsonists and shoot to maim looters." Thus, when the city determined on the night of Saturday, August 24, to sweep Lincoln Park (the headquarters and campground of the protestors) clear of demonstrators, the stage was set for violent confrontation.

Beginning that night and continuing until the following Thursday, pitched battles erupted with regularity on the streets of Chicago. Protestors hurled everything from epithets to rocks and bottles at the police. Policemen, acting both singly and collectively, chased, clubbed, and beat demonstrators. Innocent bystanders were subject to assault by the police, and newsmen, particularly those from what were perceived as the more liberal organs, were singled out for special attention. Reporters were beaten, equipment destroyed, film and notes confiscated. And in one last outburst, acting on the pretense that objects were being thrown out the windows of the Hilton Hotel, early on Friday morning police invaded a suite of rooms being used as working space by the McCarthy campaign organization and engaged in a final bloody frenzy of head bashing. By the time it was all over, 192 policemen reported injuries ranging from human bites to eyes burned from unknown chemicals, while an estimated 1,025 demonstrators were injured seriously enough to require first aid, and 101 were hospitalized. The number of persons arrested by police during the week of violence totalled 668, and, in its aftermath, portions of the city, not to mention the hopes of the Democratic party, were left in a shambles.[9]

Political Violence in Historical Perspective

Looking back over these incidents, and recognizing that they are to some degree representative of many others in recent memory, it seems a wonder that Americans have survived the last few years at all. Indeed, there were times when it appeared that as a nation they surely would not. For American society has been shaken to its very foundations by the onslaught of violence, and the danger of overreaction, of meeting violence with repression, has been very real.

In addition, there has been a second danger in these events, a danger, not of protective overreaction in a policy sense, but of distortion and misperception in a historical sense. For in the longer view, the events of the past years have not been so much more violent than those of earlier periods in American history, and in comparison they may even represent a trend toward moderation. Indeed, the United States has had a long and sordid record of political violence, much of it bearing remarkable similarities to the most recent experiences, and it is only in the context of that record that the events of the last few years may be properly understood. With that in mind, let us consider some of the more salient events in the nation's violent past and their implications for the present.

A CENTURY OF LABOR STRIFE

Among the most consistent sources of tension and violent confrontation in American politics over the past century have been the enduring conflict between labor and management over the role that each should play in an increasingly industrialized society and the concomitant efforts of government to promote one form or another of corporate dominance. And although it would be impossible to summarize in the available space the long history of labor violence that accompanied the industrial revolution and the attendant social reorientation in the United States, some of the more sanguinary episodes do provide a flavor of the scope and intensity with which the conflict was joined by all parties. Perhaps the most striking such illustration is to be found in the Great Railroad Strike of 1877.

In previous eras, the American economy was subject to much more violent fluctuations than has been the case in recent years, with one of the most noteworthy bottoms occurring in the mid-1870s. The depression that followed the so-called Panic of 1873 was both widespread and severe, with the railroad industry among those hardest hit. Fully one-fifth of all railroad property and investments had to be sold off under foreclosure proceedings during this period. In part, this was due to the general decline of the economy and the accompanying decrease in freight tonnage and travel, but in large measure it was attributable as well to the fact that the four principal railroads of the time, the New York Central, the Erie, the Pennsylvania, and the Baltimore and Ohio, all of which found themselves with a great deal of excess rolling stock, began in 1874 to engage in a ruinous price war. In fact, when this competition was at its peak in 1876, the cost of shipping a *carload* of cattle from Chicago to New York was one dollar. Clearly, no one was making much money at those rates, and the only beneficiary of the price war, aside from some shippers, was the city of Philadelphia, where the Centennial Exhibition was very heavily attended by tourists who found that they could travel cross-country at minimal expense. For its part, the railroad industry was rapidly approaching bankruptcy.

Finally, in April 1877, the presidents of the four railroads were able to reach a price-fixing agreement and an accompanying arrangement for the proportional division of freight tonnage, both to become effective July 1. Because of their overwhelming losses, however, and because of the continuing economic slump, they also announced that their employees would have the opportunity to share in this agreement by accepting a 10-percent cut in wages.

The railroad workers were not at the time highly unionized, with the Brotherhood of Locomotive Engineers being the only major labor organization in the industry, but their response was nevertheless spontaneous, unified, and hardly surprising. It began on the Baltimore and Ohio, where the cut was set to take effect on July 16. At first, most of the railroad's employees accepted the cut and continued to work, but the firemen refused and began that afternoon to abandon trains at Martinsburg, West Virginia. They induced other workers to join them, and the line was effectively closed at that point. The strike spread rapidly, and by midnight the workers held much of the railroad. The governor of West Virginia responded by calling out the entire state militia, but this force numbered only three companies, and it was wholly ineffective in controlling the situation. On July 18 President Rutherford B. Hayes sent 250 federal troops to Martinsburg, and these troops succeeded in dispersing the strikers. Trains were then stopped at other points along the line, notably at Cumberland, Maryland, where strikers attacked the state militia with rocks and guns. One company of militiamen was nearly overpowered by several thousand strikers, and, when 120 untrained reinforcements were sent to the militia's assistance, the heavily outnumbered reinforcements panicked and fired wildly into the crowd. Twelve strikers were killed and fourteen wounded. When federal troops arrived on the scene on July 22, they were able to restore order, but they could not lift the blockade.

The trouble on the Pennsylvania Railroad began on July 19 in Pittsburgh. Workers on the line had already suffered one pay cut of 10 percent when the panic hit in 1873, and they accepted the second 10-percent cut, which in this case came June 1, 1877, with reluctance but little opposition. But then, as if to add insult to injury, Pennsylvania Railroad president Thomas A. Scott ordered that, effective July 19, the road would run "double headers" over certain steeply graded sections of track. (Generally, each locomotive on the Pennsylvania could pull one "section" of seventeen cars up the steepest grades. A double header meant combining two locomotives to pull a train of thirty-four cars up these grades.) This move was intended to save the wages of one freight conductor, one brakeman, and one flagman on each such train. Unfortunately, it also amounted to the elimination of a significant number of jobs, and that was something the trainmen were not prepared to accept. Moreover, since the section of graded track in question was near Pittsburgh, the loss of jobs would be very localized and the impact substantial, and that was something the city of Pittsburgh was not prepared to accept.

When July 19 came and the "double header" order was implemented, a number of early trains did leave the Pittsburgh yards without incident. But at 8:40 A.M. two brakemen and a flagman refused to work on a "double header," and no other trainmen would agree to take their places. The dispatcher succeeded in recruiting a yard crew to take the train out, but these volunteers were beaten by some twenty to twenty-five strikers who took possession of the yard, got others to join them, and initiated a blockade of freight (though not passenger) service.

In part because of the potential impact of the proposed layoffs, but probably in greater measure because Pittsburgh residents felt that, due to an absence of competition, they were forced to pay unduly high freight rates, the strike received immediate support from the public, the mayor and the local police force, and, significantly, many local militiamen. For this latter reason, the commander of the state militia, acting in the absence of the governor who was out of the state, ordered troops to Pittsburgh from the rival city of Philadelphia. These troops left Philadelphia at 2:00 A.M. on Saturday, July 21, and arrived in Pittsburgh that afternoon. Without food or rest, they were immediately sent out to clear the tracks at the vital 28th Street crossing. When the mob of strikers, by that time swelled with disgruntled miners and mill and factory workers, resisted, the militia countered with a bayonet charge. The mob responded with rocks and bullets. By 5:00 P.M. it seemed that the situation had quieted, but suddenly a volley of shots rang out, and, in a brief minute of spontaneous fire, sixteen rioters were killed and many wounded.

The firing dispersed the crowd, but it also gave rise to a sense of outrage. As the troops withdrew to a roundhouse at 26th Street for food and rest, a rumor spread that some of those killed had been innocent spectators on a nearby hill and that they had included women and children. Bent on revenging these deaths, the mob reassembled and laid siege to the 26th Street roundhouse. After some shooting, they set fire to the building (as well as looting and burning other railroad property and driving off firemen) and forced the militia into retreat. The fleeing troops were allowed to pass through the crowd but were then fired upon from ambush. They returned the fire with their Gatling gun, and each side took a number of casualties. At last, the retreating militiamen reached the United States Arsenal in Pittsburgh, but the commander refused them entry because he feared an assault on the arsenal itself. The troops then fled the city across the Allegheny River to Sharpsburg. The rioting continued into Sunday, but eventually the participants lost interest and headed home.

In the meantime, Pennsylvania Governor Hartranft was hurrying back to the state aboard a special train. He ordered the entire state militia mobilized and prevailed upon President Hayes to call in a full division of federal troops. When Hartranft arrived in Pittsburgh on July 24, he found the city quiet but suffering shortages of food and fuel because of the freight boycott. Continuing on to Philadelphia, he ordered his state troops to occupy Pittsburgh. On the following Saturday, several hundred militiamen entered Pittsburgh on a special train led by a car containing a Gatling gun and thirty sharpshooters and trailed by a second car similarly equipped. But not until July 29 did freight run through Pittsburgh again, this time under guard. By July 31, though, things had begun to return to normal, and by August 10 all the approximately 4,600 state and federal troops who had, at one point or another, occupied the city were withdrawn.

These were only two of the most serious incidents in the Great Railroad Strike of 1877. Labor action spread from the East Coast to the Missouri River, with particular trouble spots in Illinois (where ten rioters were killed in a clash with police), New Jersey, Ohio, Indiana, Missouri, New York, Michigan, Kentucky, and Texas. In fact, given the widespread involvement of nonrailroad workers (parallel strikes occurred in a number of industries) and the geographic breadth of the violence and protest, the troubles of 1877 were probably the closest thing to a nationwide general strike in the history of the American labor movement.[10]

If these were among the bloodiest incidents to befall American labor, however, they were by no means the most vicious episodes of labor-related violence in American history. In all probability, that distinction must be reserved for a more geographically limited but much longer lasting conflict, a thirty-year war between miners and mine owners in Colorado that was climaxed by what has come to be known as the Ludlow Massacre.

The Ludlow Massacre took place in the spring of 1914, but, as in so many cases, its origins go back much further, in this instance to the attempts during the 1890s of the coal and metal miners of Colorado to unionize. A series of recognition strikes took place, accompanied by the assassinations of several labor leaders, leading eventually to a concerted effort in 1903 by the Western Federation of Miners (the forerunner of the International Workers of the World), representative by that time of most of the miners, to extend unionization to the nearby mills and smelters. Reaching for the economic jugular of the owners, the union ordered its miners to stop sending raw materials to the mills and smelters, in effect to shut down the mines. In response, the owners of these facilities, who were also generally the owners of the mines, formed the Mine Owners Associations of Cripple Creek and Tulleride and called upon the governor of Colorado to send in the militia at the companies' expense to force open the mines. The governor complied with this request, and there followed a period of martial law during which strikers were arrested without warrants and deported from the state, the writ of habeus corpus was suspended, and press censorship was instituted. By January 1904, an enforced peace reigned in the mining regions.[11]

Over the next several months, the mines were restaffed with more amenable (i.e., nonunion) laborers, most of whom were recent immigrants, but the working conditions that had given rise to the attempts at unionization were not altered. It took some ten years for these new workers to reach the level of dissatisfaction achieved by their predecessors, but ultimately that did happen, and by 1913 things were heating up once again, particularly in the counties of Las Animas and Huerfano.

In 1913 there were about forty small mining villages, with a total population of some 30,000, spread across these two southern Colorado counties. The overwhelming majority of the residents of these villages were immigrants, principally Italians, Mexicans, and Slavs, and together they spoke thirty-six different languages and dialects. Very few spoke English. Many of the mine workers and their families had gone directly from their ships to the mines of Colorado and knew little of American institutions or society. Moreover, because of the rugged geography of the area, each of these villages, lying some ten to thirty miles from the nearest population center, was effectively isolated from the rest of the world. Because these miners were not integrated into Colorado society, then, and because many had originally been imported as strikebreakers in the first place, they became natural objects of fear, distrust, and prejudice among the general population.

Conditions in the mining camps were about as one might expect. Illiteracy was high, sanitation was poor. The mining companies provided housing, but it was crowded, shabby, and unsightly. The water supply was pumped directly from the mines without treatment and was sold to the residents for a quarter a barrel. Disease was rampant. The only places of social contact in the camps were the saloons, most of which were company-owned, and it was estimated that the area supported one saloon for every thirty adults. Miners were paid not in currency but in scrip, and thus they were forced to purchase all their food and supplies from company-owned stores. Many of these conditions constituted violations of state law, but since the mining interests controlled a good deal of the government, the laws were not generally enforced.[12] In short, life in the Colorado mine fields was something less than ideal.

On September 16, 1913, the miners walked off their jobs at the Colorado Fuel and Iron Company, which owned about a third of the coal in the state (and was itself 40-percent controlled by the Rockefeller family). The strikers issued a series of demands, including the institution of an eight-hour day, pay for "narrow and dead" work, the hiring of "check weighmen" to assure that the company was not cheating them by understating the amount of coal they had mined, the right to trade in any store, the abolition of the mine guard system, a 10-percent increase in wages, and the recognition of the United Mine Workers of America as their bargaining agent. The strike was immediately extended to the Rocky Mountain Fuel Company and the Victor-American Fuel Company, the two other mining interests in the region, where employees adopted identical demands. The companies announced that they would meet all the strikers' terms except that for unionization, and the issue was joined.[13]

From the outset of the strike, the situation was serious. For several months leading up to the walkout, the miners had been accumulating weapons, fully cognizant that they themselves had once been brought in as strikebreakers and that the only way to spare themselves the fate of their predecessors might well be by force of arms. And for their part, as soon as the strike was called, the companies brought in a number of Baldwin-Feltz mine detectives and deputy sheriffs to protect their property. There followed a number of minor skirmishes, punctuated by numerous but uniformly unsuccessful efforts by state officials and interested citizens to arbitrate the dispute. Finally, on October 27, Governor Ammons ordered in the state militia and restored quiet to the area.

The militiamen, who were under instructions both to disarm the miners and to prevent the importation of strikebreakers, were at first welcomed by the miners, who saw them principally as protectors. But when the miners refused to surrender their weapons, the troops began to side with the companies, and the situation deteriorated once again. For six months, a war of words ensued, during which time the state militia, whose members served without pay, suffered a distressing number of desertions and vacancies. Sensing in this an opportunity, the mining companies provided the state with mine guards and detectives to fill these positions—on company pay. Under these altered circumstances, the importation of strikebreakers became increasingly effective, particularly at Ludlow, where the mines, with protection from the militia, were working at full capacity. It was against this background that John D. Rockefeller, Jr., testified before a congressional committee on mines and mining on April 7, 1914, that his companies would lose all their assets before they would agree to recognize the union.

On Sunday, April 19, not two weeks later, there were a number of random shooting incidents in the Ludlow area, and on the following morning the captain of the militia in that sector entered the camp of some 1,200 people to talk with miners' leader Louis Tikas about these incidents and the arms that his men still held. As they spoke, militiamen on a nearby hill trained a machine gun on the camp. According to one account, Tikas objected to this threat rather vehemently and was clubbed and shot. In any event, the militiamen opened fire on the camp, and a pitched battle raged for the entire day, resulting in the burning of the camp and the deaths of thirty-three persons including eleven women and children who suffocated when smoke filled the underground shelter where they had sought refuge.[14]

The next day, Tuesday, the strikers issued a call to battle in all the newspapers of the region as follows:

> Organize the men in your community in companies of volunteers to protect the people of Colorado against the murder and cremation of men, women, and children by armed assassins in the employ of coal corporations, serving under the guise of state militiamen.
>
> Gather together for defensive purposes all arms and ammunition legally available. Send name of leader of your company and actual number of men enlisted at once by wire, phone or mail to W. T. Hickey, Secretary of the State Federation of Labor.
>
> Hold all companies subject to order.
>
> People having arms to spare for these defensive measures are requested to furnish same to these local companies, and where no companies exist, send them to the State Federation of Labor.
>
> The State is furnishing us no protection and we must protect ourselves, our wives, and children from these murderous assassins. We seek no quarrel with the State and we expect to break no law. We intend to exercise our lawful right as citizens, to defend our homes and our constitutional rights.[15]

The paramilitary tone of the statement suggests the real gravity of the situation.

Over the next several days, both sides were reinforced as armed miners and militiamen poured into the area. Indeed, open warfare was averted only at the last minute when, on Saturday, April 25, more than a thousand women in Denver marched on the state capitol and prevailed upon the governor to request federal troops. President Woodrow Wilson complied with the request, and on April 28 elements of the United States Army entered the area and succeeded in restoring calm. In the end, the union was not granted recognition, and a third wave of strikes in 1927–28, this time led by the radical International Workers of the World, or "Wobblies," though less violent than the earlier efforts, was no more successful.[16]

Clearly, few labor disputes in American history have rivaled in bloodshed the Great Railroad Strike of 1877 or the Colorado mine war, but many strikes have in fact been characterized by extreme violence. In the Homestead Strike of 1892, for example, 300 Pinkerton detectives hired by the Carnegie Steel Company (now United States Steel) attempted an amphibious landing on a river bank to defend company property from striking members of the Amalgamated Association of Iron and Steel Workers and were turned back in a day of fighting that left ten dead and many wounded. Here the issue was union busting, and only the imposition of martial law and the insertion of 8,000 militiamen restored the peace.[17] Similarly, rioting, death, and massive destruction of property accompanied the efforts of employees of the Pullman Palace Car Company in Chicago to join the American Railway Union in 1894 after the ARU imposed a boycott on the handling of Pullman-manufactured equipment.[18] In 1910 there were violent streetcar strikes in Philadelphia and Columbus, which followed similar outbreaks in other cities.[19] In 1913, migrant workers on the Durst hop ranch in Wheatland, California, rioted in protest over unsanitary working conditions, killing a local district attorney and a deputy sheriff.[20] And the list goes on. In fact, at one point a dispute raged in *Outlook*, a popular journal of the day, as to whether the appropriate statistics for labor-related violence from January 1, 1902, to June 30, 1904, a period of relative calm from a long-term perspective, were 180 killed in strikes (including 116 nonunion men, i.e., strikebreakers, 51 strikers, and 13 officers), 1,651 injured (1,366 nonunion men, 151 strikers, 134 officers), and 5,533 arrested (374 nonunion men and 5,159 strikers), which was apparently management's view, or, alternatively, 904 killed, nearly 1,500 children orphaned, and 672 women widowed—as was claimed by the editor of the *United Mine*

Workers' Journal.[21] It goes without saying that labor-management relations during the period were less than amicable.

Virtually all these strikes had in common an effort either to obtain union recognition (and of course better working conditions), or, as in the case of the Homestead Strike, to prevent union busting by management. The unions themselves lacked legitimacy, and, as a result, the economic situation of the dissatisfied laborer was at best tenuous. But during the 1930s, the New Deal and the pressures of the Great Depression brought forth not only a series of new labor laws and economic policies that responded to both these needs but also a recognition on the part of both business and government that unions were around to stay. As a result, disputes over recognition have come more and more to be handled by the courts and by the National Labor Relations Board established in the mid-1930s, and the temptation to resort to violence has generally been stayed. Indeed, the last major riotous recognition strike, the so-called Little Steel Strike of 1937 that culminated in the Memorial Day Massacre in South Chicago in which ten were killed and fifty-eight injured,[22] appears almost as an anachronism, and, although violence has remained a part of subsequent labor activities, it has been considerably and consistently more subdued in recent years.

It is in this context, then, that the significance and indeed the irony of the hardhats' rampage through the streets of New York becomes clear. For although it is undoubtedly true that some of the motivation for this outpouring of frustration and dissatisfaction was provided by the increasing threat posed by minority workers seeking to enter the construction trades in the city, a phenomenon whose more specific antecedents we shall explore shortly, it is also true that nowhere in this incident may be found even the slightest hint of a struggle between management and labor (sympathetic employers actually provided alibis for their workers, claiming none had left their jobs at the time of the incident).[23] In fact, that struggle had been won by New York's construction workers long before. Thus, the construction workers who rioted in May 1970 were expressing less an economic or a social grievance than a political one, and their union ties were less an object of the demonstration than its instrument. As an electrician who led one of the workers' rallies put it, "This isn't the 30s.

Labor is middle class and has middle-class attitudes. We don't like students coming to tell us that everything that has made us that way has to be destroyed. . . . The basic agreement among the workers is a protest against a small elite group who are bent on changing things regardless of majority opinion."[24] Only in 1970 could workers stage a riotous demonstration carrying placards that bore the legend: "God Bless the Establishment."[25]

A CENTURY OF RACIAL STRIFE

If the United States has a long history of violent labor disputes, it has an equally long history of violence based on racism and nativism. In fact, the two histories are inexorably intertwined in that in many instances it was economic deprivation or the perceived threat of economic deprivation that gave the impetus to riotous outbreaks, but it was racism or nativism that gave them direction. And until the mid-1960s, it was generally not the oppressed minorities that rebelled, but rather the white majorities. Thus, the wars to clear the American continent of its Indian inhabitants, much of the violence of the Colorado labor dispute and other similar strikes, the antioriental pogroms of the late nineteenth century, and the race riots of the first half of the twentieth century can be seen to have much in common, and the true significance of the 1965 Watts Riot that we described earlier, the fact that it involved blacks rioting against whites and white-owned property rather than whites raping black neighborhoods, can be made clear. Let us consider this proposition at some length.

The pattern for most antiblack race riots in the present century was actually set in the nativist reaction to the influx of Chinese and other oriental immigrants in the latter half of the last century. From 1850 to 1870, Chinese immigrants provided plentiful and cheap labor for the mines and railroads of the Pacific region and significant competition for white labor in that area (even, occasionally, in the form of strikebreakers). As a result, feelings among white workers ran high against the Chinese, and, when the Panic of 1873 and the subsequent depression hit, it was an easy step for organized labor to pin the blame on cheap "coolie" labor and to clamor for restrictive legislation. Ever alert for attractive issues, both the Democratic and Republican parties took forthright anti-Chinese stands during the period to attract the support of the newly emerging forces of organized labor, with the result that in 1882 Congress passed the Chinese Exclusion Act, which barred all Chinese workers from entering the United States. Much to the chagrin of the Knights of Labor and other labor groups, however, Congress made no provision for the deportation of the one hundred thousand or so Chinese already in the country. The issue continued to simmer but became less important when economic conditions improved and more jobs became available.

Then, in the mid-1880s, another depression struck, wreaking havoc on employment and wages and giving renewed vigor to labor's anti-Chinese activities. In perhaps the most notorious incident of the period, thirty Chinese were massacred by white miners at Rock Springs, Wyoming, in 1885, and this was followed by similar incidents at Eureka, California, and Tacoma and Seattle, Washington.[26]

The Seattle incident, instigated, as were so many others, by the economic arguments of the Knights of Labor and furthered by the blatantly racist editorial policies of the local newspapers, came on the heels of a two-pronged political attack on the Chinese by the white workingmen of the city. The first element of this political effort consisted of a series of torchlight parades and mass meetings, the purpose of which was simply to frighten Chinese residents into leaving Seattle. In November 1885 several of the leaders of these anti-Chinese demonstrations were indicted on charges of conspiring to deprive the Chinese of their rights, but, following ten minutes of jury deliberation on January 10 of the following year, all were acquitted. At the same time, a parallel effort was being pressed in the Washington state legislature to restrict the Chinese with regard to employment, operation of businesses, and ownership of land. In mid-January, however, these proposals, which had passed the lower house, were stalled in the state senate, and by the end of the month they had been effectively shelved.

Thus, by February 1886 it was apparent to the workers in Seattle that legal efforts to restrict the Chinese had been stymied and that extralegal methods aimed toward the same goal were likely to go unpunished. At this point, the workers decided to take matters into their own hands. On Sunday, February 7, several "inspection committees" began moving through the Chinese quarter of the city advising all residents that they should be aboard the ship *Queen of the Pacific*, then anchored in Seattle harbor, by one o'clock that afternoon. Hundreds of frightened Chinese took this advice to heart and fled to the ship, but local authorities, who had supported the Chinese in the earlier indictment and trial, attempted to intervene. There followed a period of negotiation among the Chinese, the "inspectors," and local officials, after which 196 Chinese actually left (by choice) on the ship. As the remainder of the Chinese community left the docks to return home, they were attacked by a mob of whites. The state militia and later federal troops had to be called in to quell the outburst. In the wake of the Seattle violence, all the white rioters were acquitted of charges filed against them, and most Chinese left the city voluntarily.[27]

Other instances of antioriental violence could be cited, but we should note that this particular type of agitation has proven over the long run to be of relatively limited scope, at least in part because the number of Asians in the United States has never been especially high. Limited as it has been, however, this agitation is of considerable significance for at least two reasons. First, antioriental violence arose from the same combination of economic uncertainty and racist-nativist sentiment that gave rise to violence against blacks in later years. And second, antioriental violence set a pattern that would be followed with striking closeness in those subsequent outbreaks. Thus, the two different sets of events may be seen to have a great deal in common.

Before we leave our discussion of antioriental violence in the United States, it might be of interest to note two related, if somewhat random, facts. First, it was during an 1874 anti-Chinese episode in San Francisco that today's much-touted union label, the mark that identifies goods manufactured by union labor, came into use. At the time, however, the label was seen principally as a means by which consumers might identify goods, in that particular instance cigars, that were made by white as opposed to Chinese labor.[28] And second, during World War II literally thousands of resident Japanese and Americans of Japanese ancestry living on the West Coast were interned in detention camps away from the coast and deprived of numerous constitutional rights for the duration of the war, ostensibly to prevent them from signaling Japanese warships that might be lying offshore. No German- or Italian-Americans were similarly interned. Thus, the vestiges of nativist inclinations are not buried especially deep in the American past.

All this antioriental activity notwithstanding, however, the most vicious and extensive racial clashes of the past century (with the possible exception of those few western Indian wars that continued into the time period in question) have occurred in the area of black-white relations, and it is to these that we must now turn. One student of American race relations has identified seven distinct stages in black and white conflict dating from the earliest beginnings of the nation up to the early 1960s.[29] The first two of these stages, 1640 to 1861, a period of slave insurrections and resistance, and 1861 to 1877, the Reconstruction period in which blacks came to be seen by whites as more of a racial group than an economic asset, generally fall outside the period of our present analysis, but the remaining periods offer much that is of interest.

The first of these, the Second Reconstruction and the period of the great migration of blacks from the rural South to the urban North, covers the years 1878 to 1914. This was generally a period of Jim Crow laws, numerous lynchings (of which we shall have more to say in a later section), private racial violence, and repression of blacks in the South, but is also notable for two major outbreaks of collective racial violence. The first of these took place in Atlanta in 1906, the second in Springfield, Illinois, some two years later.

The Atlanta riot began, as did so many race riots in the first half of this century, when a large group of whites congregated informally in a downtown section of the city on the evening of Saturday, September 22, discussing, among other things, a rash of recent assaults upon white women by black men. As the liquor flowed, the crowd grew larger and more rowdy. Finally, at about 8:30 P.M., a man climbed onto a dry goods box and began to exhort the crowd to action. There followed a rampage through the nearby black quarter that was quieted only when the local fire brigade turned its hoses on the participants and forced them out of the area. This action, however, may have been a tragic error, for it split the mob into several groups which proceeded to attack small groups of blacks all over town. In one such instance, three black men were pulled from a passing trolley and beaten to death; in another, two black barbers were dragged from their shop and murdered. In all, between six and sixteen blacks were killed, and twenty were injured seriously enough to require hospitalization. Finally, shortly after noon on Sunday, fifteen slow strokes sounded on the central fire bell to call out the militia, and within an hour the crowd had dispersed. The incident was followed by several related disturbances in the suburbs of Atlanta in which further casualties, including one white woman who reportedly died of fright at the sight of a lynching, were suffered.[30]

A more clearly economic motive was apparent in the violence at Springfield, but the actual incident that touched off the riot was remarkably similar. Around the turn of the century, there was a major influx of blacks into Illinois, especially into the cities of Chicago, East St. Louis, Peoria, and Springfield. This influx threatened not only white jobs in these areas but white control of the ballot box as well. The result was rising tension between the races, tension that was exacerbated during 1898–99 when blacks were hired as strikebreakers in the mines at nearby Williamson and that was by no means dissipated over the succeeding decade. The area was ripe for violence, and violence finally came in 1908 on the eve of the celebration of the centennial of Abraham Lincoln's birth. It is, in fact, quite possible that Lincoln's close association with the cause of black freedom served in ironic fashion to accentuate the racial aspects of the local economic situation.

On a Friday in August 1908, two black prisoners were being held in the Springfield jail, one charged with murder and attempted rape of a white woman, the other with a more successful attempt on the virtue of another white women. A crowd of some 4,000 that had gathered outside the jail was little quieted by the headlines in the local newspapers that day: "NEGRO'S HEINOUS CRIME" and "DRAGGED FROM HER BED AND OUTRAGED BY NEGRO." By 5:00 P.M. Sheriff Charles Werner was so concerned that he diverted the attention of the crowd with the town fire engine and, with the aid of a local restaurateur, whisked the prisoners away to safety. Learning of this, half the crowd attacked and burned the restaurant owned by the man who assisted the sheriff, while the remainder pelted the police station with bricks and insults. The crowd then ripped through the black section of the city, shooting wildly and destroying property. Several blacks were lynched, and their bodies mutilated. By 1:00 A.M., when the mob tired of its folly and dispersed, much of the city was in flames. Of the several leaders of the riot who were subsequently indicted by a grand jury, one pleaded guilty, one committed suicide, one was acquitted, and the rest were never brought to trial. In the wake of the riot, blacks were refused food and jobs, and most of them migrated from Springfield.[31]

The second period in race relations, from 1915 to 1929, which saw World War I, the postwar economic boom, and a period of racial readjustment, was typified by an intensification of collective racial violence in the North and by a continuation of lynching in the South. The most notable race riot of the period occurred virtually next door to Springfield in East St. Louis, Illinois (an industrial suburb of St. Louis), and is of interest because it suggests the continuity of social pressures from one period to the next.

In the decade from 1900 to 1910, the number of blacks in East St. Louis tripled to 10 percent of the entire population of 59,000, but there was remarkably little racial tension in the city until 1916, when the Democratic party tried to win a congressional election by charging that the Republicans had imported black voters from the South. (It should be noted that, at the time, blacks generally voted overwhelmingly for the Republican party, the party of Abraham Lincoln, when they went to the polls.) The issue was heatedly debated on the stump and in the local press and was fresh in the minds of the voters the following year. Then in the spring of 1917, a local facility of the Aluminum Ore Company began, in effect, to replace some of its white workers with blacks. The whites correctly perceived this as a blatant recrimination for their union activities during a strike a year earlier. With this provocation, the white-dominated union called a second strike for April 18. At this point, the company announced that these strikes at its facilities were simply manifestations of a German plot to hinder the Allied war effort (World War I was then in progress) and promptly brought in strikebreakers, detectives, and militiamen. Within a week, the union had literally been broken, and the workers, recalling a similar series of events a year earlier at a local meat packing plant, blamed the black workers for its dissolution.

By May, tensions were at a peak. Labor leaders asked the mayor of East St. Louis to inform the local black population that there were no jobs available for them in the city, but the mayor demurred. The city's two newspapers, the *East St. Louis Journal* and the *St. Louis Republic*, began to fan the flames, and a series of racial clashes followed. In the most serious, on May 28, a crowd leaving a labor rally was swept by a rumor that a black had just shot a white man in a robbery attempt. Large numbers of people surged through the downtown area beating every black in sight. But eventually the disturbance was quieted.

Then, a little over a month later, the dam burst and the pent-up hatreds of the city took command. On Sunday evening, July 1, there were several assaults by whites on blacks, including one incident in which shots were fired into black homes from a passing Ford automobile. The Ford returned for a second run but was driven off by angry blacks. Unfortunately, the white plainclothesmen who were sent to investigate the incident arrived on the scene shortly afterward in a Ford of similar description. In what may well have been a case of mistaken identity, the blacks opened fire on the car as it arrived, killing two detectives.

As morning broke on the following day, a crowd began to form around the bloodstained, bullet-riddled car as it sat parked outside the police station. Members of the crowd carried copies of that day's *Republic*, which described in less than candid fashion the murder of the detectives by black rioters. The crowd emerged from a meeting at a nearby labor hall bent on revenge, formed ranks, and began to march in military formation. They stopped streetcars, beat and shot blacks, set fire to black homes, and shot the fleeing occupants. When the violence ended, a sixteen-block area had been effectively leveled.[32]

The summer of 1919 was, as we shall see, a period of widespread rioting similar to that in East St. Louis, but eventually things settled down, and the subsequent period, the Depression years from 1930 to 1941, was marked by only one major disturbance, the Harlem Riot of 1935. With the rising economic expectations that accompanied World War II, however, came a period of renewed racial conflict and the harbinger of the modern-type urban riot such as occurred in Watts some two decades later. Most notable during this period was the outbreak in Detroit in 1943.

The Detroit riot had much in common with those we have already discussed. Its roots can be traced, in fact, to the same World War I and postwar period when labor agents convinced large numbers of black workers in the South to come to the industrial North and find "real freedom." Many heeded the call, and the black population of Detroit climbed from 23,000 in 1917 to 200,000 in 1943. Throughout this period of growth, however, racial conflict in the city persisted in the critical areas of housing and jobs. Restrictive covenants and mob violence became established techniques by which whites controlled black housing, and in the spring of 1943 blacks were denied access to government-built wartime housing even though they were employed in war-related industries. On the job front, there existed in the factories an informal division of "black jobs" and "white jobs," with the result that blacks were often underemployed. And when, under federal pressure, the companies began to redress this situation by hiring black workers for "white" jobs, the white workers, spurred on by such rabblerousers as Gerald K. Smith, Frank Norris, and Father Coughlin, many of whom made their headquarters in Detroit, began a series of what were actually termed "hate strikes" that stopped production. Management then used these strikes as an excuse to reestablish the old hiring patterns. Between January 1, 1943, and the fall of that year, a number of these strikes took place at the Hudson Naval Arsenal, Dodge Truck, Timken Detroit Axle, U.S. Rubber, Vickers Incorporated, and the Packard Motor Car Company. In fact, only three weeks before the riot Packard was shut down for almost a week by some 20,000 white workers protesting the upgrading of three blacks in the Packard aircraft division. Finally, on June 20, 1943, a fight between a black and a white at a local amusement park touched off an explosion of rape, murder, and pillage that left thirty-four dead.[33] The Detroit riot is less significant for its violence, however, than for the fact that, as the last of the major white pogroms against blacks, and, together with the Harlem riot of the same year, as the first in which blacks made a concerted effort to attack white businesses in black neighborhoods, it marked a significant point of change in the structure of violent confrontations between blacks and whites.[34]

During the postwar years from 1946 to the early 1960s, racial conflict was rather muted, focusing on housing, education, and political rights; it was dominated by the rise of a multifaceted civil rights drive that received encouragement from Presidents Truman and Eisenhower, but especially from President Kennedy. Although there was racial violence during this period, it tended to be of relatively limited scope and duration. All that changed, however, in the mid-1960s. It is impossible to gauge the impact of the Kennedy assassination on the civil rights movement and on the political perceptions and expectations of blacks in general, but it was shortly after this event that cities across the nation erupted in waves of racially based violence. The Watts Riot of 1965, the widespread urban insurrection of 1967 (which we shall discuss below), and the flurry of riots following the King assassination all reflect years of pent-up anger and frustration that found a spontaneous and violent outlet.[35]

Although many explanations have been set forth for the lengthy list of racial disturbances we have just traversed, one cannot help but be struck by the close ties, particularly up until 1943, between these race riots and the labor violence we described earlier. Migration by racial or ethnic subgroups often influenced the level of white unemployment in a given area or the ultimate success or failure of a strike by white workers. Economic conditions repeatedly heated or cooled racial tensions. Thus, need and prejudice have frequently combined to provide both the impetus and the direction for a resort to political violence. Indeed, even the form that that violence has taken in both racial and labor disputes, not to mention the form of the response to the violence by the larger community, has remained more or less consistent over the years. Such observations help lead one to conclude that the specific group tensions from which political violence arises may be of far greater significance to the American political culture and to the fate of the nation than the violence itself.

POLITICAL MURDER IN AMERICA

Labor and racial confrontations account for only part of the history of violence in the United States. Still another form of political violence common to the American experience is assassination. Assassination has been defined as "the deliberate, extralegal killing of an individual for political purposes," a murder in which the motive of the perpetrator derives, not from any personal relationship with his victim, but rather from the victim's political status.[36] The term originated in the methods used by a military and religious order that migrated from Persia to the mountains of Syria toward the end of the eleventh century. Agents of the order were sent out to various parts of the known world to murder social and political leaders who were seen as a threat to its interests. In preparation for their suicide missions, these agents were drugged with hashish and came to be known by the Arabic word *hashashin*, or hashish eater. The term was subsequently converted by the French to the form that we now employ.[37]

Unlike the race riots and labor struggles reported above, and notwithstanding the fact that it is popular to associate each with a more extensive conspiracy, assassinations are generally much less collective acts than individual ones. That is, assassinations result more directly from the actions of individuals under conditions of appropriate motive and opportunity than from the actions of groups working in concert. For that reason, it is the assassins themselves who must interest us here rather than the systematic development of events that we have emphasized in earlier sections. Still, a brief summary of some of the more notable assassinations and assassination attempts of the past century may prove worthwhile.

During the past 100 years, five incumbent American presidents have been the victims of would-be assassins. The first of these was James Garfield, the twentieth president of the United States, a Republican from Ohio. On July 2, 1881, four months after his inauguration, Garfield rode in the carriage of his secretary of state, James G. Blaine, to the Baltimore and Potomac Railroad depot in Washington and entered the women's passenger room. He was approached from behind by Charles Guiteau, an itinerant lecturer and evangelist, who shot him twice in the back. Garfield clung to life for more than two months but succumbed on September 19.[38] Some twenty years later, on September 6, 1901, President William McKinley was standing in a receiving line at the Pan American Exposition in Buffalo, New York, when he was fatally wounded by a twenty-eight-year-old mill worker, Leon Czolgosz. McKinley died a week later. Then, in October 1950, President Harry S Truman escaped unharmed but one secret service agent was killed and two others wounded when two Puerto Rican nationalists, Oscar Collazo and Griselio Torresola, stormed Blair House in Washington, where the president was living at the time. The next assault on a president came on November 22, 1963, when, while motorcading through downtown Dallas, Texas, President John F. Kennedy fell victim to a rifle bullet believed to have been fired by Lee Harvey Oswald, a worker in a nearby book depository. Oswald was himself murdered before details of the assassination could be ascertained, a fact which has given rise in subsequent years to widespread suspicion of a broad assassination conspiracy. Finally, as recently as September 1975, President Gerald R. Ford was the target of two separate assassination attempts, both in the state of California, both by distraught women, and both unsuccessful.[39]

Four aspirants to the presidency have also come under attack during this period. On October 14, 1912, Theodore Roosevelt, who was then seeking his return to office, was leaving his hotel in Milwaukee, Wisconsin, to make a campaign speech when he was shot by John Schrank, a thirty-six-year-old bartender. In a rather dramatic display, the wounded Roosevelt continued on his way and delivered his speech (he displayed the typescript of the speech, which had a bullet hole and bloodstains, to the crowd) until he was finally weakened by the loss of blood. Roosevelt survived the assault, though not the election.[40] In 1933 President-elect Franklin D. Roosevelt, Theodore's cousin, was speaking at a political rally in Miami, Florida, when an Italian immigrant construction worker, Giuseppe Zangara, opened fire on the speakers' platform with a pistol. Roosevelt escaped injury, but Mayor Anton Cermak of Chicago, who was standing nearby, was killed in the assault. Then in June 1968, Senator Robert F. Kennedy, brother of the recently slain president and himself a candidate for the presidential nomination of the Democratic party, had just issued his victory statement in the California presidential primary and was exiting through a hotel kitchen when he was shot to death by a Jordanian, Sirhan Sirhan, who disapproved of the candidate's positions on Middle Eastern policy.[41] And in May 1972, Alabama Governor and presidential candidate George C. Wallace was left paralyzed after being shot by Arthur Bremer while on a campaign appearance at a Laurel, Maryland, shopping center.

Nor, as the earlier-described murder of Martin Luther King, Jr., illustrates, is assassination by any means restricted to presidents or would-be presidents. In addition to King and the others whom we listed before, assassins have claimed the lives of such prominent figures as John R. Clayton, a Republican congressional candidate who was murdered in 1889; Colonel Albert Fountain, a leading New Mexico Republican who was slain during a series of political murders in the state in 1896; William Goebel, governor of Kentucky, killed in 1900; Frank Steunenberg, former governor of Idaho, who was blown up by a labor union's hired dynamiter in 1905; Huey P. Long, senator and political boss from Louisiana, who was shot to death in 1935; and George Lincoln Rockwell, leader of the American Nazi party, who was murdered in 1967. Even those not directly involved in politics may become targets of assassins, as in the cases of Henry Clay Frick, president of Carnegie Steel Corporation, who was the object of an unsuccessful assassination attempt by a Russian-born anarchist during the Homestead Strike of 1892, and of Joseph Yablonski, challenger for the leadership of the United Mine Workers union, who, along with his wife and children, was killed by hired assassins in 1970.[42]

Thus, we can see that, although a rash of assassinations and attempts has taken place in our own time, these assaults are hardly an anomaly in American history. On the contrary, although assassination has not become a socially acceptable instrument of political action in the United States as it has in some nations at some points in history, it has been exercised as an option in American politics with some regularity. (The United States ranked thirtieth out of 89 nations in assassinations and attempts between 1918 and 1968, fifth of 84 nations since World War II.)[43]

But who are these assassins and what can be said of their

motives? Most of these men (all except Ford's two assailants were men) appear to have been marginal members of society who had achieved little success. Among the presidential assailants, none except Collazo held a steady job or had a stable family life at the time of his attack, and almost all were mentally unstable.[44] For example, a doctor called in by the defense to examine Charles Guiteau before he stood trial for the death of Garfield found him to be "responsibly insane," which he defined as being able to have an organized plan for murder.[45] Schrank reported having seen an apparition of the late William McKinley pointing an accusing finger at Theodore Roosevelt, his successor in the presidency, and calling upon Schrank to avenge his death. And Zangara is quoted as having announced to his captors, "I have trouble with my stomach and that way, I make my idea to kill the President—kill any president, any king."[46] Even the two women who separately assaulted President Ford have displayed similar characteristics of instability and social marginality. Lynette Fromme, whose pistol failed to fire at point-blank range in Sacramento on September 5, 1975, was a member of the so-called Manson Family, whose leader, Charles Manson, and several of his followers had earlier been convicted in the sensational ritual murders of actress Sharon Tate and others; Fromme had lived for years on the very fringes of society. Similarly, Sara Jane Moore, whose pistol shot was deflected when a bystander grabbed for her gun as the president emerged from a San Francisco hotel on September 22, had suffered an unhappy childhood (she was raised in Charleston, West Virginia, the same city, incidentally, that produced both Manson and McKinley assassin Leon Czolgosz), a case of amnesia, and several unsuccessful marriages and was remembered by many as a loner. She had become involved in the radical left during the attempt to ransom kidnap victim Patricia Hearst, daughter of newspaper publisher Randolph Hearst, by distributing millions of dollars worth of food to the poor in 1974, and she had been recruited as an FBI informant shortly afterward. It has been suggested, in fact, that the attempt on Ford's life represented an effort to atone for the guilt she felt at having spied on her leftist friends on the government's behalf.[47]

It is interesting to note, by the way, that, although assassination is generally the act of an individual, the public response to assassination is often to suspect the existence of a broader conspiracy. This was true, as we have noted, in the case of James Earl Ray's attack on Martin Luther King, Jr.; it was true as well, though later evidence seems to have put the suspicion to rest, regarding the Sirhan Sirhan murder of Robert F. Kennedy. Nowhere is the belief in conspiracy more intense or more enduring, however, than in the shooting of John F. Kennedy. Films of the event, fifty-two eyewitness reports, and even some of the physical evidence not only fail to confirm absolutely the official finding of the Warren Commission, the presidentially-appointed investigatory body charged with sifting the evidence, that a single assassin, Lee Harvey Oswald, acting alone, murdered the president but actually seem to point to precisely the opposite conclusion. When one considers as well the fact that Oswald himself was shot to death two days after the assassination, the apparent coincidence that seventeen witnesses to the deaths of Kennedy, Oswald, or police officer J. D. Tippit (who was allegedly shot by Oswald before his arrest) also died within three years of the assassination (five of so-called natural causes, twelve of murder, accidents, or suicide), and the fact that a principal dissenter within the Warren Commission, Representative Hale Boggs of Louisiana, was killed in the crash of a light plane in Alaska in 1972 when he was said to be on the eve of reopening the issue, it is little wonder that suspicions of conspiracy have been aroused.[48] Although such notions may, in the final analysis, arise from nothing more than shock, insecurity, and an unwillingness to accept the most apparent explanation for a great tragedy, they nevertheless cannot help but undermine the basic trust and support that the American people give to their political leaders and weaken the ties between government and citizen.

In any event, all these assailants have had in common the fact that they appear to have struck at the presidency or at the position of other victims at an institutional level rather than at the incumbents to those positions at a personal level, and it is this symbolic element that sets their deeds apart and gives them political significance. Moreover, it is this same unpredictable combination of unstable, threatened, or dissatisfied assailant with visible, symbolic victim that gives the threat of assassination its continuing role in American political life.

VIOLENCE: THE RESPONSE TO VIOLENCE

Having arrived at this point in the narrative, one can scarcely help but be impressed by the persistence and perniciousness of the forces of social upheaval and the violence that they have unleashed on the American public. It seems that everywhere one looks in the annals of American social, economic, and political development one encounters strikers, rioters, and even assassins ravaging the civilization. Yet if one looks more closely, one also finds that perhaps more often than not, and particularly in the areas of labor and racial violence, it is not the opponents of the status quo so much as its supporters who frequently resort to violence. It is not, in many cases, the resistance to societal orthodoxies so much as the perception of a threat to those orthodoxies brought on by resistance that gives rise to bloodshed.

We have seen evidence in a number of the strikes and riots that we have described that the forces of legal order, be they police, sheriffs, or militiamen, have frequently wrought more violence than they have quelled. In Ludlow, Colorado, it was the state militia that engaged in a bloody massacre of men, women, and children. The miners were perceived as foreigners and outsiders, which in fact they were, and as a threat to the economy and society of the state, and they were treated accordingly. In Springfield, Illinois, blacks were seen as imported troublemakers who were causing economic and political dislocations, and they were driven from the community as the Chinese had been from Seattle some years earlier. In Chicago in 1937, it was a police assault on strikers at Republic Steel that brought on the Memorial Day Massacre. Even in Watts in 1965, no deaths occurred until riot police and the National Guard arrived on the scene.[49] And the list goes on. It would seem that the typical response of our society to threat or violence is a still higher order of threat or violence.

But if a heightening of tensions is frequently our most immediate response to conflict situations, there is, over the longer term, a more complex organization response as well. Thus, at least one scholar argues that the development of formal policing agencies in the United States has been in direct response, not to the rise in crime, but to the kinds of essentially political events we have been describing. As we shall note in chapter 3, for example, the establishment of modern urban police systems in this country followed very closely a series of urban riots that began around 1830 and culminated in what was undoubtedly America's bloodiest three days (in excess of 300 deaths), the New York Draft Riot of 1863. Similarly, when the inadequacies of the state militias became apparent after the violent strikes of 1877, the National Guard was established, at first in precisely those central and northeastern states such as Illinois and Pennsylvania that had suffered serious rioting, and by 1892 on a nationwide basis. In those early days, the guard was commanded mostly by businessmen and professionals, and it was sometimes subsidized by industrialists. It was frequently employed to restore order in labor disputes from the period of its inception until World War II; since that time it has been used most often in calming racial disorders.[50]

Moreover, there developed during this same period in the late nineteenth century a variety of quasi-legal detective organizations that played an active and violent part in a number of labor disputes. In addition to the Baldwin-Feltz Agency, whose operatives played such a catalytic role in the Colorado Mine War, the Pinkertons, who are perhaps better known today, and a number of other detective firms, many corporations set up their own police forces, such as the Coal and Iron Police of Pennsylvania, paid their guards and detectives to serve in the state militia (as in Colorado), or used their not inconsiderable influence to have deputies' badges or other symbols of legitimacy pinned to the chests of their private patrols.[51]

And finally, there has developed in the United States a tradition of collective self-defense known as vigilantism. The phenomenon of vigilantism appears to have begun in South Carolina in the latter half of the eighteenth century and to have spread rapidly in the absence of effective local law enforcement agencies. In its earliest stages, it was a necessary and effective response to frontier lawlessness. The high point of vigilantism was probably reached in San Francisco in 1856, when a coalition of leading merchants organized to combat crime and political corruption,[52] but the inclination toward vigilante action endures to the present in the form of a variety of self-protection groups such as the Jewish Defense League, ultrapatriotic defense organizations such as the modern day Minutemen, and enforcers of local social mores such as the Ku Klux Klan.

The powerful emotional pull and the distinctly American philosophical overtones of vigilante rhetoric are perhaps best illustrated in the words of William Tell Coleman, leader of the San Francisco vigilante movement.

> Who made the laws and set agents over them? The people.
>
> Who saw these laws neglected, disregarded, abused, trampled on? The people.
>
> Who had the right to protect these laws, and administer them when their servants had failed? The people.
>
> The people are the power; it is theirs by birthright, and when they delegate it, it is expressed and implied that upon wrong-doing the servants shall be pushed aside formally or informally, and their places promptly filled by other and better agencies.[53]

In general, vigilante movements in the United States have been dominated by conservative, even elite, elements of the community and have been ardent defenders of social orthodoxy.[54] Combine this fact with the nativist and antiunionist sentiments of their supporters, and it is not particularly surprising to find within them a consistent tendency to operate to the detriment of racial and ethnic minorities and other societal outgroups. Thus, in a sense the mixed economic and racial outbreaks such as those at Rock Springs in 1885 and East St. Louis in 1917 can be seen as prototypical vigilante outbreaks, as attempts to drive those who were socially different and economically dangerous from the community. Still more longlasting and widespread than these occasional outbursts, however, has been another outgrowth of the vigilante spirit, the practice commonly referred to as lynching.

Since the technique has most frequently been employed by whites against blacks, it is tempting to consider lynchings as more nearly race riots than vigilante actions, but closer inspection suggests that the latter description may be more generally appropriate. The origins of the term lynching are in some dispute, but one of the more likely explanations traces the word to Judge Charles Lynch of Bedford County, Virginia, who, during the period of the American Revolution, headed what has been described as an "uncourteous" court, which meted out rude punishments to suspected Tories. The judgments of this court, termed "Lynch Law," generally took the form of public whippings, and it was not until much later, probably during Reconstruction, that "lynching" came to be associated with hanging and other less enjoyable forms of death.[55] But whatever its origins, the event itself could be rather gruesome. In one of the most widely declaimed of such episodes, for example, the Coatesville (Pennsylvania) lynching of 1911, a black man named Zach Walker killed a private policeman at the local mill. (The connection between vigilante action and industrial police forces is more than incidental here.) Upon his arrest, Walker made an unsuccessful attempt at suicide—as a result of which he was hospitalized. On Sunday, August 13, Walker was taken by force from his hospital room, dragged a half mile, thrown on a pile of wood, covered with oil, and put to the torch as several hundred onlookers watched approvingly. When he broke loose and attempted to flee, the crowd forced him back into the fire with pitchforks and fence rails. And when the screams ended and the fire died down, large numbers of spectators cut off fragments of Walker's body to retain as souvenirs of American justice.[56]

Although it is true that Walker and hundreds of other lynching victims were black, it is not true that lynching was employed solely by whites against blacks. In fact, particularly during the post-Reconstruction era, increasing numbers of whites became victims of lynch mobs. According to one tally, of 3,300 total lynchings between 1882 and 1903, fully 1,169 involved white victims.[57] And although the great majority of these lynchings took place in the South, a significant number (376 between 1885 and 1903), and, if the Coatesville incident is any indication, some of the most brutal, took place in the North. In fact, during the period just noted, lynchings occurred in all but five states. Of the victims, 1,099 were lynched for committing murder; 564 for "criminal assault" (rape or attempted rape); 106 for arson; 326 for theft, burglary, or robbery; 96 purely as a result of racial prejudice; and 134 for unknown causes. Fifty-three blacks were lynched for simple assault, eighteen for insulting whites, and sixteen for threatening whites. Seventeen people were apparently lynched simply because they were unpopular in their neighborhoods, while other justifications included slander, miscegenation, informing, drunkenness, fraud, voodooism, violation of contract, resisting arrest, elopement, trainwrecking, poisoning livestock, refusing to give evidence, political animosity, disobedience of quarantine regulations, passing counterfeit money, introducing small pox, concealing criminals, cutting levees, kidnapping, gambling, rioting, testifying against whites, seduction, incest, and forcing a child to steal. One poor fellow was lynched for jilting his girlfriend (she married another man shortly afterward, but there is no word on whether he was one of the lynchers), a reformer was lynched for advocating colonization, a black for enticing a servant away from her mistress, and a mountaineer for making moonshine. The gentleman who compiled these statistics was, however, able to find the proverbial silver lining, noting that

> there is a brighter side to the picture. While there is a decrease in lynchings [from 210 to 1885 to 104 in 1903] there is an increase in legal executions, and this increase is specially noticeable in those states where lynching has been most common. . . . [Thus] there is no reason to be discouraged. The outlook is hopeful.[58]

We can see, then, that violence has indeed begotten violence and that American society has, from time to time, resorted to a variety of legal, quasi-legal, extralegal, and illegal means of purging itself of perceived threats and evils. And as the Chicago police riot of 1968 and the hardhat rampage of 1970 make clear, the tendency to do so is still very much with us.

Regularities in American Political Violence

We have now reviewed at some length not only the violent tendencies inherent in modern American society but also the historical context in which those tendencies have been nurtured. We have acquired a sense of the tenuous balance between domestic tranquility and domestic turmoil. And that in itself is a noble accomplishment. Yet, we would surely be remiss were we not to seek from this history of sordid and bloody deeds some deeper understanding, some sense of the regularities, if any, that may be noted in the litany of facts presented above. Before concluding, therefore, let us consider some of these recurrent patterns.

THE TIMING OF VIOLENCE

Two of the most notable patterns in much that we have described have to do with the timing of violence. In the first place, there is a distinct tendency for American political violence to erupt in relatively brief but intense paroxysms, sweeping the country from one end to the other and then all but completely dissipating. One such outburst, fundamentally economic in character, accompanied the railroad strikes of 1877 and included not only a large number of violent strikes but labor-related racial pogroms as well, most notably in San Francisco, where labor activist Denis Kearney led local workers in rioting against some 150,000 Chinese laborers who had, in effect, been dumped on the San Francisco economy upon the completion of the transcontinental railroad. Interestingly enough, when local political leaders and police were unable to end the disturbances, they called upon former vigilante leader William Tell Coleman and 5,500 volunteers to do the job.[59]

Another such period was the so-called Red Summer of 1919, when an unprecedented wave of labor troubles and race riots swept the country in the aftermath of World War I. Between April 14 and October 1 of that year, race riots occurred in twenty-two cities including Chicago, Washington, Knoxville, St. Louis, Memphis, and Birmingham. During that period, seventy-four blacks were lynched. Housing was especially tight because of a decrease in building during the war, and competition for jobs was particularly intense, in part because of the massive black migration to northern urban centers of which we have spoken earlier, and in part because large numbers of veterans were returning to the civilian economy. These economic and social pressures mixed with the Red Scare xenophobia, of which we shall have more to say later, to produce what was, for all practical purposes, an economically inspired, nationwide race war.[60] Add to this a phenomenal number of strikes and one has a picture of a rather unsettled year.[61]

Again in 1967, violence swept our urban centers like an epidemic. In that year there were forty-one racial disorders judged serious or major by the National Commission on Civil Disorders and fully 123 other outbreaks. In Newark, New Jersey, for example, rioting that followed the forceable arrest of a black cab driver raged for five days in July and resulted in twenty-three deaths (twenty-one of them blacks) and more than $10 million in property damage.[62] The following week, in Detroit, scene of the largest outbreak, rioting followed a series of police raids on black-owned drinking and gambling clubs and led to forty-three deaths (including thirty-three blacks) and 7,200 arrests.[63] Unlike the 1919 racial rioting, however, these uprisings were found not to involve interracial skirmishes between whites and blacks so much as concerted black action against white authority and white-owned property, the twin symbols of black subjugation. They thus bore many similarities to the Watts riot of two years earlier.[64]

The recurrence of these concentrated periods of conflict has given rise to a "contagion" theory of political violence. In this view, the concept of riot, once translated into concrete reality in one place, takes on not only an aura of realizability but perhaps even a certain inevitability as it is transmitted to other locations. As people in different areas come to accept the possibility of rioting, an actual outbreak of violence becomes more likely. This theory is particularly impressive when applied to the 1967 urban rebellions because of the rapidity with which news of the events was thoroughly disseminated both within the riot cities and across the country by television, but it also receives apparent support from earlier events. In 1919, for example, the same dissemination function was performed so well by the newspapers of the day, particularly with regard to the Chicago riot, that between 1919 and the mid-1960s there was actually an informal effort by certain newsmen to suppress news of rioting for fear that such news would help foment further violence.[65] The events of 1877 are also illustrative in this context in that the principal locus of strike action across the country was the railroad, a nationwide transportation and communication nexus of the first magnitude. Even the recent flurry of assassinations and attempted assassinations, which is similar to an earlier and more localized flurry in New Mexico before the turn of the century, lends credence to this notion of contagion.[66] Thus, when one speaks of an epidemic of violence, one might be closer to the truth than simple analogy.

The second pattern discernible in the timing of American political violence has to do with its distribution *within* a given year, that is, the seasonal character of such occurrences. The data here are less impressive to date since they have thus far been developed for only a fairly short time span, but a study of the years 1965 to 1968 does suggest, and the frequent appearance of summer dates in our own analysis tends to confirm, that a disproportionate share of violence or potential violence occurs during the months of June, July, and August. This was found to be the case with regard to antiwar protests, urban riots, labor strikes, and even violent crime.[67] No conclusive rationale for this phenomenon has yet been put forward, but it would seem that the "long hot summer" of which we have heard so much during the past decade in connection with racial disturbances may in some degree be a permanent feature of American political life.

THE ORGANIZATION OF VIOLENCE

A second consistency in the pattern of American political violence may be found in the extent to which that violence is *not* systematically planned and carried out. With only a few notable exceptions, the instances of violence that we have described, though not necessarily the conditions out of which they developed, are most striking, not for the detail of their central planning and coordination, but precisely because such planning and coordination seem to have been altogether lacking. Indeed, many of these outbreaks of violence have resembled random occurrences rather than organized action, accidents of circumstance rather than purposive or controlled campaigns. A troop of militiamen, overtired and underprepared, lost its composure under pressure, and a bloody massacre followed. A black taxi driver was arrested, and a ghetto exploded. A mentally unbalanced man had a pain in his stomach, and a public figure was assassinated.

In such cases, and they have been many, the most apt analogy by which to describe American political violence may be that of spontaneous combustion. The conditions for violence may develop over an extended period, but the conflagration itself may be triggered by events that are at best only marginally related to them. Thus, the real question underlying the role of violence in American society may pertain less to the *propensity* of the population toward violent behavior, or its inclination to act, than to its *capacity* for violence, or its ability to act. And the ultimate impact of the conditions that underlie political violence may be either magnified or reduced by the random distribution of historical circumstance.

THE PSYCHOLOGY OF VIOLENCE

Finally, some scholars have argued that there exist certain regularities in the operational psychology of collective violence and that these regularities may be seen to apply to the American experience. According to one such argument, each individual within a society has a personal set of social needs that are organized in hierarchical fashion. Basic among these are the so-called physiological needs such as hunger, thirst, or the need for sleep. These physiological requirements are followed in decreasing order of significance by the needs for safety or a sense of security; love, in the general sense of social acceptance and affection; self-esteem or a sense of one's own dignity and worth; and, finally, self-actualization or the pursuit of one's social goals and desires. According to this theory, it is the drive to meet various of these needs that leads a person to engage in social or political activity. Each level of need gratification is seen as providing the basis for the creation and the perception of all subsequent levels, and, it is argued, only when the needs manifested at one level have been satisfied can one progress to the next level. That is to say, one perceives a need for security only after he has met his needs for food or drink, one perceives a need for social acceptance only after having achieved a sense of security, and so forth.[68]

The importance of this argument for understanding the occurrence of violent social behavior becomes apparent if we carry the analysis one step further and suggest that violent behavior is brought about when a discrepancy is perceived between one's needs at one or another level (but most especially at the lower levels of the need hierarchy), on the one hand, and one's realistic expectations of what he may actually attain, on the other. That is, if a person's need for food is strong but his perceived capability to obtain it under a given social structure is relatively low, that person may react violently against that social structure because satisfaction of his need is frustrated by maintenance of the status quo. Thus, strike violence that arises out of the inability of workers to earn a living wage or the continuation of dangerously unsanitary working conditions (e.g., the farm workers' strike in Wheatland, California) can be seen to result from the realization that the workers' capability to obtain physiological necessities is impaired by the continuation of existing practices. Similarly, a perceived threat to the satisfaction of safety needs could be argued to have underlain portions of the mine war in Colorado and certain vigilante movements, the threat to self-esteem to have sparked many of the ghetto uprisings of recent years, the threat to self-actualization to have set off the activities of the construction workers in New York City, and so forth. Indeed, certain levels of both need and expectation may actually be incorporated over time into the underlying political culture of our society, so that a true mark of the social development of the United States may be the progression of its people along the need hierarchy from basic physiological requirements to the more social demands of self-actualization as a basis for political behavior. Similarly, the present-day limits of that development may be indicated by the fact that Americans still feel the need from time to time to resort to violence, presumably because not all their personal and social needs have yet been satisfied. Thus, the objects of political violence may reflect social progress, but the existence of that violence suggests a continuing pressure for change.

This discrepancy between a person's needs and his expectations regarding his capability to meet those needs is generally referred to as "relative deprivation," and can arise from a variety of circumstances. For example, relative deprivation can result from an increase in an individual's wants and needs relative to fixed capabilities (as in the numerous drives for union recognition where the attainment of unionization and its presumed benefits for the worker are effectively resisted by management); from a decrease in realistic expectations relative to a constant level of wants and needs (as in the withdrawal of recognition from an established union such as the action that brought on the Homestead Strike of 1892, or as in the increased black migration and the accompanying economic competition that touched off the rioting in Springfield and East St. Louis); from an increase in wants and needs that outpaces an accompanying increase in perceived capabilities (as in the property-oriented urban race riots of the 1960s); or from a constant level of wants and needs that are paralleled but never satisfactorily met by a constant level of expectations (as, perhaps, in the lengthy mine war in Colo rado).[69] In each instance capability failed to match need, and ir each instance violent or protoviolent behavior developed.

But if these complex theories of need and relative deprivation help explain the general underlying psychology of collective violence and perhaps even the creation of incendiary situations, they tell us considerably less about the specific factors that actually result in collective violence. As presently formulated, in other words, these theories can tell us in a broad sense why a strike took place in the steel industry in 1937 and why a crowd formed in Chicago on Memorial Day (or some alternative date), but they cannot tell us why the first shot of the Memorial Day Massacre was fired. They can tell us why blacks in Watts were angry and alienated and ready for violence in 1965, but they cannot explain why the routine arrest of a young man for a minor traffic violation touched off a major insurrection. For, as we have noted, these events were not long-planned, rational actions undertaken in systematic order by conspirators bent on violence; they were merely chance occurrences that touched off spontaneous upheavals out of all proportion to the events themselves. And although the structures of many episodes of collective violence bear striking similarities to one another, whether in regard to the role of rumor in spreading dissatisfaction, the role of inadequate rest or preparation of forces sent to maintain or restore order, the importance of overreaction in magnifying the violent aspects of a confrontation, or some other apparent consistency, there remains an element of uncertainty in all potentially violent situations that serves to reduce the degree of control that may be effectively exercised over the flow of events. Perhaps it is just that element of uncertainty that is the most troubling characteristic of contemporary American political violence.

Conclusion

We can see, then, that several continuities are present in the history of American political violence. In the first place, violence tends to be concentrated in a few relatively brief but intense outbreaks such as the racial and economic conflicts of 1919, the urban warfare of 1967, and the epidemic of assassination attempts from 1963 to 1975. In such periods, violence becomes accepted as a realistic form of political expression and, with the apparent exception of the assassinations, as a quasi-legitimate tool of influence. Similarly, political violence tends rather consistently to reflect underlying psychological insecurities or discontents both at the individual level (as in the cases of virtually all of the would-be assassins) and among collectivities (as with the widespread perception of relative deprivation among urban rioters). The intergroup tensions, the distrust of the unknown, the fear of competitive disadvantage, the misunderstanding of those who are different—these and other factors contribute to a universal uneasiness that prepares Americans for violence. Indeed, as we have seen in numerous instances, even the structures and processes of violent political behavior in the United States remain relatively constant through time. Thus, the capacity for violence and disruption is very much a part of the American political culture, and it is, in a sense, only natural that violence occurs with considerable regularity.

At the same time, according to at least one study, the United States is by no means the most violent country in the modern world. In fact, during the mid-1960s, a period of substantial violence, it ranked twenty-fourth of 114 countries in the overall level of domestic strife, twenty-seventh in the proportion of the population actually participating in violence (an estimated 1.1 percent), and fifty-third in the proportion of casualties in domestic violence.[70] According to a second study, the level of American violence today is markedly below that at some periods in the past (notably the years around 1880) and, as measured by some indicators, has even been declining for about a century.[71] These figures, however, are relative rather than absolute—and, in fact, are relative to what might be considered a rather high base. For violence seems to be a widespread phenomenon not only in the national history of the United States but also throughout the history of the countries of the modern world. Thus, while we may in fact live in violent times, both the historical record and cross-national comparison suggest an important context within which contemporary American political violence must be judged—and one without which it cannot be properly understood.

NOTES

1. Ramsey Clark in the preface to Irving J. Sloan, *Our Violent Past: An American Chronicle* (New York: Random House, 1970), p. xi.

2. Fred J. Cook, "Hard Hats: The Rampaging Patriots," *The Nation*, 15 June 1971; "Sudden Rising of the Hardhats," *Time*, 25 May 1970, pp. 20f.

3. "Watts: The Forgotten Slum," *The Nation*, 30 August 1965, pp. 89f.

4. "Trigger of Hate," *Time*, 20 August 1965, pp. 13–19.

5. Ibid.

6. Thomas R. Dye, *The Politics of Equality* (Indianapolis: Bobbs-Merrill, 1971), pp. 176–77; Irving J. Sloan, *Our Violent Past: An American Chronicle* (New York: Random House, 1970), p. 62.

7. Murray Clark Havens, Carl Leiden, and Karl M. Schmitt, *The Politics of Assassination* (Englewood Cliffs, N.J.: Prentice-Hall, 1970), pp. 62ff, 70f.

8. See Richard Hofstadter and Michael Wallace, eds., *American Violence: A Documentary History* (New York: Alfred A. Knopf, 1970) for a discussion of several of these incidents.

9. Daniel Walker, *Rights in Conflict*, a report submitted to the National Commission on the Causes and Prevention of Violence (New York: New American Library, 1968), passim.

10. James Ford Rhodes, "Railroad Riots of 1877," *Scribners Magazine*, July 1911, pp. 86-96.

11. Ray Stannard Baker, "The Reign of Lawlessness: Anarchy and Despotism in Colorado," *McClures*, May 1904, pp. 43–57.

12. W. T. Davis, "Strike War in Colorado," *Outlook*, 9 May 1914, pp. 67-73; "Tent Colony of Strikers Swept by Machine Guns," *Survey*, 2 May 1914, pp. 108–110; "Colorado Appeals to the President for Help," *Current Opinion*, June 1914, pp. 413–16.

13. "Colorado Appeals"; Helen Ring Robinson, "War in Colorado," *Independent*, 11 May 1914, pp. 245–47.

14. "Colorado Appeals"; Robinson, "War"; Davis, "Strike War."

15. Davis, "Strike War," p. 69.

16. Robinson, "War"; "Industrial War in Colorado," *Review of Reviews* 49 (June 1914): 732–34; Charles J. Bayard, "1927-1928 Colorado Coal Strike," *Pacific Historical Review* 32 (August 1963): 235–50.

17. Sloan, *Our Violent Past*, pp. 187-93.

18. Philip Taft and Philip Ross, "American Labor Violence: Its Causes, Character, and Outcome," in *The History of Violence in America*, ed. Hugh Davis Graham and Ted Robert Gurr (New York: Bantam, 1969), pp. 297-99; and Grover Cleveland, "The Government in the Chicago Strike of 1894," *McClures*, July 1904, pp. 226–40.

19. Taft and Ross, "American Labor Violence," pp. 311-14; Harold J. Howland, "War in Philadelphia," *Outlook*, 5 March 1910, pp. 522-25; "Anarchy in Columbus," *Outlook*, 27 August 1910, pp. 908-911.

20. Carleton H. Parker, "Wheatland Riot and What Lay Back of It," *Survey*, 21 March 1914, pp. 768-70.

21. Slason Thompson, "Violence in Labor Conflicts," *Outlook*, 17 December 1904, pp. 969-72; S. M. Sexton, "Strike Violence," *Outlook*, 21 January 1905, pp. 198-99.

22. Donald G. Sofchalk, "Chicago Memorial Day Incident: An Episode of Mass Action," *Labor History* 6 (Winter 1965): 3-43.

23. Cook, "Hard Hats."

24. "Sudden Rising of the Hardhats."

25. Ibid.

26. Herbert Hill, "Anti-Oriental Agitation and the Rise of Working-Class Racism," *Society* 10, (January-February 1973): 43-54.

27. Jules Alexander Karlin, "Anti-Chinese Outbreaks in Seattle, 1885-1886," *Pacific Northwest Quarterly* 39 (April 1948): 103-130.

28. Hill, "Anti-Oriental Agitation," p. 48.

29. Allen D. Grimshaw, "Lawlessness and Violence in America and Their Special Manifestations in Changing Negro-White Relationships," *Journal of Negro History* 44 (January 1959): 52-72.

30. Thomas Gibson, "The Anti-Negro Riots in Atlanta," *Harpers Weekly*, 13 October 1906, pp. 1457-59.

31. James L. Crouthamel, "Springfield Race Riot of 1908," *Journal of Negro History* 45 (July 1960): 164-81.

32. Elliot M. Rudwick, *Race Riot at East St. Louis* (Carbondale, Ill.: Southern Illinois University Press, 1964), pp. 3-57.

33. L. Martin, "Prelude to Disaster: Detroit," *Common Ground* 4 (Autumn 1943): 21-26.

34. August Meier and Elliot Rudwick, "Black Violence in the Twentieth Century: A Study in Rhetoric and Retaliation," in *History of Violence*, ed. Graham and Gurr, p. 405; Morris Janowitz, "Patterns of Collective Racial Violence," in *History of Violence*, ed. Graham and Gurr, pp. 412-43, passim; Joe R. Feagin and Harlan Hahn, *Ghetto Revolts: The Politics of Violence in American Cities* (New York: Macmillan, 1973), pp. 89-90.

35. For a discussion of the expectations of violence among blacks and whites, see David Street and John C. Leggett, "Economic Deprivation and Extremism: A Study of Unemployed Negroes," *American Journal of Sociology* 67 (July 1961): 53-57.

36. Havens, Leiden, and Schmitt, *Politics*, p. 5.

37. James M. Buckley, "Assassination of Kings and Presidents," *Century* 63 (November 1901): 136-42.

38. Ibid.; William J. Crotty, "Presidential Assassination," *Society* 9 (May 1972): 23.

39. Crotty, "Presidential Assassination."

40. Ibid.; "Attempted Assassination," *Independent*, 24 October 1912, pp. 963-65.

41. Crotty, "Presidential Assassination."

42. Richard Maxwell Brown, ed., *American Violence* (Englewood Cliffs, N.J.: Prentice-Hall, 1970), p. 115; Richard Maxwell Brown, "Historical Patterns of Violence in America," in *History of Violence*, ed. Graham and Gurr, p. 58; Hofstadter and Wallace, eds., *American Violence*, p. 420; David G. Phillips, "Assassination of a Governor: William Goebel," *Cosmopolitan*, April 1905, pp. 611–24.

43. Crotty, "Presidential Assassination," p. 20.

44. Ibid., p. 25.

45. Buckley, "Assassination," p. 139.

46. Crotty, "Presidential Assassination," pp. 25, 28.

47. "The Two Faces of Sara Jane Moore," *Newsweek*, 6 October 1975, pp. 22–24; Henry Weinstein, "A Strange Encounter with Sara Jane Moore," *New Times*, 17 October 1975, pp. 35–37.

48. Robert Sam Anson, "The Greatest Cover-Up of All," *New Times* 18 April 1975; Robert Blair Kaiser, "The JFK Assassination: Why Congress Should Reopen the Investigation," *Rolling Stone*, 24 April 1975.

49. Hofstadter and Wallace, eds., *American Violence*, p. 263.

50. Brown, "Historical Patterns," pp. 60–61.

51. Ibid.; Michael Wallace, "The Uses of Violence in American History," *The American Scholar* 40 (Winter 1970–71): 91-92.

52. Brown, "Historical Patterns," pp. 67–68.

53. Freeman Champney, "Justice of the People," *Antioch Review* 7 (June 1947): 238.

54. Richard Maxwell Brown, "The American Vigilante Tradition," in *History of Violence*, ed. Graham and Gurr, pp. 192–96; Robert Moats Miller, "Protestant Churches and Lynching, 1919-1939," *Journal of Negro History* 42 (April 1957): 118–31.

55. Albert Bushnell Hart, a review of "Lynch Law: An Investigation into the History of Lynching in the United States," by J. E. Cutler, *American Historical Review* 11 (January 1906): 425–28. See also Albert Mathews, "Lynch Law," *Nation*, 4 December 1902, pp. 439–41.

56. Albert Jay Nock, "What We All Stand For: Coatesville Lynching," *American Magazine*, February 1913, pp. 53–57.

57. James Elbert Cutler, "Practice of Lynching in the United States," *South Atlantic Quarterly* 6 (April 1907): 125–34. See also "30 Years Record in Lynching," *World's Work* 39 (March 1920): pp. 433–44.

58. George P. Upton, "Facts about Lynching," *Independent*, 29 September 1904, pp. 719–21.

59. Champney, "Justice," p. 238f.

60. William Tuttle, Jr., "Views of a Negro during the Red Summer of 1919," *Journal of Negro History* 51 (July 1966): 209–218; "Our Own Race War," *North American Review* 210 (October 1919): 436–38.

61. "The Labor Crisis and the People," *Outlook*, 29 October 1919, pp. 223–29. On a single day in October 1919, it was estimated that in New York City alone some 60,000 longshoremen, 25,000 building-trades workers, 16,000 millinery workers, 15,000 cigar makers, 10,000 laundry workers, 10,000 piano makers, 5,000 expressmen, 5,000 paper box makers, 4,600 printers, 3,000 tailors, 3,000 shipbuilders, 1,000 coppersmiths, 1,000 ash-can makers, 700 box makers and sawyers, 650 chandalier makers, 500 mattress makers, and 175 micrometer workers were on strike.

62. Cited in Brown, ed., *American Violence*, pp. 150–52.

63. Hofstadter and Wallace, eds., *American Violence*, p. 267f.

64. From the Report of the National Commission on Civil Disorders as cited in Dye, *Politics of Equality*, p. 179.

65. Janowitz, "Patterns," p. 440f.

66. Brown, "Historical Patterns," p. 59f.

67. Raymond Tanter, "International War and Domestic Turmoil: Some Contemporary Evidence," in *History of Violence*, ed. Graham and Gurr, pp. 558, 564, 565.

68. A. Maslow, "A Theory of Human Motivation," *Psychological Review* 50 (1943): 370–96.

69. Ted Robert Gurr, "A Comparative Study of Civil Strife," in *History of Violence*, ed. Graham and Gurr, pp. 597–602. See also idem, *Why Men Rebel* (Princeton: Princeton University Press, 1971); James C. Davies, "The J-Curve of Rising and Declining Satisfactions as a Cause of Some Great Revolutions and a Contained Rebellion," in *History of Violence*, ed. Graham and Gurr, pp. 690–730.

70. Gurr, "A Comparative Study," pp. 575–78.

71. Sheldon G. Levy, "A 150-Year Study of Political Violence in the United States," in *History of Violence*, ed. Graham and Gurr, pp. 86–94.

3

A Nation of Cities: The Urbanization of the United States

The Twentieth Century opens with two distinguishing features—the dominant city and militant democracy. . . . These features are permanent. This is assured by the nature of things. The life, the industry, the culture of the future will be urbanized. . . . The city may change in many ways—undoubtedly it will. . . . But in a historical sense, the city has resumed the commanding position which it enjoyed in the days of Athens, Rome, and the mediaeval towns.

Frederic C. Howe, *The City: The Hope of Democracy*, 1905

New York is:

The city that disposes of its garbage by dumping it into the ocean, where any prolonged south wind blows it back to cover New York and New Jersey beaches with vegetables, bottles, domestic animals, and insecticide tins.

The city that transports the bulk of its population in accommodations that Armour and Swift would not offer to their swine.

The city that, in order to protect the bathers on its beaches, employed life guards fifteen of whom did not know how to swim. . . .

The city in which bribery is a stepping-stone to the judiciary; the city in which a police detective has been demoted on the ground that he disgraced the Police Department by associating with the friends of a judge; the city which chuckles at the musical comedy line, "We have the best judges that money can buy"; the city in which a decent private citizen on being hailed as "Judge" whirled round and snarled, "When you call me that, smile."

The city which, although free from smoky industries and blessed by nature with a clear atmosphere, has succeeded, by sheer civic slackness, in making itself one of the murkiest and grimiest cities on the continent. . . .

The city which deliberately educates its masses to a boorishness unknown elsewhere. . . . New York exacts homicidally bad manners of its inhabitants.

Alva Johnston, 1931[1]

We are not strangers to an urban world. We began our national life gathered in towns along the Atlantic seaboard. We built new commercial centers around the Great Lakes and in the Midwest, to serve our westward expansion. Forty million came from Europe to fuel our economy and enrich our community life. This century has seen the steady and rapid migration of farm families—seeking jobs and the promise of the city.

From this rich experience we have learned much. We know that cities can stimulate the best in man, and aggravate the worst. We know the convenience of city life, and its paralysis. We know its promise, and its dark foreboding. What we may only dimly perceive is the gravity of the choice before us. Shall we make our cities livable for ourselves and our posterity? Or shall we by timidity and neglect damn them to fester and decay?

Lyndon B. Johnson, 1966[2]

In 1920, the United States Bureau of the Census announced that for the first time in the nation's history the majority of Americans resided in urban areas. A nation that in 1790 had numbered only 5 percent of its citizens as urban dwellers, and that would in 1970 see almost 75 percent of its population living in or around cities, had passed a significant mark. In many ways, the history of the United States is a history of urban development, and the political culture of the American people is an urban political culture. In the present chapter we shall explore that history and that culture as we trace the process of urbanization and its effect on American politics and policy.

The American City: An Early History

Almost since the beginning, the United States has been, in effect, a nation of cities. The growth and development of the American urban center traces its origins to the very arrival of the earliest European colonists. Although it is true that, out of both necessity and preference, most of the newly arrived settlers devoted the bulk of their attention to agriculture as a means of survival, it is also true that one of the first goals of any group that landed was to establish some sort of urban community around which they could organize their social life, their mutual protection, and their economic forays into the nearby countryside. Though these early settlements were quite small by modern standards, they compared favorably in terms of both size and wealth with English provincial cities of the same period.

As the years passed, these American urban centers gained significantly in commercial importance. They became marketing centers for the exchange of local agricultural produce; focal points for the import of such essential English manufactured goods as hardware, tools, firearms, medicines, and books; and organizing loci for the establishment of regional commercial empires. Such cities as Boston, New York, Philadelphia, and Charleston engaged in vigorous competition for spheres of economic influence and for shares of trans-Atlantic and intracoastal commerce. By the end of the eighteenth century, these and other rival cities had begun to solidify their economic positions and to establish an effective hegemony over their surrounding regions. American urban development was well under way.[3]

So also, it would seem, was the rise of American urban problems. These early cities suffered from poor lighting, inadequate fire protection, crime, unhealthy water treatment, and inadequate sewage disposal, to name only a few of their more noticeable shortcomings. Police protection was left to volunteers, though in some places such "volunteerism" was mandatory, and garbage disposal was generally left to herds of goats and pigs that roamed freely through the streets. Only the fire hazard, probably the most real and frightening threat to the common good, was met with early and concerted action through the development of strict building codes for chimneys, the licensing of chimney sweeps, the adoption of ordinances requiring that filled water buckets be kept in every building, and the formation of numerous volunteer fire departments.[4]

Slowly, but only slowly, governments in the urban centers began to respond more or less effectively to this plethora of problems as citizens began not only to accept but to demand a greater role for the political system in their everyday lives. A case in point is the development of municipal water services in Philadelphia around the turn of the last century. In the 1790s a deadly yellow fever epidemic swept the Northeast, hitting Philadelphia especially hard and leaving in its wake a heightened public concern about cleaning up municipal water supplies. The common practice at the time was for citizens to obtain their water from spring-fed wells through a system of private and public pumps. But as the demand for water grew with the expansion of the urban population, the springs that supplied the water were drawn down and often became polluted with sewage from nearby outhouses and contaminated seepage from graves. As the city continued to grow, it became clear that the shortage of acceptable water would become increasingly acute. In 1798, therefore, responding to public pressure, the city council of Philadelphia retained an engineer-architect named Bernard Latrobe to design and construct the nation's first major public waterworks. Latrobe's system, which pumped water from the Schuylkill River to a high-ground reservoir from which it flowed through wooden pipes to various sections of the city, eventually became a model for municipal water supply in other cities (sixteen such systems were in operation by 1860) and even served as the impetus to the development of that ultimate convenience of modern life, indoor plumbing.[5] Were it not for the yellow fever epidemic and the accompanying public outcry, however, the development of these systems might have been postponed indefinitely.

Other civic advances were also made during the years before the Civil War. In 1822, for example, Boston installed the first system of gas lights, and the next year the city followed with the nation's first publicly owned sewage system. Regular stagecoach service was begun in New York in the same decade, with the introduction of railbound horse-car lines following shortly afterward. And in 1837 Boston established the first nonvolunteer municipal fire department.[6]

These varied municipal services were less quick to spread, however, than another roughly contemporary advance, the development of the municipal police force. We have already seen in chapter 1 that race- or labor-related mob violence in later years gave rise to detective forces, the National Guard, and other police organizations. The same point may be argued with respect to the creation of municipal police forces during this earlier period, for it was a continuing wave of urban disorder between 1830 and 1855 that helped develop the middle- and upper-class constituency that first demanded, and later supported, the establishment of an effective urban constabulary to maintain order and protect life and property. In that twenty-five-year period of rapid growth, Philadelphia, Providence, and Cincinnati were the scenes of major race riots, while antiabolitionists rampaged in New York and Boston; anti-Catholic and anti-Irish outbreaks occurred in Philadelphia, Boston, Baltimore, St. Louis, and Louisville; and bread riots hit New York. Boston responded by creating a municipal police force in 1838. New York followed suit in 1844, Philadelphia in 1850, and Baltimore in 1857.[7]

Despite all these efforts at improvement, however, American cities in the years before the Civil War were scarcely showplaces of urban efficiency. Perhaps the sense of the period is best captured by Daniel MacLeod in his description of the city that greeted incoming New York Mayor Fernando Wood in 1855.

> He found the streets of this great metropolis ill paved, broken by carts and omnibuses into ruts and perillous gullies, obstructed by boxes and signboards, impassible by reason of thronging vehicles, and filled with filth and garbage which was left where it had been thrown, to rot and send out its pestiferous fumes, breathing fever, cholera, and a host of diseases all over the city. He found hacks, carts, and omnibuses choking the thoroughfares, the Jehu drivers dashing through the crowds furiously, reckless of life; women and children were knocked down, trampled on, and the ruffians drove on uncaught. Hackmen overcharged and were insolent to their passengers; baggage-smashers haunted the docks, tearing one's baggage about, stealing it sometimes,

and demanding from timid women and strange men unnumbered fees for doing mischief or for doing nothing at all; emigrant runners, half bulldog and half leech, burst in crowds upon the docks of arriving ships, carried off the poor foreign people, fleeced them and set them adrift upon the town; rowdyism seemed to rule the city; it was at the risk of your life that you walked the streets late at night; the club, the knife, the slungshot [*sic*] and revolver were in constant activity; the Sunday low dram shop polluted the Sabbath air, disturbed the sacred stillness, and in the afternoon and night sent forth its crowds of wretches infuriate with bad liquor to howl and blaspheme, to fight or lie prone on the sidewalk or in the gutters.[8]

It was during the decades following the Civil War that the city really came into its own as the true center of American life and the dominant force in the political culture of the nation. Three principal factors contributed to this development. The first of these was the creation and expansion of mass transit systems not only within cities but among them. The development of urban mass transit had begun, as noted above, with the introduction of the omnibus, a large horse-drawn coach that carried passengers over fixed routes for fixed fares, in Manhattan in 1827. Within twenty-five years almost 700 such vehicles were in operation in New York City alone. As the *New York Herald* described the experience of riding in such a conveyance in 1864,

Modern martyrdom may be succinctly defined as riding in a New York omnibus. The discomforts, inconveniences, and annoyances of a trip on one of these vehicles are almost intolerable. From the beginning to the end of the journey a constant quarrel is progressing. The driver quarrels with the passengers, and the passengers quarrel with the driver. There are quarrels about getting out and quarrels about getting in. There are quarrels about change and quarrels about the ticket swindle. The driver swears at the passengers and the passengers harangue the driver. . . . Respectable clergymen in white chokers are obliged to listen to loud oaths. Ladies are disgusted, frightened, and insulted. Children are alarmed and lift up their voices and weep. Indignant gentlemen rise to remonstrate with the irate Jehu and are suddenly bumped back into their seats, twice as indignant as before, besides being involved in supplementary quarrels with those other passengers upon whose corns they have accidentally trodden. Thus the omnibus rolls along, a perfect Bedlam on Wheels.[9]

This obvious discomfort notwithstanding, some 120,000 persons boarded New York's omnibuses each day.

As transportation technology advanced, the omnibus was replaced in New York and elsewhere by alternative vehicles. In 1870, for example, New York opened its first elevated railway, while San Francisco and Chicago followed with cable cars shortly afterward. Cleveland, Kansas City, Richmond, Atlanta, Montgomery (Alabama), Appleton (Wisconsin), and Scranton all claim the first electric street railway, with dates ranging from 1884 to 1889. Whichever claim is valid, total mileage of such railways exceeded 8,000 by 1890, and reached 29,830 by 1904. (It was the system in Richmond, incidentally, that gave rise to the common term for such street railways, "trolley," which was a corruption of the word "troller," the name given to a device invented by electrician Frank Sprague to transfer electricity to the vehicle from overhead wires.) Boston opened the first American subway, a one and two-thirds mile stretch under Tremont Street, in 1897, and New York, which had been planning such an undertaking since 1891, contracted for its first subway in 1900. And since the 1850s when the Chicago and Milwaukee Railroad (now the Chicago and Northwestern) had constructed a depot in Evanston, Illinois, north of Chicago, rail links with outlying areas had provided commuter service for a number of cities. In short, urban transit was beginning to weave cities together (as well as facilitate the flight of those who could afford to leave them), to make possible the social, economic, and political integration of urban society on a scale previously unimagined. Largely because of the development of urban mass transit, the city remained a viable entity.[10]

Intercity rail service, which also saw its greatest growth during this period, contributed to urban development as well. In the East this was true in two ways: first, this service provided increasingly efficient links for shipping and commerce among the various urban centers; and second, the needs of the railroads for capital equipment fired the furnaces of many an industrial city. Thus, commerce and industry were both stimulated and facilitated in established population centers by the extension of the railroads. In the West these roads were more important still. Not only did the railroads make the cities of the West accessible, but in many instances they were decisive in the very creation and ultimate survival of these fledgling urban areas. The Northern Pacific Railroad, for example, in effect created the city of Tacoma, Washington, as its western terminus in 1873, and the company attempted to destroy the rival city of Seattle in order to assure Tacoma's regional dominance. (Seattle was rescued from obscurity twenty years later by the arrival of the Great Northern Railroad.) Similarly, Colorado Springs was built by General William J. Palmer out of his profits from the building of the Denver and Rio Grande Railroad. Other cities, such as Duluth, Minnesota, however, faired considerably less well. When the Northern Pacific went bankrupt in the Panic of 1873, more than half the businesses in Duluth closed, the city forfeited its charter and became a village, tax receipts dropped by some 75 percent, and the municipal debt was written down to fifty cents on the dollar.

But nowhere was the importance of the railroads more clearly illustrated than in California, where the Southern Pacific Railroad was dominant not only in the politics of several cities but at the state level as well. In 1872, for example, in exchange for $100,000 worth of waterfront property, the Southern Pacific agreed to make Oakland its western terminus. That same year, in exchange for a subsidy of $610,000 and control over a small railroad that served the city through the harbor of San Pedro, the Southern Pacific agreed not to bypass Los Angeles on its main line. The railroad then used its positions in Oakland and Los Angeles to gain a foothold in San Francisco. Once that foothold was obtained, however, the company used its position in San Francisco to discriminate in freight rates against Los Angeles—even to the extent of entering into agreements to restrict competition with the steamship companies operating between the two cities. The Southern Pacific subsidized newspapers, provided judges and other officials with free rail passes, and attempted to control street railroads, ferries, and shipping. The railroad controlled both California political parties, two of the three railroad commissioners who served from 1879 to 1882, and local political machines in Los Angeles and San Francisco. The names of its organizers, Collis P. Huntington, Leland Stanford, Mark Hopkins, and Charles Crocker, remain familiar to Californians and others to this day. The enormity of the profits of the Southern Pacific is suggested by the fact that, from his share alone, Stanford founded the university named for his son with an endowment that was, at the time, more than double those of Harvard or Columbia.[11]

If mass transit was the first contributing factor to the quickening pace of urbanization in the United States, a second and no less vital element was the rapid industrial development that marked the latter part of the nineteenth century and the early years of the twentieth. To some extent, the nation's cities benefited directly from advances in technology, particularly from Brush's outdoor arc lamp, Edison's incandescent bulb, Bell's telephone, or even, eventually, the automobile. The development of apartment buildings and department stores helped simplify the meeting of housing and commercial needs, while steel-framed skyscrapers contributed to the efficient use of the limited space available in central areas.[12] Through its pioneering efforts in these and other methods to improve the quality of urban life, the United States began to assume a role of leadership in the development of modern technologies.

Far more important for the development of urban centers, however, was the basic impact that industrialization had on movement within the population, for the virtual explosion of factories of all kinds upon the urban scene created unprecedented economic opportunities that began to attract people to the cities like flies to honey. Rochester and Philadelphia became famous for shoe manufacturing, New York City for clothing, the mill towns of Massachusetts for textiles, Minneapolis for flour, Omaha and Chicago for beef, Milwaukee for beer, Cleveland and Pittsburgh for coal and iron, Houston and Oklahoma City for oil, Detroit for automobiles, Akron for tires, and so forth. Each of these cities and others as well built upon a commercial base to develop capital, upon the availability of labor, upon transportation provided largely by the railroads, and upon product specialization to draw to themselves increasing numbers of workers and consumers whose arrival would in itself create both the demand and the means for still further economic expansion. In this way Denver, which established itself as a mining and minerals center, grew from nothing to a city of 134,000 between 1860 and 1900, and Memphis, a cottonseed oil center, expanded from 23,000 to more than 100,000 in the same period. Between 1860 and 1910, the number of American cities whose populations exceeded 100,000 rose from nine to fifty, those with populations between 25,000 and 100,000 from twenty-six to 178, and those with populations between 10,000 and 25,000 from fifty-eight to 369. By 1890, New York and Brooklyn, with a combined population of nearly two and one-half million, rivaled Paris in size, while Chicago and Philadelphia, each with more than one million residents, ranked sixth and seventh, respectively, among the cities of the Western world.[13]

The third and final factor contributing to the growth of cities during this period was the large number of migrants and immigrants who sought opportunity in the burgeoning urban centers of the United States. Migration from South to North, East to West, and rural areas to cities contributed to the development of the labor pools that were essential to the nation's rapid industrialization, as did the waves of immigrants from Europe who literally poured into the country by the millions during the Industrial Revolution. The migrants were generally unskilled workers who settled into low-paying positions with little expectation of advancement. However, many of the immigrants were skilled workers with visions of upward mobility. Glassmakers from Britain and Holland vitalized the economies of Corning, New York, Pittsburgh, and other cities; German brewers helped bolster St. Louis, Chicago, and Milwaukee; and skilled mechanics from England and Germany were welcomed in many cities.[14] To the immigrant, America was truly a land of opportunity, a nation that was greater than all its contributing elements, yet a nation of which the newcomer could nevertheless be a part. Nowhere is this more clearly illustrated than in the words of David Quixano, a character in Israel Zangwill's play *The Melting Pot*, which was first performed on Broadway in 1908 and whose title became a byword of American social thought. Proclaimed Quixano:

> America is God's Crucible, the great Melting Pot where all the races of Europe are melting and reforming! Here you stand, good folk, think I, when I see them at Ellis Island, here you stand in your fifty groups with your fifty languages and histories, and your fifty blood hatreds and rivalries, but you won't be long like that brothers, for these are the

fires of God you've come to—these are the fires of God. A fig for your feuds and vendettas! German and Frenchman, Irishman and Englishman, Jews and Russians—into the Crucible with you all! God is making the American. . . .[15]

Bosses and Gangs: The Shame of the Cities

Not all the immigrants, of course, considered themselves to be as fortunate over the long run as the fictitious Mr. Quixano, and not all Americans, as should be abundantly clear from our analysis of the preceding chapter and as will become more so as we proceed, welcomed the influx of the foreign born with open arms. To the contrary, conflict, friction, prejudice, and distrust were as much the order of the day as was optimism, and the increasing disillusionment of the newest arrivals was matched by the continuing resentment of the "native" Americans. This was particularly true with regard to the Irish, who became the objects of distrust and discrimination in part because they entered the United States in such tremendous numbers (several million between 1840 and 1890 alone), in part because they were poorly educated and generally unskilled, and in part because they were Catholics entering (and frequently altering the religious and political balance within) an overwhelmingly Protestant nation. Typical of the outrage expressed by those on the receiving end of this influx were the comments of William S. Bennett, a member both of the Congress and of the Immigrant Commission, who noted in 1909:

> Our friends on the other side of the Atlantic took advantage of that [the absence of United States immigration restrictions], and thirty years ago societies were actually organized for the purpose of sending to this country criminals, paupers, old people, and the class that we call unfortunate women. They advertised in the newspapers for subscriptions. People left them legacies in their wills and they used that money to bring to this country the unfortunate from the lands across the sea. . . .
>
> It went so far that the British government, about twenty-six or twenty-seven years ago, chartered a ship called the "Formosa" and sent it around Ireland, and from the workhouses in Ireland filled that ship and then started it straight for New York. There was instance after

> instance where the people from that ship were in the workhouse in New York City with British workhouse clothes still on them within twenty-four hours after the ship landed.[16]

There was, it should be pointed out, a certain validity to the claim that immigrant populations, though surely not the Irish alone, contributed their share to what was seen at the time as a serious increase in urban crime. This crime wave was summarized and put in contemporary perspective in 1908 by Professor Charles D. Bushnell.

> Murder and homicides in the twenty years between 1885 and 1904 have increased more than three times as fast the population. . . . Their growth has been almost steady, showing it is not the resultant of accidental causes, but of some sinister evil in the nation, which is steadily working increasing wrong.
>
> Of professional criminals, such as burglars, footpads, gamblers and other crooks, there are now known and estimated to be some 300,000 in the country, getting an average income each of perhaps $1,500 a year, and causing an additional national expense for police protection, to say nothing of extra expenses for locks, safes, alarms, etc., of $2,000,000 more, making a total annual loss to the nation from this source, more than counterbalancing the value of all our annual exports of manufactures, or nearly equal to the annual running expenses of all our churches, benevolent institutions, public schools, institutions of higher education and home missions of every kind.[17]

And while the immigrant was far from the sole participant in this rapidly expanding "industry," his role was undeniably substantial. The police commissioner of New York City at the time, Theodore Bingham, estimated that some 85 percent of the criminals in the city were of what he termed "exotic origin," that is, immigrants, but he argued that this should not be taken as a condemnation of the immigrants, since fully 85 percent of the city's population was either foreign-born or of foreign parentage. Thus, in Bingham's view, the immigrants' share of criminal activity was proportionate to their share of the population.[18]

Among the most conspicuous manifestations of the presumed criminality of the immigrants were the street gangs that were formed in the slum neighborhoods where the most recent, and as yet least successful, arrivals on the American urban scene were forced to live. In the older cities of the United States, slums had begun to appear as early as the 1840s, and it was at about that time as well that gang activity first attracted the attention of the public. The development of gangs on the East Side of New York was fairly typical. In the mid-nineteenth century the East Side gangs were mostly Irish, and their activities consisted largely of frequent brawls with weapons ranging from fists to lead pipes. With names such as the Rabbit Foot Gang or the Gas House Boys, these small bands of youths survived on petty crimes such as theft or purse snatching, and they benefited from close relationships with Irish politicians, for whom they performed such tasks as distributing circulars and election literature, spotting unreliable voters, spying on rival candidates, augmenting the applause and cheering for favored street speakers, and disrupting opposition rallies. In return, each group was in effect granted some degree of neighborhood hegemony and received help from the politicians when problems arose with the police. These Irish street gangs were important participants on the side of the police (and against the city's black population) in the draft riots of 1863, but otherwise their violence was less organized and generally less political in content.

Toward the end of the century, as the sources of immigration shifted, the principal population of the slum districts—and as a consequence the dominant force in East Side street gang activity—turned increasingly Italian. During this period, the weaponry of gang war escalated, with knives the most common arms, and the number of violent crimes committed by gang members rose substantially. More importantly, however, it was during this relatively brief period of Italian domination that the gangs began to focus their attentions on the remainder of the community instead of being satisfied simply to fight among themselves. And where the Irish hooligans (the word derives from the name of a New York gang leader) had eventually graduated into the political associations and Irish-controlled urban political machines that rose to prominence during the middle to late nineteenth century (and of which we shall have more to say below), the Italian youths graduated in significant numbers into the ranks of the professional criminals who gained prominence in the 1920s and 1930s.

By 1920, however, the East Side of New York was populated mostly by Jews from Russia and Eastern Europe, members of yet another wave of newcomers, and the street gangs, too, reflected the change. Led by such colorful figures as "The Kid Dropper," who got his nickname because as a youngster he had gotten money by knocking over children who were leaning over sidewalk dice games and stealing their pennies, the gangs of this period initially consisted of some twenty to forty members who generally held low-paying jobs (driving laundry wagons, pressing trousers, cleaning windows) and who engaged in petty crime in their spare time.

This pattern was altered, though, when the gangs were hired by building contractors to protect strikebreakers in labor disputes. Members of the gangs began to carry firearms, and the gangs themselves began to compete with one another for the lucrative protection business. Such a situation led naturally to dangerous rivalries, and an East Side gang war finally broke out in 1922, when the leader of a rival gang, Jacob (Little Augie) Augen, unwisely made advances to The Kid Dropper's girlfriend. In retaliation, The Kid Dropper issued a warning that Little Augie would be killed. Augen went into hiding, but when he emerged a week later he was the object of a shotgun attack from a passing automobile that claimed the life of a fellow gang member. The Kid Dropper was immediately arrested, but when the police were unable to prove a case against him, an agreement was reached that he would be given safe conduct to Grand Central Station in return for which he would join his brother in Omaha and never return to New York. The police took elaborate precautions, cordoning off streets, putting The Kid Dropper in a taxi cab with two detectives, positioning four additional detectives with drawn pistols in a second cab in front, and assigning fifty uniformed policemen to protect the procession, but a small youth named Louis Cohen managed to conceal a gun under a newspaper, reach into the cab, and shoot The Kid Dropper three times in the back. The gang war that followed lasted several years.[19]

Nor was New York alone in its gang violence. A sociological study published by the University of Chicago Press in the mid-1920s, for example, identified 1,313 distinct gangs in that city with a combined membership estimated to be in excess of 25,000. Here the progression of events was similar to that on Manhattan's East Side. In the area of Maxwell Street, for instance, the Irish dominated from the 1850s until about 1900, when they were displaced by Germans and Jews, who were themselves later displaced by Lithuanians. In the Bridgeport section, the Irish gave way to Germans, who in turn gave way to Poles. The various all-white gangs of Chicago, often called "athletic clubs," were active participants in the race riots of 1919, though the black participants in the riots were not at the time organized into gangs.[20]

A rather different type of urban gang extant during this period was found in the Chinese communities of such cities as Chicago, New York, and San Francisco. Known as tongs, the Chinese word for protective societies, these organizations originated in California and Nevada during the Gold Rush in order to guarantee the protection of their members against enemies in rival tongs and against members of other races. As secondary activities, the tongs engaged in gambling, extortion, blackmail, slave dealing, drug smuggling, and similar pursuits. The most fearsome aspect of the groups, however, was their maintenance of rosters of paid killers who willingly engaged in carefully planned and executed murders. It was this institutionalized preparation for homicide that made the so-called Tong Wars in New York and other cities during the early years of the present century among the bloodiest gang conflicts in the nation's history.[21]

But if gangs and criminal activity were one province of the immigrants who settled in America's urban centers, politics, which some, of course, would argue to be little different, was another. Indeed, it was principally through the control and manipulation of urban political systems that many of these immigrant groups, most notably the Irish, gradually assured their success in the new land. For it was during the period of rapid urban growth and virtually unlimited immigration, and in no small way precisely because of those two closely related forces, that there arose in cities all across the United States a system of political bosses and machines whose principal function, aside from graft and corruption, was to serve the downtrodden urban masses. Building on the support of immigrant slum dwellers and organizing around such protopolitical groups as the still numerous volunteer fire departments and the Irish street gangs, immigrant politicians took advantage of the growing demand for expanding city services (and the associated flow of public funds) to improve their own personal positions as well as those of their various ethnic groups. Writing in 1914 of the effectiveness of the Irish in particular in such undertakings (and reflecting as well the anti-Irish sentiments common at the time), sociologist Edward Alsworth Ross suggested both the breadth of this phenomenon of control of city government and what he saw as the reasons for its success. In 1912, Ross noted,

> of the eighteen principal personages in the city government of Chicago, fourteen had Irish names and three had German names. Of the eleven principal officials in the city government of Boston, nine had Irish names, and of the forty-nine members of the Lower House from the city of Boston, forty were obviously of Hibernian extraction. In San Francisco, the mayor, all the heads of the municipal departments, and ten out of eighteen members on the board of supervisors, bore names reminiscent of the Green Isle. As far back as 1871, of 112 chiefs of police from twenty-two States who attended the national police convention, seventy-seven bore Irish names, and eleven had German names. In 1881, of the chiefs of police in forty-eight cities, thirty-three were clearly Irish, and five were clearly German. . . .
>
> United by strong race feelings, [the Irish] held together as voters, and, although never a clear majority, were able in time to capture control of most of the greater municipalities. Now for all their fine Celtic traits, these Irish immigrants had neither the temperament nor the training to make a success of popular government. They were totally without experience of the kind Americans had acquired in the working of democratic institutions. . . .
>
> Warm-hearted, sociable, clannish, and untrained, the naturalized Irish failed to respect the first principles of civics. "What is the Constitution between friends?" expresses their point of view.[22]

Beginning in the early to middle nineteenth century and continuing well into the twentieth—or in some cases even to the present day—these immigrant-based political machines constituted the dominant feature on the urban political landscape in the United States. And although it is true that such organizations raided the public treasuries and reduced to its lowest common denominator the quality of political exchange in the nation's cities, it must also be noted that they served some distinct and relatively necessary purposes that earlier urban administrations and other institutions had, in fact, failed to serve. For it was these political machines, and not the established political order, that successfully brought about the political integration of the immigrant classes in the United States; and it was these political machines, and not the established but morally too self-righteous social and charitable institutions of the day, that saw to the basic welfare of the masses and provided for their social and economic needs. In this way, the political machines responded to their constituents in ways that were beyond either the will or the abilities of the "proper" authorities.[23] If the machines endured and themselves became, in effect, the establishment, it was not because they were corrupt, which they most assuredly were, but rather because they were more effective and more reliable in meeting the needs of the people than were any of the available alternatives.

Machines and bosses ruled in many cities across the country. Boston had its "Czar" Martin Lomasney, who built upon the organizational base provided by his leadership of a gang (he had once had a "job" smashing baggage at a railroad depot) to play a major role in the politics of both the city and the State of Massachusetts around the turn of the century. Philadelphia had first its "King" James McManes, whose empire building started when he was trustee of the municipal gas works (from which position he was able to fashion a patronage army), and later its "Duke" Edwin H. Vare, who rose from a ward politician in South Philadelphia to the powerbroker who held effective control of the city by 1916. Cincinnati had its "Old Boy" George B. Cox; Chicago its Frederick Lundin, "Big Bill" Thompson, and Roger C. Sullivan; and San Francisco its Abraham Ruef. Later still, Jersey City had its Frank Hague, Albany its four O'Connell brothers, and Chicago its Kelly-Nash Machine. The list could go on literally for pages.[24]

One of the more powerful bosses at the turn of the century was William Lorimer, the so-called Blond Boss of Chicago, who controlled the Republican party in both the city and the state of Illinois for some ten years. Lorimer was an English immigrant whose power was centered in the immigrant neighborhoods of Chicago's west side, where he was admired for his solid family life, his loyalty to his friends, and, not incidentally, the political favors he was able to dispense. In 1909 Lorimer was elected (by the state legislature) to the United States Senate, but sometime afterward the *Chicago Tribune* published the confession of a state assemblyman that he had been paid $1,000 to vote for the Chicago boss. After a lengthy proceeding that included two Senate investigations, Lorimer was expelled from the Senate, though upon his return to Chicago he was met with a hero's welcome. He was later tried for banking violations (Lorimer and a downstate businessman had established a bank shortly after the bribery charge had been raised; they had been granted a charter on the strength of the fact that Lorimer was a United States Senator) relating to such practices as giving inadequately secured loans to his political friends in return for the deposit of public monies, but he was acquitted of the charges (though his partner was convicted). Lorimer shook the jurors' hands, promised to reimburse all those who had suffered losses when his bank failed, and announced that he would run for Congress that fall. He never kept the promises, but in the late 1920s he did regain much of his previous influence in Chicago politics. Lorimer died in September 1934.[25]

Lorimer, Cox, McManes, and the others notwithstanding, however, the most notorious, and hence the most noteworthy, of all the urban political machines was New York's Tammany Hall. Tammany Hall, or the Society of Saint Tammany, was formed around 1789 by William Mooney as a benevolent and patriotic society; it first became an active political organization on the Democratic side in 1799 at the urging of Aaron Burr, who used the group as a personal power base.[26] Its first victory came in 1800, when Tammany forces captured both houses of the New York state legislature, thereby handing the first significant defeat to the then-dominant Federalists and establishing Tammany (and its ally, Thomas Jefferson) as the political refuge of the less-favored classes.[27] As the voting strength of its working-class constituency grew in the early years of the nineteenth century, Tammany's influence expanded as well. When the Panic of 1837 and its attendant depression struck the city, Tammany saw to it that New York's poor received food, fuel, and clothing, a relief mission that was extended to the growing numbers of Irish immigrants during the succeeding decade. The society then built upon its charity and its well-deserved reputation of concern with the well-being of the common people to move closer and closer to control of the machinery of the Democratic party, a plum that promised not only opportunities for future public service but a great potential for patronage and self-aggrandizement as well.

William Marcy Tweed was the first scion of Tammany to put it all together. Tweed was a former neighborhood gang leader and later head of a volunteer fire company who worked his way up through Tammany politics until he achieved control of New York City in the late 1860s. Working with a crew that included the likes of "Slippery Dick" Connolly and "Brains" Sweeney, Tweed operated on two levels for his and the organization's benefit. First, to assure that they would retain political hegemony over the city, Tweed's operatives sought to control the electoral process. Their efforts included multiple voting in the names of falsely registered citizens, bribery of opposition electoral judges and falsification of election results, and the rapid naturalization of immigrants who promised to vote the Tammany line. In October 1868, for example, a single Tweed judge naturalized an average of 718 potential Democrats per day, and three years later *The Nation* estimated that—through offices, sinecures, contracts, public works, pending indictments, suspended sentences, penalties, licenses, ordinances, and the like—the Tweed Ring controlled not less than 60,000 votes, no mean total when counted as a bloc.[28]

At the same time, Boss Tweed and his henchmen were busy on a second front, the milking of the city treasury through padded bills, kickbacks, and other devices. During the Tweed years, the costs of public construction were inflated to at least double to allow for skimming, and bills from tradesmen doing business with the city were split, with 35 percent going to the tradesmen and 65 percent to the Tweed Ring. In 1870 alone, the city's debt increased from $36 million to $97 million, and by the end of the following year it exceeded 12 percent of the total value of real estate in the city. In addition, Tweed used his control over judges and court injunctions to give Jay Gould, of whom we shall hear more in the next chapter, control of the Erie Railroad, in return for which Tweed was named a director and legal advisor of the company at an annual salary of $100,000. In the meantime, the lesser lights of the machine gathered in bribes, protection money, and even stock tips. For a suitable fee, one could obtain from the Tweed Ring anything from prior knowledge of municipal real estate dealings to informal licenses for gambling or prostitution.[29]

After investigations by a special committee, an exposé by the *New York Times*, and a spate of damaging cartoons by former schoolmate Thomas Nast (which prompted Tweed to comment, "We must stop them damned pictures. My constituents can't read but they can see pictures."), and after he had had ample opportunity to destroy substantial amounts of evidence, Tweed was finally arrested in October 1871 on a warrant issued in a civil suit for malfeasance. He was released, though, when his bail of $1 million was met by Jay Gould. In 1873 Tweed was convicted on twelve counts of fraud, for which he served a prison sentence of one and one-half years. Upon his release, Tweed found himself the subject of still other legal actions, and when he was unable to make the $3 million bail, he was locked up in the Ludlow Street jail. His jailors permitted him to make periodic visits to his family, however, and on one such visit in December 1875, he escaped, going first to Florida, then to Cuba, and finally to Spain. There he was recaptured when a Nast cartoon that pictured Tweed as a policeman dragging two young boys toward a placard reading "Reward. No Questions Asked" came into the possession of authorities in the town of Vigo. Recognizing Tweed from the caricature, but mistaking him as a kidnapper, they arrested the fugitive and sent him back to the United States. Tweed died in jail in 1878.[30]

Tweed's successor at Tammany Hall was "Honest John" Kelly, a longtime foe of the Tweed Ring who, after choosing leadership of Tammany over entry into the priesthood, displayed an intriguing blend of boss tactics and reform rhetoric. The first of a long line of Irish Catholic Tammany leaders (Tweed had been a Scottish Protestant), Kelly reconstructed and revitalized the coalition of firemen, local Irish gangs, and immigrant families upon which Tammany power was based, created a formal organizational arrangement within the society covering all authority relationships from the voters to the boss himself, and streamlined the mechanisms for dispensing personal favors that served to maintain the loyalty of Tammany's following. He even established patronage quotas for his district leaders and neighborhood bosses so as to reduce the competition and friction within the machine. Even so, Kelly was not able to control everyone around him. His first mayor, William Havemeyer, for example, unable to understand why Kelly should have influence over mayoral appointments merely because he had been instrumental in the mayor's election, once commented, "Men who go about with the prefix of 'honest' to their names are often rogues." Honest John sued Havemeyer for libel, but the issue was never settled since the mayor died of apoplexy on the opening day of the trial. His successor, William Wickham, named Kelly to the post of city comptroller in recognition for his services.[31]

When John Kelly retired from Tammany in 1884, the power vacuum he left behind was quickly filled by his most trusted aide, Richard Croker. Croker had risen through Tammany's ranks in typical fashion, first by fighting his way to the top of a gang of Irish toughs, the Fourth Avenue Tunnel Gang, later by joining a volunteer fire department and being given a city job by Boss Tweed's comptroller, Richard Connolly, and finally by astutely playing one faction against another as he worked his way up the hierarchy of the society. But Croker, of whom reformer Lincoln Steffens once wrote, "Richard Croker never said anything to me that was not true unless it was a statement for publication," differed significantly in style from Tweed and Kelly. Where these earlier political bosses, and especially Tweed, had encouraged and participated in direct raids on the public treasury, Croker practiced more subtle forms of corruption once described by the erstwhile philosopher of Tammany Hall, George Washington Plunkitt, as "honest graft." ("Everybody is talkin' these days," Plunkitt once noted, reflecting on his own experience, "about Tammany men growin' rich on 'graft,' but nobody thinks of drawin' the distinction between honest graft and dishonest graft. There's an honest graft, and I'm an example of how it works. I might sum up the whole thing by sayin': 'I seen my opportunities and I took 'em.'") Honest graft, it seems, consisted of receiving stock in corporations doing business with New York City in exchange for the letting of contracts and franchises; and the practice of such graft, particularly during the term of Mayor Hugh Grant, when Croker served as city chamberlain (the official charged with overseeing the investment of city funds), made the Tammany chief a wealthy man. This financial success, in turn, contributed to Croker's popularity with the immigrant masses, who saw him as something of an Irish version of a Horatio Alger hero. At the same time, however, Croker also allowed the customary abuses of "dishonest" graft to continue at lower levels of the organization, and he was, in fact, the first Tammany leader to give control over local patronage wholly to local leaders. This served to retain the loyalties of lower echelon leaders, but it also served to create a number of lesser machines within Tammany that ultimately weakened the power of Croker and his successors. It was the breakdown of the coalition thus created that led in 1901 to Croker's own retirement to a castle in Ireland, where he died in 1922.[32]

It was during this period in the history of Tammany, incidentally, that various of the Hall's spokesmen were most candid in their assessment of the role of the political machine in New York City. We have already seen one example of this candor in George Washington Plunkitt's analysis of honest graft, but that was only one of many similar statements. On another occasion, for instance, commenting on a reform that promised considerable difficulty for his beloved society, Plunkitt observed, "The Civil Service law is the biggest fraud of the age. It's the curse of the nation. There can't be no real patriotism while it lasts. I know more than one man in the past years who worked for the ticket and was just overflowing with patriotism, but when he was knocked out by the Civil Service humbug he got to hate his country and became an anarchist."[33] On a related point, William S. Devery, still another Tammany stalwart, once noted that "the graft belongs to the people, and youse is the people. When youse give me the office, youse get the graft."[34] Or, as it was put rather succinctly in a 1905 campaign ditty that played upon the "Indian rites" employed by the society,

Big Chief sits in his teepee
Cheering braves to victory
Tammany, Tammany
Swamp 'em, swamp 'em
Get the wampum
Taammanee![35]

There followed, interspersed with periods of reform such as the era of Fiorello LaGuardia, a number of other Tammany bosses including "Big Tim" Sullivan, "Silent Charlie" Murphy, and Carmine De Sapio and Tammany mayors such as "Gentleman Jim" Walker. But although the faces changed over the years, and although different factions within the Society of Saint Tammany struggled for control, the reasons for Tammany's success remained relatively constant. For Tammany Hall had, since the early decades of the nineteenth century, professed to be the one true friend of the immigrant in a city of immigrants, the source of comfort and assistance that could always be counted upon. Tammany had leaders who understood the common man and who always put the Hall in the forefront of movements to increase the privileges of the masses. Tammany Hall took its politics seriously, espoused only the most popular of causes, and, although openly contemptuous of what it viewed as "idealistic" reform, always supported practical reform, which it saw as molding the government of New York City to best serve the interests of the majority of its inhabitants. For all its corruption, Tammany Hall was a genuinely populist urban political organization, and its effectiveness as such is amply evidenced by the extended period of its influence.[36]

Not everyone, of course, was charmed with the bosses of Tammany Hall and the other city machines around the country, and there occurred from time to time a number of reform movements aimed at ousting one or another corrupt political machine in favor of such alternative devices as nonpartisan elections, citywide as opposed to ward balloting, and the employment of nonelected city managing experts.[37] The leaders of these reform movements generally assumed that, once given the opportunity, most citizens would, in fact, do their part to "throw the rascals out" in favor of good government slates. That this assumption was of at best questionable validity, however, is suggested by Brewster Adams, a journalist who in 1903 recounted the story of a friend prominent in the reform movement in New York who told

> of a men's club in which he became greatly interested. He spent several evenings before election explaining to them the significance and value of a vote. Later he was thunderstruck to find that the club had voted Tammany to a man. It was explained to him as follows:

"You see, we never knew what a vote was worth until you told us, and so we all struck for five dollars for our votes instead of two dollars, being what they had always given us, and we got it."[38]

One of the more notable of these efforts at reform was that spearheaded by another journalist, Lincoln Steffens, shortly after the turn of the century. In a series of articles published by *McClure's* (and later compiled in a book entitled *The Shame of the Cities*), Steffens attacked the practice of government and politics in St. Louis, Minneapolis, Pittsburgh, Philadelphia, Cincinnati, San Francisco, Chicago, and New York, arguing in each case that the real culprits were not the grafting politicians but the citizens who permitted them to get away with their manifold corrupt practices. When, in the light of these arguments, the public was eager to begin the task of reform, however, and turned to Steffens for advice, he found that he had none to offer, and as a result the movement degenerated into little more than a passing wave of indignation.[39] Indeed, it was not a reform movement of any sort that finally succeeded in bringing down many of the nation's urban political machines—but rather a much more fundamental shift in the conditions of their existence. This is perhaps best exemplified once again by the case of Tammany Hall, in which urban historians have identified six principal factors that appear to have contributed to the decline and fall of the New York Democratic machine.

The first of these six factors was an act of Congress passed in 1921 that, for the first time, established a quota system for immigration and that had the net effect of substantially reducing the number of persons arriving in the United States each year. This legislation was, in effect, a "time bomb" under Tammany Hall, for it meant that the legions of immigrants upon whom Tammany power rested must, over the long run, find their numbers depleted and their impact on New York politics significantly diminished. Thus, as the years passed, Tammany was destined to lose its primary constituency and, as a consequence, its power.

Had this been the only misfortune to befall the Hall, of course, and had Tammany's leaders recognized the danger in time, an alternative power base might have been constructed and the organization itself rescued. But that was not to be the case. For in

1930 and for two years afterward, the leaders of Tammany were to be distracted and the public alternately entertained and incensed by the revelations that poured forth from a series of three investigations of Tammany activities conducted by Samuel Seabury, one each on behalf of the state's judges, Governor Franklin D. Roosevelt, and the Republican-controlled state legislature, respectively. Seabury found corruption in city government from top to bottom, and the pressure that his charges created forced several Tammany politicians, including the popular Mayor James Walker, to resign their positions. The public indignation that accompanied Seabury's investigations, however, was something quite new (Tammany graft had, after all, never been much of a secret) and no doubt resulted from a third factor in the decline of the machine, the Great Depression. The years of prosperity, particularly in the 1920s, had enabled people to turn their backs on municipal wrongdoing (as a New York union man had told Lincoln Steffens some years earlier, "I know what Parks [a Tammany politician] is doing, but what do I care. He has raised my wages. Let him have his graft!"), but the Depression brought with it a change of perception. Suddenly the protectors of the working man of earlier days were seen as crooks taking money from workers and shopkeepers who didn't have any. The practices had not changed, but the circumstances had, and the cost in political support for the machine was almost more than it could bear.

But there was still more to come. In the 1930s, President Franklin D. Roosevelt and the nation's labor unions combined to deprive Tammany and other similar political machines of their place and their strength in the political life of American cities. Under Roosevelt, for example, the federal government began to take on precisely those social-welfare functions that Tammany and others had used to such great advantage. No longer was it necessary to give loyal service to a ward boss or a district leader if one was in need. Now one could simply turn to that collective relative, Uncle Sam. Thus, not only were the nation's Tammanies being slowly deprived of their constituencies but those constituencies were being offered an alternative source of succor.

On top of this, local political machines were being supplanted within the very political parties (particularly, but not exclusively, the Democratic party) that they had so long manipulated to gain and hold power by yet a second creature of the Roosevelt years, the newly legitimized and rapidly expanding labor unions. Once their economic power was accepted, these labor organizations began to turn their not inconsiderable skills, experience, and resources to acquiring political power, and during the 1930s and 1940s they demonstrated that they, too, could mobilize electoral support on a large scale. In this way, organized labor constituted a direct threat to the claims of the machines upon the parties.

Finally, Roosevelt's unprecedented electoral strength, while a short-run blessing to Democratic political machines such as Tammany Hall, proved in the long run to be yet another cause of their demise. For the Roosevelt landslides substantially increased the number of persons who chose to vote and more generally created a widespread norm of participation in politics that carried over to nonpresidential elections as well. As voter turnout increased, however, the limited blocs of votes controlled by the various urban machines, which had earlier been sufficient to throw victory to the preferred side, now proved unequal to the task. Thus, the machines were, in effect, overrun at the ballot box even as Roosevelt carried their chosen candidates to victory. And when, after Roosevelt's death, the norm of participation was maintained, the machines suffered the consequences.[40]

The New Federalism: Cities and the Federal Government

Political machines, however, were not the only victims of the economic hardships and social and political readjustments of the 1930s. Indeed, the Depression years, and the demands for increased social services that accompanied them, found America's cities themselves caught between the proverbial rock and a hard place. At the same time that they were being pressed to provide increased welfare and housing aid to the needy, municipalities saw their tax bases shrinking and their tax delinquency rates rising sharply, both because of the decline in business activity. In 1930, for example, the delinquency rate among 145 cities with populations in excess of 50,000 was just under 11 percent, but by 1933 the rate had climbed above 25 percent. Some cities, such as Dayton and Des Moines, agreed to accept late tax payments without penalty, but others borrowed against uncollected (and largely uncollectible) revenues, thereby driving themselves still deeper into debt. Out of desperation, many cities turned to the sales tax as a new source of revenue. By 1940, for instance, New York City's sales tax of 3 percent brought in some $60 million each year.

Added to these demands for services and to the difficulties in generating funds to meet them was yet another problem, for during the early years of the century, and especially during the 1920s, many cities had issued bonds to finance large-scale civic improvement projects. Unfortunately, many of these bonds came due during the 1930s, at precisely the time when these same cities were suffering the worst of their financial crises. Many defaulted on their bond payments, while others were able to meet their obligations only by using their emergency reserves. By 1933, for example, bonds issued by Detroit and by Greensboro, North Carolina, were worth only forty cents on the dollar, and in its 1934–35 fiscal year Los Angeles paid fully 78 percent of its budget for debt service. Nowhere was the situation more desperate than in Philadelphia, which faced municipal bankruptcy in 1939. "Philadelphia is broke," wrote journalist Alan Frazier at the time. "The third largest city in the United States is caught behind the eight-ball. . . . The City Treasury is empty; what hasn't been stolen is in hock. To meet payrolls . . . it has even been proposed that the city sell Independence Hall, birthplace of the nation." The holders of these cities' municipal bonds, needless to say, were less than pleased with the course of events. Many called for state intervention in local affairs to review budgets, limit debt, and supervise the levying of taxes, a call in which they were joined by conservative politicians.

Municipal belt-tightening was widespread. Some cities, with the notable exceptions of Detroit and New York, ended all borrowing and adopted pay-as-you-go budgets. Others consolidated departments and functions and eliminated those they regarded as unnecessary. Milwaukee imposed a 10 percent pay cut on all municipal employees. But as the Depression deepened, the problems of the cities worsened, and their ability to provide increased social assistance out of decreased revenues was diminished. Some state aid was forthcoming (in New Jersey and New Hampshire, for example, state agencies assumed the welfare burden), but it, too, was proving inadequate to the task. So it was that the cities began to look to Washington.

In May 1932, a number of mayors met in Detroit to appeal to the federal government for $5 billion in financial assistance for capital projects. Their plea was rejected by President Hoover, though he did agree to establish the Reconstruction Finance Corporation, which, among other things, could make loans to municipalities for projects that would pay for themselves. This limited response, of course, was woefully inadequate, and even as the election of 1932 approached, the plight of the cities deteriorated almost daily. It was in this context, then, that Franklin D. Roosevelt determined shortly after his election that the federal government should assume primary responsibility for the economic and social well-being of the American people. Through a variety of alphabet-soup administrations which included the likes of FERA (Federal Emergency Relief Administration), CWA (Civil Works Administration), PWA (Public Works Administration), and WPA (Works Progress Administration), millions of Americans were put on the public payroll to engage in municipal (and other) improvement projects ranging from building roads and dams to painting murals in public buildings. Billions of federal dollars poured into such programs, and between 1936 and 1941 the WPA alone employed almost one-fifth of the entire American labor force in the building of some 600 airports, 500,000 miles of roads and streets, 100,000 bridges and viaducts, 500,000 sewer connections, and 110,000 libraries, schools, and other public buildings. Other Roosevelt legislation provided federal assistance for housing as well, with several billion dollars more being spent to modernize existing structures and subsidize the building of new ones. Thus, during the years of the New Deal, the cities received not only financial salvation but also a much-needed facelift, and the traditional reluctance of the federal government to involve itself in urban problems gave way to a new philosophy of more or less willing intervention.[41]

With the outbreak of World War II, of course, the economic health of the nation, and as a consequence that of its cities, was renewed, but in the postwar years the role of the federal government in dealing with urban problems has continued to expand. Beginning in 1949, for example, the government encouraged a program of urban renewal under which local agencies, with federal funds and the power of eminent domain, were able to condemn slum neighborhoods, tear down all the buildings, clear the land, and either build public housing or, as was more often the case, resell the land to private developers at a reduced rate for the construction of upper- and middle-class housing. Unfortunately, the program often failed to give due consideration to the needs and rights of residents of the renewal areas, as suggested in an analogy by sociologist Herbert J. Gans. Suppose, wrote Gans in 1965,

> that the government decided that jalopies were a menace to public safety and a blight on the beauty of our highways, and therefore took them away from their drivers. Suppose, then, that to replenish the supply of automobiles, it gave these drivers a hundred dollars each to buy a good used car and also made special grants to General Motors, Ford, and Chrylser to lower the cost—although not necessarily the price—of Cadillacs, Lincolns, and Imperials by a few hundred dollars. . . . Change the jalopies to housing, and I have described, with only slight poetic license, the first fifteen years of . . . urban renewal.[42]

Urban renewal sites were often chosen not because they had the worst slums but because they offered the most desirable sites for luxury housing. Entire neighborhoods were destroyed in the name of improvement, and tenants were dispossessed and asked to select among alternative housing units that they often could not afford. Countless small businesses were destroyed and friendships and extended families (common among the Italians and Puerto Ricans who were often the victims of urban renewal) broken apart.[43] Many of the tensions that gave rise to the urban violence of the 1960s that we discussed in chapter 2 were seriously aggravated by the seemingly impersonal and racially biased actions of government in urban renewal projects. In 1964 Congress passed the Housing Act, which required that government agencies provide relocation information and assistance, as well as additional financial aid, to those displaced by urban renewal, and in 1966 it required the inclusion of a proportion of low-income housing in any project built on renewal sites. But even these actions have proven inadequate to meet the needs of those who are forced from their homes.[44]

At the same time that the federal government was pressing for urban renewal (or "Negro removal" as it was generally referred to by black residents of the affected areas), it was also seeking to assist low- and middle-income families in purchasing their own homes. A cabinet-level Department of Housing and Urban Development (HUD) was established in 1966 (its first secretary, Robert C. Weaver, was also the first black to serve in the cabinet), and under its auspices literally hundreds of thousands of home mortgages were guaranteed by the government, thereby assuring qualified homeowners of reduced interest rates and loan availability and banks of a certain return on their investment. This ambitious effort to aid those needing housing was, in fact, a cornerstone of Lyndon Johnson's Great Society. Yet in the end, even this program has proven a failure as HUD has been forced to foreclose on more than 200,000 mortgages, a total that grows by some 3,700 units each month. Indeed, as the owner of some 64,000 abandoned homes, most of them in central urban areas where they are ready targets for vandals, HUD finds itself in the ironic position of being the nation's biggest slumlord. Recently, the department has been trying to divest itself of its holdings by selling its properties "as is" at a substantial loss to families willing to move in and repair them.[45]

The one major new response to the urban dilemma that the federal government put forward during the 1970s, revenue sharing, began in 1972 under the administration of Richard Nixon when Congress passed the State and Local Fiscal Assistance Act, which called for the return of some federal tax revenues to local governments to be applied in such areas as public safety, transportation, health, environmental protection, and social services. Several billion dollars have subsequently been distributed through the program, but since the basis for distribution rests primarily on the population of each locality rather than on relative need (which is difficult to determine), revenue sharing has in many cases helped suburbs and small towns more than it has aided central cities.[46]

The effectiveness of action by local governments to improve living conditions in the cities has also been limited in the years since World War II, not so much out of mismanagement or fiscal weakness per se, but because of a long-term demographic trend, that toward suburbanization, that has gradually deprived many American cities of their tax bases and, as a consequence, of their economic lifeblood. For as conditions in the central urban areas worsened, crime increased, the quality of education declined, traffic congestion grew, and poverty spread, those who could best afford it—and those whose support the beleaguered cities could least afford to lose—fled to the suburbs by the tens of thousands. Encouraged by the federally subsidized spread of superhighways in the 1950s and 1960s, developers opened to settlement new areas beyond the reach of urban governments from which commuters might take from the city its employment and entertainment but leave behind its trials, its travails, and, significantly, its taxing powers. So great was the outward movement, in fact, that by 1970 more Americans lived in suburbs surrounding the nation's cities than lived in the cities themselves. Where some thirty million people had lived in suburban areas in 1950, more than seventy-six million were suburbanites just twenty years later.[47] And although this flight from the cities was nothing new, the ability of the cities to cope with it was suddenly lessened as the urban centers came up against walls of already incorporated territory. Thus deprived of their traditional political response of annexation of outlying areas to counter loss of population, American cities at last faced the possibility of irreparable erosion of their economic bases.

This massive but selective (in terms of social class, age, skills, and education) migration to the suburbs has left the cities in an especially difficult position. The populations that remain in most large American cities are disproportionately young and old (as opposed to middle-aged), disproportionately rich and poor (as opposed to middle-class), and disproportionately nonwhite. Young people are attracted to the cities in their search for opportunity, while many older citizens on fixed incomes are unable or unwilling to leave. The very rich regard the city as a cultural Mecca and are able to afford the amenities of urban life, while the very poor regard the city as a prison from which they are unable to escape. Blacks, Puerto Ricans, and others find that they are relegated to the city by subtle patterns of discrimination in housing, while whites seek refuge in the suburbs. There are, of course, exceptions, but these are the general patterns that prevail, and they suggest an increasing polarization of the urban population the consequences of which bode ill for the future of American cities.

When one puts all these population characteristics together, the nature of the new urban crisis becomes apparent. For it is precisely those who remain in the cities—the young with their need for good schools for their children, the old and the poor with their need for increased social services—who place the most demands upon urban political systems. And it is precisely those who leave the cities—the middle classes, and, increasingly, the corporations that employ them—whose tax dollars might have provided the means to respond to those demands. Moreover, because those intermediate groups around whom compromises might be fashioned have departed the city, and because economic differences and mistrusts tend to be paralleled by racial differences and mistrusts, the difficulty in establishing a meaningful dialogue to resolve urban conflicts continues to mount. Thus, once again, as they were in the 1930s, a number of cities around the country are being faced with the possibility of political and financial collapse, and once again the response has been to seek outside assistance. Nowhere is this more clearly the case than in New York City, which, faced with rising costs for social services and the increasing demands of powerful municipal employees' unions during the 1960s and 1970s, borrowed immense sums against anticipated tax revenues that were at times knowingly overstated by city officials. As bankruptcy approached in 1975, the State of New York sought through a specially created agency, the Municipal Assistance Corporation (or Big Mac, as it was dubbed in the press), and through a series of grants and loans to help the city avoid default on its debt and restore fiscal responsibility by reducing the budgetary discretion of city officials. This was accompanied by calls for the federal government to guarantee bonds issued by the city and to take other steps within the financial community to ease the situation, calls that ultimately led to the lending of several billions in federal funds to help the city through its crisis.[48] In the final analysis, however, any such solution that fails to take into account the larger factors contributing to the plight of the cities is destined to create as many difficulties as it resolves.

Conclusion

There is much about urban life in the 1970s that has changed from earlier years, and many of the changes, though not all, are unpleasant. Although urban planning and such urban systems as transportation and health care have in many instances improved significantly over the years, poverty and squalor are still apparent. In several cities, including New York, Boston, Chicago, Milwaukee, Houston, and New Orleans, persons displaced by redevelopment programs and overlooked or overrun by the government have even gone so far as to assert squatters' rights to new and abandoned housing. And in the South Bronx neighborhood of New York City, despair has reached such a level that an average of thirty-four fires a day (or 12,300 a year in an area of only a few square miles), at least 30 percent of which are believed to have been deliberately set, have reduced whole city blocks to rubble.[49] Urban school systems have failed to meet the needs of their students, thereby perpetuating their inferior status in the social system, and even welfare recipients have found it necessary to organize to protect their interests. Such events are without precedent in American history and reflect nothing so much as the political environment of the past decade.

And yet, there is much about urban life in the 1970s that is reminiscent of the more distant past. Despite the exodus to outlying suburbs, America's cities remain the hubs of her economic and cultural life, much as they have been since the arrival of the earliest settlers centuries ago. The cities of the nation still harbor the lion's share of opportunity and the means for personal advancement within American society. But the same cities also harbor a new generation of criminals and gangs (whose weaponry has now escalated to rifles, machine guns, and even homemade bazookas), and even a few of the old political machines still survive. Chicago, with its Blackstone Rangers (later known as the Black P. Stone Nation), who evolved from a street gang into a quasi-legitimate social organization seeking to improve the black community in much the manner of the Irish street gangs of an earlier era, and with its Cook County Democratic machine headed by Richard J. Daley, who had, in customary style, risen from the Irish neighborhood of Bridgeport to control an Irish-dominated urban political organization, provides perhaps the clearest latter-day example of both.[50]

But whether we look for change or continuity, for growth or decay, for advancement or decline, one point stands out with regard to the nation's cities today: what happens in America's urban centers is in many ways simply a reflection of what is happening in the United States in general. The problems of the cities cannot be separated from the conditions of contemporary political life. The cities and their surrounding metropolitan areas, after all, are home to three out of every four Americans. It must come as no surprise, therefore, that when the city sneezes, the nation feels the chill.

At the same time, just as the nation changes through time, so must the city. Indeed, the solutions to the urban problems of one era often become themselves the problems of the next. This was as true of the political machines that served the immigrant but stifled participation in politics as it was of the reform movements and federal programs that swept away the machines and imposed unrealistic and impersonal programs in their place, and it will no doubt prove true of contemporary approaches to the urban crisis as well. Still, the problems cry out for solution; still, the effort must be made. But we must recognize that circumstances change, often in long-term, systematic, and discoverable ways, and we must remain flexible and innovative if our urban policy is to keep pace.[51]

NOTES

1. Alva Johnston, "Scandals of New York," *Harper's*, March 1931, pp. 409–410.

2. Lyndon B. Johnson, "The Rebirth of Our Cities: A Message to Congress," in *A Nation of Cities,* ed. Robert A. Goldwin (Chicago: Rand McNally, 1968), p. 1.

3. Arthur M. Schlesinger, "A Panoramic View: The City in American History," *Mississippi Valley Historical Review* 27 (June 1940): 43–45; Arthur M. Schlesinger, "The City in American Civilization," from *Paths to the Present* (New York: Macmillan, 1949), pp. 210–33, as reprinted in

Alexander B. Callow, Jr., ed., *American Urban History*, 2d ed. (New York: Oxford University Press, 1973), p. 36.

4. Schlesinger, "Panoramic View," pp. 45–46; Schlesinger, "The City," p. 36.

5. Howard P. Chudacoff, *The Evolution of American Urban Society* (Englewood Cliffs, N.J.: Prentice-Hall, 1975), pp. 36–37.

6. Schlesinger, "Panoramic View," pp. 45–46.

7. Chudacoff, *Evolution*, p. 38.

8. Quoted in Everett P. Wheeler, "History of Tammany Hall," *Outlook*, 13 September 1913, pp. 73–74.

9. Quoted in Chudacoff, *Evolution*, p. 69.

10. Ernest S. Griffith, *A History of American City Government: The Conspicuous Failure, 1870–1900* (New York: Praeger, 1938, 1974), pp. 183–84; Schlesinger, "The City," p. 45; Chudacoff, *Evolution*, pp. 70–76.

11. Griffith, *American City Government*, pp. 23–30.

12. Schlesinger, "Panoramic View," pp. 45–46.

13. Blake McKelvey, "The Emergence of Industrial Cities," from *The Urbanization of America, 1860–1965* (New Brunswick, N.J.: Rutgers University Press, 1965), pp. 35–46, reprinted in Alexander B. Callow, Jr., ed., *American Urban History*, 2d ed. (New York: Oxford University Press, 1973), pp. 160–71; Chudacoff, *Evolution*, pp. 84–87; Schlesinger, "Panoramic View," pp. 56–57.

14. McKelvey, "Industrial Cities," pp. 163–64.

15. Quoted in Nathan Glazer and Daniel P. Moynihan, *Beyond the Melting Pot* (Cambridge, Mass.: M.I.T. Press, 1963), p. 289.

16. William S. Bennett, "Immigrants and Crime," *Annals* 34 (July 1909): 118.

17. Quoted in George Allan England, "The Harvest: A Brief Inquiry into the Conditions of Crime in the United States," *Arena* 40 (October 1908): 294–95.

18. Theodore Bingham, "Foreign Criminals in New York," *North American Review* 188 (September 1908): 381.

19. Morris Markey, "Gangs," *Atlantic*, March 1928, pp. 296–99; Brewster Adams, "The Street Gang as a Factor in Politics," *Outlook*, 22 August 1903, pp. 986–87.

20. Frederic M. Thrasher, *The Gang: A Study of 1,313 Gangs in Chicago* (Chicago: University of Chicago Press, 1927), pp. 199–203.

21. Ibid., pp. 208–212.

22. Edward Allsworth Ross, "Immigrants in Politics: The Political Consequences of Immigration," *Century* 87 (January 1914): 392–93.

23. Robert K. Merton, *Social Theory and Social Structure* (New York: Free Press, 1957), pp. 72–82.

24. For discussions of various of these political machines see, for example, Harold Zink, *City Bosses in the United States* (Durham, N.C., Duke University Press, 1930); Charles Van Devander, *The Big Bosses* (Howell, Soskin, 1944); idem, "O'Connell Machine in Albany," *American Mercury* 59 (October 1944): 408–415; Dayton D. McKean, "Worst American City: Jersey City," *American Mercury* 52 (February 1941): 211–18; Ted Leitzell, "Chicago, City of Corruption," *American Mercury* 49 (February 1940): 143–51.

25. Joel Arthur Tarr, *A Study in Boss Politics: William Lorimer of Chicago* (Urbana: University of Illinois Press, 1971), pp. ix, 308–316.

26. Wheeler, "Tammany Hall," p. 73.

27. Alfred Connable and Edward Silberfarb, *Tigers of Tammany: Nine Men Who Ran New York* (New York: Holt, Rinehart & Winston, 1967), pp. 53–54.

28. Alexander B. Callow, Jr., *The Tweed Ring* (New York: Oxford University Press, 1966), p. 117; Chudacoff, *Evolution*, pp. 133–34.

29. Griffith, *American City Government*, pp. 70–71.

30. Connable and Silberfarb, *Tigers*, pp. 167–72; "What Are You Going to Do About It?" *Independent*, 22 October 1921, pp. 82–83.

31. Connable and Silberfarb, *Tigers*, pp. 173–96.

32. Ibid., pp. 197–230.

33. "Plunkitt of Tammany," *Literary Digest*, 3 January 1925, p. 44.

34. Brewster Adams, "The Street Gangs as a Factor in Politics," *Outlook*, 22 August 1903, p. 985.

35. Quoted in Connable and Silberfarb, *Tigers*, p. 231.

36. William L. Chenery, "So This Is Tammany Hall?" *Atlantic*, September 1924, pp. 310–19.

37. Stephen M. David and Paul E. Peterson, *Urban Politics and Public Policy: The City in Crisis* (New York: Praeger, 1973), pp. 13–14.

38. Adams, "Street Gangs," p. 985.

39. C. C. Regier, *The Era of the Muckrakers* (Chapel Hill, N.C.: University of North Carolina Press, 1932), pp. 59–82; Louis Filler, *The Muckrakers: Crusaders for American Liberalism* (Chicago: Regnery, 1950, 1968), pp. 90–101.

40. Warren Moscow, *The Last of the Big-Time Bosses: The Life and Times of Carmine De Sapio and the Rise and Fall of Tammany Hall* (New York: Stein and Day, 1971), pp. 23–29. The quote from Steffens may be found in Lincoln Steffens, *The Shame of the Cities* (New York: McClure, Phillips, 1904), p. 13.

41. Chudacoff, *Evolution*, pp. 211–21; Alan Frazier, "Philadelphia: City of Brotherly Loot," *American Mercury* 47 (July 1939): 275.

42. Herbert J. Gans, "The Failure of Urban Renewal," *Commentary* 39 (April 1965): 29–37.

43. Ibid.

44. Chester Hartman, "The Politics of Housing: Displaced Persons," *Society* 9 (July-August 1972): 53-60.

45. "Dreams for Sale," *Newsweek*, 22 September 1975, pp. 68-70.

46. Chudacoff, *Evolution*, pp. 260-61.

47. Ibid., p. 238.

48. Robert Sam Anson, "Down to the Core," *New Times*, 3 October 1975, pp. 16-22; "New York's Big Gamble," *Newsweek*, 22 September 1975, pp. 27-28.

49. Rob Hollister, "The Politics of Housing: Squatters," *Society* 9 (July-August 1972): 50-52; "The Bronx Is Burning," *Newsweek*, 16 June 1975, p. 30.

50. With regard to street gangs see, for example, R. Lincoln Keiser, *The Vice Lords: Warriors of the Streets* (New York: Holt, Rinehart & Winston, 1969); "Son of 'West Side Story,'" *Newsweek*, 21 July 1975, p. 20. For information on Richard J. Daley and his political machine, see Mike Royko, *Boss: Richard J. Daley of Chicago* (New York: New American Library, 1971); Len O'Connor, *Clout: Mayor Daley and His City* (Chicago: Regnery, 1975); Sidney Lens, "Mayor Daley's Last Hurrah," *Progressive*, April 1975, pp. 13-18.

51. For a unique and significant point of view on urban problems and their solution see Edward C. Banfield, *The Unheavenly City Revisited* (Boston: Little, Brown, 1974).

4

The President's Men: Lessons in Executive Malfeasance

One . . . misconception is that the successful political leader is necessarily a fellow of great shrewdness, subtlety and resource. The fact is that the amazingly adroit political mind exists only in fiction. Except in the imagination of hard-pressed political writers and credulous sideline observers, there are no deep plots in politics, no dark and diabolically ingenious schemes. The clever explanations of political tactics are almost always completely false. When stories of craft and cunning are unfolded they are usually so fascinating and plausible that the temptation to believe them is almost irresistible. The disposition to romanticize politics is strong in all of us and it is hard to avoid yielding to it. Yet the fact remains that in nine hundred and ninety-nine cases out of a thousand what appears to be super-human strategy is actually either accident or blunder.

Frank R. Kent

Men do not blame a great leader for making a mistake; they blame him for refusing to acknowledge it.

William E. Dodd[2]

People have got to know whether or not their President is a crook. Well, I'm not a crook.

Richard M. Nixon[3]

Three times in the last hundred years the American presidency has been rocked to its very foundations by scandals surrounding the discovery of conspiracies against the public interest. First in the days of Reconstruction, later at the outset of the Roaring

Twenties, and most recently in the years preceding the Bicentennial celebration, the faith of Americans in their national leaders has been severely tested. And if the nation has emerged from each such period with its legal and constitutional systems more or less intact, it has emerged as well with its confidence shaken, its trust disabused, and its cynicism predominant. Indeed, in each instance the greatest cost of scandal has been, not the dollars lost through corrupt practices or the disservice to the national interest resulting from improper policies, but rather the decline in political interest and regime support among the American population. The greatest cost of political corruption, in other words, has been to the political system itself.

Yet, although it is common to attach to each of these scandalous eras the name of the president within whose administration corruption was practiced, this natural tendency to blame the most prominent political personage can be somewhat misleading. In point of fact, the so-called Grant Scandals were generally not perpetrated either by or for President Grant, and the "Harding Scandals" were generally not perpetrated either by or for President Harding. In each case, as we shall see, elements in a president's disposition or in the nature of his relationships with his associates helped make possible the development of rampant corruption, but in each case evidence of direct presidential involvement or approval is lacking. Even in the case of the more recent "Nixon Scandals," though there is some evidence of apparent presidential involvement the validity of which can be judged only with the passage of time, the president stood accused in large measure of creating an atmosphere within the circles of government that led his associates to engage in corrupt practices for his benefit, in which end they saw a high moral purpose.

In the present chapter we shall investigate in turn each of these periods of moral breakdown within the executive branch of government and shall then direct our attention to the common elements in each and to the lessons that those commonalities suggest for the future.

Knavery and Naiveté: The Grant Scandals

When Ulysses Simpson Grant took office as the eighteenth president of the United States on March 4, 1869, he had already established himself as a national leader of the first merit. Grant, of course, had led the Northern armies to final victory in the Civil War and had accepted General Lee's surrender in the courthouse at Appomattox. These actions, needless to say, did little to endear him to Southerners, but then, Southerners were not permitted full political participation during the years of Reconstruction, so their voices counted little. In fact, it was precisely because Grant possessed proven Union credentials that many Northern voters looked to him as a man strong enough to complete the political reunification of the nation that had been undertaken by Andrew Johnson but effectively stymied by the so-called Radical Republicans in the Senate.

Grant had been the last in a lengthy succession of generals named by President Lincoln to bring the war to an end, and his accomplishment was in large measure attributable to the fact that Grant was able to tighten the organization of the Union armies and gather around him aides and advisors of the highest quality. Thus, when the American people elected him to the presidency, they assumed that they had selected a capable organizer and a good judge of character. It is an irony of history that Grant was done in by those whom he trusted precisely because he could neither organize nor judge.

Interestingly enough, the scandal for which the Grant era is best remembered did not involve the president or the executive branch of government at all. Rather, it involved several prominent members of the Congress. This was the so-called Crédit Mobilier Scandal, which revolved around some shady financing in the building of the Union Pacific's transcontinental rail line. The idea for such a rail line dated to sometime in the 1840s and had gained support for a number of reasons, ranging from fears that without such a link the western territories would seek independence and develop as a separate nation to the hopes expressed by the Reverend Calvin Colton in a lecture at the Smithsonian Institute in 1850 in which he lauded the railroad proposal "as a door for Christian missions. I do not hesitate to say," proclaimed Colton on that occasion, "that since the day when Christ commissioned his Twelve Apostles to go forth and teach all nations, there has no such door as this been opened. You observe, by a map of the world, that it [the railroad] will connect the darkest regions of paganism with the brightest lights of

Christianity—that it will put all Asia . . . in immediate connection with Christian Europe and Christian America. Both Europe and America teem with Christian people who are earnestly desirous of evangelizing the world, and who are only waiting for the opportunity."[4] (The Reverend Colton, whose somewhat overstated sentiments, we shall see in a later chapter, were echoed elsewhere, seems in his exuberance to account neither for the Atlantic and Pacific oceans nor for the fact that access from Europe to Asia had for some time been both quicker and easier than it ever could be by way of Chicago.) The rail project was actually begun early in the Civil War, when debate over whether the line would follow a northern or a southern route became moot, but it was not until 1864, when the government offered a grant of twenty million acres of land and a loan of $55,000,000, that enough private capital was attracted to allow significant progress. It was, in fact, the generosity of this grant that enticed a group of railroad developers to defraud the government of vast sums through an intricate corporate conspiracy centered in a company known as Crédit Mobilier of America.

To initiate the conspiracy, Thomas C. Durant, the president of the Union Pacific Railroad, purchased the charter of a Pennsylvania corporation known as the Pennsylvania Fiscal Agency, which had been established in the 1850s to assist in the construction of railroads and public works, and renamed his prize Crédit Mobilier of America. Each Union Pacific stockholder (they were few in number) received from Durant stock of the new corporation on a share-for-share basis. Thus, in the wake of this acquisition and distribution, there existed two corporations, separate but with identical ownership, both of which possessed the legal right of limited liability (the corporation, not its individual owners, is legally responsible for its actions) that attaches to all corporations. As soon as this dual mechanism was in place, the fraud commenced.

As the scheme developed, directors of the Union Pacific would award construction contracts at inflated rates to various individuals who would in turn assign these contracts (in return for certain financial considerations) to a major contractor, none other than Crédit Mobilier of America, which, of course, consisted of the very men who had let the contracts in the first place. For example, one Oakes Ames, a millionaire shovel manufacturer and holder of Crédit Mobilier stock, received a contract to build 667 miles of railroad for $42,000 a mile—including a stretch of 238 miles *that had already been built,* and for only $27,000 a mile. The enormous profits that resulted from transactions of this sort were hidden by a complex manipulation of the books of the two corporations. Union Pacific directors were not permitted by law to use stocks or bonds to pay for construction work or to sell these securities except for cash and at par value. So the railroad directors issued to themselves *as directors of Crédit Mobilier* checks for work completed, then returned the checks to themselves as directors of the Union Pacific to purchase stocks and bonds. Their transactions thus appeared on Union Pacific's books as legal cash sales, but the directors of the railroad were obtaining substantial amounts of the company's securities as dividends from Crédit Mobilier. (Crédit Mobilier paid an astonishing 595 percent dividend in the period from December 1867 to December 1868 alone.) In all, the railroad was saddled with $90,000,000 to $100,000,000 in construction charges, though the actual costs of construction were closer to $50,000,000. The difference was the net take of Crédit Mobilier.[5]

While all this building of railroads and siphoning of funds was progressing, it became evident to the perpetrators of the fraud that they would have to keep the government out of their affairs. They accomplished this in two ways. First, they simply bribed the government commissioners whose job it was to oversee the building of the railroad. Thus, for example, one government member of the Union Pacific board, James Brooks, who also happened to be a member of Congress, received 100 shares of Crédit Mobilier stock, $5,000 in Union Pacific bonds, and $20,000 in Union Pacific stock, all conveniently listed in the name of his son-in-law. And second, the directors distributed some 343 shares of Crédit Mobilier stock (with a par value of $100 per share but a market value of roughly twice that) to a number of influential members of Congress. In this latter pursuit, they were no doubt aided by the fact that the abovementioned Oakes Ames, a major partner in the conspiracy, was not only a member of the House of Representatives but was in addition a member of the Pacific Railroad Committee. Those of Ames's colleagues who could not afford to purchase their shares at par were told to keep the shares and pay for them out of their dividends. Two weeks later, Crédit Mobilier of America paid a 100 percent dividend. The point of all this largesse, it appears, was not to obtain any particular new legislation but merely to assure that any potentially adverse legislation or investigation would be effectively blocked. As Ames himself put it in a private letter later made public, "We want more friends in this Congress. There is no difficulty in getting men to look after their own property."[6]

All this, of course, took place well before Ulysses S. Grant became president. It did not become public knowledge, however, until the election year of 1872. In that year, a citizen named McComb brought suit against the directors of Crédit Mobilier to compel delivery of shares of stock to which he claimed he was entitled. Certain documents in the suit, as well, possibly, as the Ames letter quoted above, were leaked to the *New York Sun*, and the public outcry that followed disclosure forced a congressional investigation that tainted the vice-president, the vice-president-elect, the chairmen of nearly all important congressional committees, future President James Garfield, and presidential hopeful James G. Blaine. The worst damage of all was done to the reputation of Vice-President Schuyler Colfax, who flatly denied holding Crédit Mobilier stock or receiving dividends. Congressman Ames, who was not about to take all the blame for the affair, produced for the congressional investigators a cancelled check in the amount of $1,200 for a dividend on twenty shares that Colfax had cashed through the sergeant-at-arms of the House. A cashier at Colfax's bank confirmed a deposit of like amount on the date in question. Faced with these charges, Colfax went off on a religious lecture tour for two weeks. Upon his return he claimed that he did remember receiving $1,200 but that $200 of this sum was from his father and the remaining $1,000 had been a gift from wealthy philanthropist George F. Nesbitt, who, Colfax said, admired him because he had started life as a printer. Nesbitt had asked that the gift remain a secret, claimed the vice-president, and hence he had been reluctant to divulge the name of his benefactor. Since Nesbitt had, in the interim, passed away, however, Colfax had decided that no harm could be done by revealing his name. Nor, one might add, for the same reason, could Colfax's claim be substantiated. Colfax also noted, incidentally, that he had received other such gifts from Nesbitt, but the investigators never followed up on these, despite the facts that Nesbitt had made his fortune as a manufacturer of envelopes with lucrative government contracts and that Colfax, while in the House of Representatives, had chaired the Post Office Committee, which oversaw many of those contracts.[7]

When the investigating committee issued its report, its findings became the subject of a debate that could only be described as a gala event. Responding to the crush in the galleries, notes a later student of the event, "the gallant congressmen voted to admit lady visitors to the floor and, as soon as their permission was given, the ladies swarmed down the aisles, perched on chair-arms, climbed upon desks, filled the steps leading up to the Speaker's desk, and pulled available law books into the aisles and sat upon them. A basket of flowers presented by a feminine admirer filled Ames's desk. In such an atmosphere the House could scarcely be vindictive."[8] Nor was it. In a report that in essence said that dishonest practices had been committed but that no one was guilty of them, the House whitewashed the entire affair.[9] Ames and Brooks were singled out for a motion of censure but were not otherwise held accountable, and Colfax escaped impeachment thanks to the fact that his term had all but expired anyway. A second congressional committee, which looked at Crédit Mobilier itself rather than at other congressmen, found evidence of massive fraud, and on the basis of the evidence developed by this committee the Attorney General brought suit in September 1873 against the Union Pacific Railroad and a number of individuals. The government lost the case, however, when both the circuit and the Supreme courts held that it had no legal standing against Crédit Mobilier of America (whose contracts were with the railroad and not with the government) and that the defendant in the case (the Union Pacific) should actually have been the plaintiff. There was, of course, no one among the directors of the Union Pacific who saw reason to cause any legal difficulties for the directors of Crédit Mobilier, so all escaped without punishment.[10]

Although President Grant was clearly not involved in this whole affair, he did suffer from it by association in two ways. First, though it was quite apparent that the president himself was above suspicion of wrongdoing, it was equally clear that members of his party, including his vice-president (in whose total innocence Grant publicly proclaimed his confidence), were not nearly so guiltless. In an election year, voters tend to be unusually cognizant of such connections. On top of this, the Crédit Mobilier Scandal roughly coincided in time with the first evidences of far more pervasive graft and corruption within the *executive* branch of government, and thus could be seen, as time passed, as part of a much larger pattern of improper behavior—some of which was in fact laid much closer to the president's doorstep. Crédit Mobilier thus contributed to a set of public expectations described at the time by a Wisconsin politician as creating the impression "that our whole public life is debased[,] that our legislation is essentially corrupt and that honesty in official circles is the exception and not the rule."[11]

If Grant was merely an interested but innocent bystander to the financial shenanigans of the railroad barons in the Crédit Mobilier Scandal, however, it was the president's own judgment that was more clearly at issue in the second great scandal of the period, the Gold Conspiracy. In this incident, two businessmen of wide repute but questionable ethics, Jay Gould and James Fisk, Jr., set out to control the gold supply of the United States by manipulating government policy regarding the price of gold. At the time, there existed a relatively limited supply of the metal in the country other than that held by the Treasury, yet businessmen depended on gold as a medium of exchange for all foreign and some domestic transactions. There was thus a steady or growing demand for a commodity that was in short supply. And it was the policy of the Treasury to regulate economic growth and stabilize the price of gold by selling off some small portion of its holdings on a monthly basis to increase the supply of the metal in the private sector. Gould and Fisk determined that, if they could somehow bring to an end these Treasury sales and thus limit the supply, they could force the price of gold up and, through the simple expedient of buying low and selling high, could become immensely wealthy. The "somehow" upon which they settled was a gentleman named Abel Corbin, an elderly real estate operator who was not averse to profiting from a little speculation in gold. Corbin also happened to be married to President Grant's sister.

Corbin introduced Gould and Fisk to the president in June 1869, and he provided other social occasions later in the summer at which the discussion frequently turned to the government's gold policy. Gould sought to convince the president, who greatly admired both wealth and those able to accumulate it and was thus open to persuasion, that both the balance of trade and the American farmer would benefit from an increase in the price of gold, an increase that would follow immediately if only the Treasury would stop dumping $2,000,000 of the metal on the market each month. He apparently succeeded, for in August of 1869 President Grant ordered Treasury Secretary George S. Boutwell to reduce gold sales, justifying his action on precisely the grounds argued by Gould. Boutwell, who was largely ignorant of the complexities of high finance, failed to warn the president of the dangers inherent in this change in policy. At that point, the president, convinced that he had taken a proper and important position, left for a country vacation in the remote town of Washington, Pennsylvania, aboard a special train provided by none other than Jay Gould, who, as we saw in chapter 3, held a controlling interest in the Erie Railroad.

With the Treasury's policy changed and the president off to an isolated vacation spot, the conspirators got down to business. Gould and Fisk began buying gold and by mid-September held contracts for roughly twice the available supply. As their corner on the market became evident, the price rose sharply. Merchants, who needed the gold for their business transactions, rushed to get what they could, and the rumor spread that high government officials were active in the market. Knowing that news of a gold panic on Wall Street would soon reach the president even in Pennsylvania, Corbin wrote to his brother-in-law (the president) urging that he keep the government out of the situation. By this time, Grant had caught on to what was happening, however, and, through an exchange of letters between his wife and his sister, warned Corbin to end his gold speculations. Corbin showed the letter to Gould and asked Gould to purchase his share of the corner on the market. Gould agreed, but only on the condition that Corbin keep the contents of the president's message secret. At this point, Gould could see the writing on the wall and began to dump his holdings. Privately, he sold, but he continued to buy lesser amounts publicly to mask his intentions, and he made sure that none of his sales were to Fisk, whom he was in the process of double-crossing.

On Friday, September 24, a day remembered long afterward as Black Friday, Wall Street was in a panic as merchants and speculators scrambled for whatever gold was available. By late morning, the price had soared to $162, and Fisk's boast to push it to $200 seemed realizable. But Grant had privately instructed Secretary Boutwell to respond to the crisis, and at about noon the Treasury announced that it would sell $4,000,000 in gold immediately. As news of the Treasury sale spread, gold prices collapsed, falling in a single half hour from $162 to $135, with the result that Fisk, a number of brokers, and many businessmen who had taken late positions in gold found themselves facing bankruptcy.[12] Panic and a period of economic deprivation followed, and the public came to see Grant both as the willing associate of men who would engage in such actions and as a man who had been deceived by a relatively simple and straightforward conspiracy against the public interest.[13] The president had simply been done in by his brother-in-law, and the public's faith in his judgment had been significantly lessened.

But it was really the third major incident of the Grant era, the attempt by the government to break up the so-called Whiskey Ring, that focused primarily on the president's official family, that displayed most clearly of all the nature of Grant's naive culpability in scandal, and that cost both the president and the presidency most dearly in terms of political capital. The Whiskey Ring was a sizable group of distillers, shippers, and dishonest government inspectors who conspired to deprive the government of tax revenues on a substantial portion of the whiskey produced in several major cities including Milwaukee, Chicago, and St. Louis. Early efforts to investigate the ring were hampered by a group of paid informers in the Treasury Department and the Bureau of Internal Revenue who would warn the conspirators of any impending danger. Finally, Treasury Secretary Benjamin H. Bristow and an assistant put together a special secret force of trusted agents who infiltrated the distilleries and helped break the conspiracy.

Most notable of the Whiskey Ring operations were those in St. Louis, where Grant's appointee as collector of internal revenues,

John McDonald, was a moving force in the conspiracy, and where the President's own personal secretary, Orville E. Babcock, was found to have received some $25,000 in cash as well as diamonds, rare liquors, and the companionship of a "sylph" in return for services rendered. Indeed, the most interesting feature here is not the conspiracy itself but the president's continuing refusal to accept the evidence of Babcock's guilt, his efforts to impede the trial of his secretary, and his growing distrust of Secretary Bristow, who had broken the Whiskey Ring but whom Grant suspected of using the Babcock prosecution to further his own presidential ambitions. When Babcock was indicted by a grand jury for his role in the conspiracy, Commander-in-Chief Grant approved a request by his secretary (who still held the military rank of colonel) that he face a military court of inquiry to determine his guilt or innocence rather than a civilian court, and the president appointed a friendly tribunal for that purpose. When that failed to forestall a civilian criminal trial, Grant issued an order that essentially denied the use of plea bargaining and trades of immunity from prosecution to obtain testimony for the government's case against Babcock. And when the trial commenced regardless, the president went so far as to file a deposition assuring the jury of the integrity of his aide. This deposition, combined with the apparently perjured testimony of defense witnesses, resulted in Babcock's acquittal.[14] Nor did the matter rest there, for Grant was not one to take such affrontery passively. In the wake of the trial, Secretary Bristow was forced to resign, the federal attorney who had prosecuted the case was dismissed, and the treasury agent who had headed the investigation of the Whiskey Ring was framed for extortion and then subsequently dismissed.[15] The lesson, for those who had missed it earlier, was quite clear. One simply did not cross the president or his friends.

If these were the most infamous of the scandals of the Grant years, however, they were far from the only ones. Indeed, it was a rather free and easy time for those who would take advantage of government positions. There was, for example, the Treasury scandal of 1873, in which Assistant Treasury Secretary William A. Richardson, who succeeded Boutwell as secretary, appointed one James Sanborn to a contract for the collection of delinquent taxes, the proceeds of such collection to be equally divided between

Sanborn and the Treasury. Although the contract itself was legal and in line with the practice of the day, its execution was unique in that Sanborn used his contract and a letter from Richardson to collect taxes that the government would have received anyway, to have his collections payable to himself (he would then pay the government its share), and, it was suspected, to use some of his $213,500 profit to fatten the purses of certain politicians. Congressional attention in the matter focused on Richardson, who resigned before he could be censured by the House.[16] Still, Grant performed in what was becoming typical style by coming to the defense of his appointee. As one historian summed up his response, "Mr. Richardson's resignation was soon after reluctantly accepted by the President, and his nomination to the Court of Claims confirmed with equal reluctance by the Senate."[17] Richardson became a federal judge.

In yet another instance, Grant's secretary of war, W. W. Belknap, was discovered, first by the *New York Herald* and shortly afterward by a congressional committee, to have been augmenting his government salary of $8,000 a year by selling appointments to War Department positions, most notably those as traders on Indian posts, for as much as $20,000 apiece. Indeed, the president's brother Orvil seems to have been in on this action as well, having used his influence to obtain in 1874 the rights to four traderships and having placed "partners" in each so that he invested little capital but received a substantial income. Belknap, who, it turned out, had also made some $90,000 on the side through the letting of contracts for national cemeteries, resigned his cabinet post but was impeached by the House nevertheless. On a subsequent near-party-line vote in the Senate, only thirty-seven of the sixty-two votes, four short of the required two-thirds, were cast for conviction, but of the twenty-five who voted not guilty, fully twenty-three said they did so only because they doubted the right of the Senate to impeach an officer who had already resigned. No action was taken against Orvil Grant or against a relative of the president's wife who was also found to have had an interest in Indian affairs.[18] There is, incidentally, a little-known but interesting sidelight to this matter that offers some additional insight into Grant's tendency to protect those close to him and to lash out at their detractors. It seems that one of the principal witnesses before the House Committee on War Department Expenditures that investigated the Belknap case was none other than General George A. Custer, who testified about waste and abuse in the Indian Bureau. For giving such testimony, Custer was removed from his command by Grant just before a planned expedition against the Sioux in the Dakota Territory and, after some public outcry, was put in charge of a regiment of some 600 men with the rank of major. It was thus an angry, disgraced, and humiliated Custer who led his troops rather incautiously into the valley of the Little Big Horn.[19]

The list of Grant's travails, however, by no means stopped with Richardson and Belknap. Presidential appointees to direct the customs houses in New York (Tom Murphy) and New Orleans (James F. Casey, another of Grant's brothers-in-law) were found to be using their positions for personal and political gain. Grant responded by declaring Murphy's innocence and reappointing Casey for an additional term.[20] And when a friend of the president, General T. B. Van Buren, was appointed to head a commission to a trade fair in Vienna, that "friend" *sold* other positions on the commission as well as restaurant and liquor concessions for the American exhibit hall. When the plot was uncovered, Grant rushed to the defense of Van Buren as he had to the defense of the others.[21] And in still other scandals of the Grant era, the American minister to Great Britain, Robert C. Schenck, allowed his name to be used in connection with the sale of shares in a speculative Utah silver mining company to the British public, the failure of which company caused great embarrassment to the United States Government.[22] The wife of George Williams, Grant's third attorney general (he had five), apparently with her husband's knowledge and consent, accepted a bribe of some $30,000 to halt a suit that her husband was bringing against a large New York merchant firm; she was also found to have used government funds to meet household expenses and to purchase a carriage. When these pecadillos were discovered, Williams resigned.[23] Columbus Delano, secretary of the interior, was rumored to have issued land warrants in response to fraudulent claims in the names of veterans of the Revolution and the War of 1812 where the names of such veterans were supplied to the claimants by someone within the Interior Department. Grant accepted Delano's resignation only with great reluctance.[24] George M. Robeson, secretary of the navy, used his influence to the advantage of a Philadelphia grain firm with which he was connected and himself became wealthy in the process.[25] And even Grant's appointee as head of the Board of Public Works for the District of Columbia, Alexander R. Shepherd, who singlehandedly converted Washington from a mud pit to a stately metropolis, was found to have engaged in some questionable practices regarding the letting of contracts. Grant's response to the accompanying public outcry was to name Shepherd governor of the District.[26]

Given even this limited series of events (there were still other scandals), it is little wonder that the term "Grantism" became one of cynicism and derision and that even today we look back on the Grant era as one of the most corrupt in our history. Still, there is little indication that the president himself was less than honest. Indeed, if he were guilty of anything, it must be that he chose his associates poorly and that he refused to believe that any of them could be less honest than he. Time after time, Grant came to the aid of an appointee under fire, regardless of the evidence of guilt or the political cost of a defense, and on some occasions he even forced out exemplary public servants when they displayed the audacity to attack his official family and, through them, Grant apparently believed, himself. Thus, Grant was guilty at worst of a misplaced sense of loyalty, and his role in the scandals that bear his name was, in almost all instances, general and indirect. It was less the fact that he engaged in culpable activity himself than that he made possible and even naively defended the distortion of duty by others that has earned for President Ulysses S. Grant his place in American political history.[27] As we shall see, this pattern was to repeat itself.

A Friend in High Places: The Harding Scandals

It was to be another fifty years before scandal on such a scale would once again touch the executive branch of government, but when it came, it came for reasons not unlike those of the 1870s. For Warren Gamaliel Harding was in many ways not unlike Grant, and his style of governing by trust led to his betrayal much as it had to Grant's half a century earlier.

Legend has it that Warren G. Harding became president because he looked like one. He was handsome and likable, and at a time when the nation needed a symbol of "normalcy," he provided it. But Harding came to the presidency straight from the Ohio political machine, or the Ohio Gang, as it was called (his was the nomination agreed to in the famous "smoke-filled room"), and he had a healthy respect for such American traditions as cronyism and patronage. It was this respect, combined with his consistent tendency to judge men by their camaraderie rather than by their abilities, that made him particularly vulnerable. Yet Harding, too, was honest to the core and, like Grant, was undoubtedly more guilty of misplaced loyalties and poor judgment than of any personal corruption. Still, in a president of the United States such characteristics can be fatal, and in Harding's case they were quite literally so.

Harding, of course, is best remembered for the Teapot Dome Scandal in which government oil reserves were leased to private developers in exchange for some very private financial considerations, but there were numerous other instances of corruption during his administration as well, several of which are worthy of note. In one such instance, Charles R. Forbes, Harding's choice to head the Veterans' Bureau, was found to be engaging in what one could only with the greatest charity describe as gross mismanagement of his office. Forbes had been a winner of the Medal of Honor in World War I and had attained the rank of lieutenant colonel, but he had earlier been a military deserter, and his wife at one point had even solicited the assistance of the army in obtaining financial support from her husband. And although his nomination to the War Risk Insurance Bureau (which he parlayed into the directorship of the Veterans' Bureau when the two were merged) had been supported by veterans' groups, it had been opposed by virtually all Harding's advisers. But Harding sincerely liked the amiable Forbes, who could play poker or trade off-color stories with the best, and pushed through his appointment without hesitation.

Once ensconced in the Washington bureaucracy, Forbes became an instant embarrassment to the administration, not so much for the extravagant parties and high-stakes poker games that became his trademark, but for his questionable handling of his official duties. For one thing, Forbes employed some rather unusual criteria for hiring assistants. One man obtained a $3,500 per year position as a mechanical engineer on the basis of his experience as a milkwagon driver—plus the probably not incidental fact that he happened to be married to Forbes's sister. Another was hired as a "special expert" at an annual salary of $4,800, for which he contributed fully two hours of work each *year.* In addition, in exchange for a fully subsidized nationwide junket euphemistically termed an "inspection tour of potential sites for veterans' hospitals" and for certain other considerations of a pecuniary nature, Forbes contrived with the St. Louis firm of Thompson and Black to purchase (from the company) sites for veterans' hospitals at greater than their market value and then to wrest from the army control over the design and construction of the buildings. These were all rather subtle forms of connivance, but the deed that finally brought Forbes's downfall was much more blatant and much more readily understood by the public. In late 1922 and early 1923, Forbes undertook to dispose of surplus hospital supplies left over from the war as well as to acquire new inventories—and to do so, not in public and by competitive bidding, but in private and under the most unfavorable (for the government) of terms. Indeed, Forbes's policy seems to have been to buy high and sell low. To this end he purchased $70,000 worth of floor cleaner and wax (estimated at the time to be a hundred-year supply) for 98 cents per gallon when it was actually worth about 3.2 cents. He sold 98,000 pairs of homemade winter pajamas that had been contributed by the public for the use of soldiers for 30 cents a pair. He sold 84,000 brand new bedsheets at 26 cents apiece (they had cost $1.37 each), *at the same time* purchasing 25,000 others at $1.03 each. Despite the fact that many of these items were needed at the time in veterans' hospitals, they were disposed of at about 20 percent of their value to a Boston firm, Thompson and Kelley.[28]

Altogether, Forbes disposed of some 125 railroad carloads of "surplus goods," or some $3,000,000 worth.[29] Still, Harding was reluctant to think the worst of his erstwhile friend. He labeled the charges against Forbes "abominable libel," and even when those charges became undeniable and when Forbes tendered his resignation, Harding demurred and offered him a position in

Europe, though one account does have the president berating and actually shaking Forbes in the White House at the time of the latter's departure.[30] After a Senate investigation and a nine-week trial, Forbes was sentenced to two years in jail and a $10,000 fine. His counsel at the Veterans' Bureau, Charles F. Cramer, had already committed suicide rather than testify in the case.[31]

In a second major scandal of the period, the Alien Property Scandal, yet another of Harding's appointees, Thomas W. Miller, was caught with his hand in the public till. This scandal centered on the case of the American Metal Company, the principal business of which was the purchase, refining, and sale of metals. At the start of World War I, American Metal had been 49-percent owned by German interests, with the remainder held by Americans and Britons. As was the normal practice, the German interest in the firm was taken over at the start of the war by the Alien Property Custodian and was later sold for $6,000,000. This sum was deposited in a bank and had grown to about $7,000,000 by 1921, when President Harding appointed Miller to the custodian's position. Shortly after Miller's appointment, a Swiss concern, the Société Suisse pour Valeurs de Méteaux, filed a claim stating that it had purchased the German interest in American Metal shortly before the outbreak of the war and was therefore entitled to the $7,000,000 on deposit. Although the American president of American Metals said that he was unaware of such a transfer; although during the war and after the supposed date of sale two Americans had, with special government permission, attempted to negotiate the purchase of the German interest and had failed only because the United States government thought the terms unfavorable; and although the head of the Swiss firm, one Richard Merton, also happened to have been one of the original German owners (indeed, the majority of the board members of Société Suisse were German), Miller approved the transfer. Attorney General Harry Daugherty gave his approval as well, and the property was transferred. It was subsequently revealed that Miller, a go-between named John T. King, and Harding-Daugherty crony Jess Smith had divided among themselves some $441,000 in cash and bonds the source of which was that selfsame Richard Merton. Smith, in fact, maintained an account in an Ohio bank that was owned by the brother of Attorney General Daugherty, and, when investigators sought the records of that account, they found that they had all been destroyed. The attorney general himself refused to testify in the matter *on the grounds of possible self-incrimination*. Miller was sentenced to eighteen months in prison, while Smith had already become the second prominent suicide of the period by the time the case was brought to light.[32]

Smith's name, in fact, came up rather often in discussions of influence peddling in Washington during the Harding years. A charter member of the Ohio Gang, he was ever a friend to both Daugherty and the president. Until his death, Smith maintained what was known as "the little green house on K Street," from which location he dispensed government positions, immunity from Justice Department prosecutions, access to government files, liquor permits for withdrawals from bonded government warehouses, and other political favors. Indeed, his suicide was apparently triggered by his increasing fear of discovery, by Harding's refusal to take him along on a grand political tour of Alaska, and by Daugherty's suggestion that the time might have come for him to leave Washington.[33] Harding, already shaken by the Forbes scandal and the Cramer suicide, took the death of his friend Smith as further evidence of corruption in his administration and became increasingly depressed.

There were other scandals during Harding's brief administration as well, some purely political and others much more personal. On the political front, the Justice Department (or the Department of Easy Virtue, as it was popularly known), which was under the pressure of constant public suspicion throughout Daugherty's stewardship for delays and failure to convict in a number of prominent cases, for failure to enforce antitrust laws, for favoritism to bankers, for questionable practices regarding pardons, for diversion of funds, for failure to recover oil lands in the wake of the Teapot Dome disclosures, for the appointment of corrupt persons to office, and even for collusion in the interstate transportation of boxing films (which had been outlawed to preserve the prestige of the white race following the winning of the world's heavyweight championship by a black boxer named Jack Johnson), was discovered to have in operation an extensive espionage network. The network, which had been established by Attorney General A. Mitchell Palmer (who had served under

President Wilson), was used to advantage by Daugherty. Congressmen were shadowed in a search for blackmail material, offices were burglarized, and telephones were tapped. And when Senator Burton K. Wheeler had the audacity to investigate Daugherty, the senator became the object of a concerted effort to discredit him.[34] This effort included harassment, threats, intimidation of witnesses, and even a trumped-up charge of bribery. Ironically, it was this unbounded defense of Daugherty by the agents of the Justice Department that, more than anything else, led Calvin Coolidge, who by then had succeeded to the presidency, to request Daugherty's resignation.[35] Harding, who owed much of his political career to his long-time friend from Ohio, had never been willing to do that.

On the personal front, Harding was subject to two charges. One, that he was part Negro, had haunted him since early in his political career and is of interest in a presidential context only because at one point a book that purported to prove such claims regarding his lineage was actually suppressed and all known copies confiscated by the Department of Justice and the Post Office.[36] The second charge centered around a woman named Nan Britton, a paramour of the president's from time to time, who claimed in a book entitled *The President's Daughter*, which was widely read and believed at the time, to have mothered an illegitimate child by Harding while he was president. This charge was rather more compelling and caused Harding considerably more difficulty than the first one. Still, when, after the president's death, Miss Britton sued for a share in Harding's estate, an Ohio jury found no cause to support her claim.[37]

All these instances of corruption and scandal notwithstanding, however, the real *pièce de resistance* of the Harding era and the one scandal that is best remembered is the so-called Teapot Dome Scandal. It was this event that put the Harding administration, in the public's mind at least, on a par with that of Grant and made Harding the president that Americans most wanted to forget.

Teapot Rock is an irregularly shaped outcropping of eroded sandstone that rises above the flats about fifty miles north of Casper, Wyoming. It sits atop a moderately extensive geological formation known to oilmen and students of politics alike as the

Teapot Dome. Although it contained no proven reserves at the time, this site was set aside by President Wilson in 1915 as Naval Oil Reserve Number Three (numbers one and two having already been established at Elk Hills and Buena Vista Hills, California, some time earlier). With war threatening and the navy in the midst of converting its vessels to oil as a principal fuel, it was feared that the then-prevalent helter-skelter development and exploitation of domestic oil resources could promise no reliable source of supply to meet military requirements. Thus, Wilson's move in establishing these reserves was primarily intended to conserve a needed military resource.[38]

Setting up these naval reserves, however, proved to be a much easier task than maintaining them. Even at the time of their establishment, government reserves were checkerboarded with privately held oil lands, and natural drainage from the reserves to the private holdings was a constant problem. This was compounded by the attempts of several private companies to purchase land or drilling rights immediately surrounding the government reserves, thus threatening still further drainage problems. And as if that were not enough, private interests decided to challenge the government directly by simply drilling on the naval reserves regardless of the absence of any valid legal claim for doing so. Against these pressures, the government struggled to create a viable policy for the development and conservation of petroleum resources.

President Wilson first responded to this problem by establishing the Petroleum Advisory Committee, one of a series of such planning groups he set up to oversee various industries, which consisted of the heads of all the major oil companies as well as three representatives of the smaller independents. This group assessed American productive capacity and allocated petroleum supplies between domestic needs and the wartime demands of the Western Allies. (The United States supplied, for example, some 85 percent of Britain's petroleum needs during that period.) When the United States entered the war, the Advisory Committee was renamed the National Petroleum War Service Committee but maintained its basic structure, personnel, and functions. Among the members of the committee at this time were E. L. Doheny of the Mexican Petroleum Company and Harry F. Sinclair of

Sinclair Oil and Refining Company, two men whose names were shortly to become household words.[39] The industry generally gave broad support to this committee, as is suggested by an editorial in *National Petroleum News,* a trade publication, which argued that "every man in the oil industry must absolutely give his entire confidence to this Oil Committee. . . . If necessary, we should put our entire businesses into the hands of this Committee, and it would be far better for the oil industry to do so than to put the oil industry directly into the hands of the government."[40] The public, however, began to view this committee-industry relationship as just a bit too cozy, and critics charged that such a committee, organized as it was around a private interest, could not properly represent the public interest. In effect, it was argued, the National Petroleum War Service Committee amounted to a powerful private cartel cloaked in patriotism.

Wilson responded to this public dissatisfaction by replacing the War Service Committee with the United States Fuel Administration, which, under the direction of Harry A. Garfield and Mark Requa, took charge of pooling production, promoting conservation, and allocating supplies. But in 1919, shortly after the war had ended, the Fuel Administration was disbanded, and the oil industry was once again put on its own. Interestingly enough, it was also in 1919 that the head of the U.S. Geological Survey announced that the country would run out of oil within a decade. With domestic demand increasing (automobiles, for example, were becoming more common), with supplies expected to be tight, and with the industry recently freed from government oversight, the scene was set for a petroleum free-for-all.[41] And for the same reasons, there developed increasing pressure on the government to free its naval oil reserves, pressure that mounted to new heights with the election of Harding because it was thought that a Republican administration would be more amenable to exploitation than the Democrats had proven.

Enter yet another of Harding's trusted appointees, Albert Fall, secretary of the interior. In June 1920, while Wilson was still president, control over the naval reserves had been vested for the first time in the secretary of the navy (such control had previously been the province of the Interior Department, but the navy had finally won a long battle to oversee its own resources) in an attempt to put these reserves above politics and to assure their proper military use.[42] Harding's naval secretary, Edwin Denby, however, was a man of limited abilities who had no particular interest in conserving petroleum supplies, and he agreed to Fall's request to transfer control of the reserves back to the Interior Department. Denby also agreed to Fall's request that he transfer an aide who objected to the change to a post far distant from Washington. A letter ordering the change of jurisdiction over the reserves and directing the secretary of the interior "to perform any and all acts necessary for the protection, conservation, and administration" of the reserves was submitted to the president by Fall on May 31, 1921, and the president, in an apparent contradiction to the expressed will of the Congress (which had ordered the original transfer), signed the letter on that date. Fall was in the oil business, and the president, who subsequently wrote of the matter to the Senate that "I think it is only fair to say in this connection that the policy which has been adopted by the Secretary of the Navy and the Secretary of the Interior in dealing with these matters was submitted to me prior to the adoption thereof, and the policy decided upon and the subsequent acts have at all times had my entire approval," was squarely behind the eight ball. Harding died before the details of Fall's "subsequent acts" became known, though there is evidence that he had begun to suspect a betrayal at the time of his death. Had he lived, these words might well have resulted in his impeachment for "high crimes and misdemeanors."[43]

Fall wasted little time in putting his scheme into effect. On April 7, 1922, the secretary announced that, by failing to develop the naval reserves, the Wilson administration had lost an estimated 22,000,000 barrels of oil through drainage and that the Interior Department would begin drilling immediately in order to conserve what oil was left. Leases were to be signed for the development of Reserves One and Two (much of Reserve One, presumed to be the richest of the three, had been leased to E. L. Doheny almost a year earlier in exchange for the construction of oil storage tanks at Pearl Harbor, Hawaii), with the government to receive *a portion* of the oil, which could be stored above ground to prevent drainage. In his announcement, Fall neglected to mention that he had also leased the entire Teapot Dome

Reserve to another oilman, Harry Sinclair.[44] The Doheny and Sinclair leases, unlike the others, had been made by private arrangement rather than through public bidding and were couched in terms that were relatively unfavorable to the government. Fall later justified these agreements as serving the national interest and security by providing for efficient conservation and development and for the establishment of a Hawaiian storage facility.[45] But on October 22, 1923, Fall's policies became the subject of congressional inquiry, and before long the dimensions of a scandal began to emerge.

Fall, it seems, had been having some financial difficulties prior to becoming secretary of the interior, and he found matters improving shortly thereafter thanks in no small measure to a $100,000 "loan" from Doheny (who then tore Fall's signature off the note that he received in exchange) and a payment of $68,000 from Sinclair. (The hearsay testimony supporting the latter was later claimed by Sinclair's personal secretary to have been misunderstood because, he said, he had in fact spoken, not of $68,000, but of "six or eight cows and . . .," a reference to a gift of livestock from Sinclair to rancher Fall.) Fall denied everything, but bit by bit the evidence piled up, ranging all the way from the testimony of Doheny to a series of mysterious telegrams coded in the secret code of the Justice Department that bore inscrutably on the roles in the affair played by Edward McLean, publisher of the *Washington Post* and erstwhile witness for Fall, Attorney General Harry Daugherty, with whose activities we are already familiar, C. Bascom Slemp, the president's private secretary, and even Calvin Coolidge, who by the time of the Fall hearings was president of the United States.[46] During the hearings all other congressional business came to a standstill. As one political pundit put it, Washington was "wading shoulder deep in oil."[47]

The congressional hearings led to the appointment by President Coolidge of two special prosecutors and subsequently to a lengthy series of trials that commenced on November 22, 1926.[48] But when the legal dust had finally settled in March 1930, the results were less than clear-cut. The Teapot Dome and Elk Hills leases were invalidated by the Supreme Court as having resulted from fraud, corruption, collusion, and conspiracy. But Fall and Doheny were acquitted on charges of conspiracy as were Fall and

Sinclair in a second trial. However, Sinclair did serve brief sentences for contempt of Congress (he had challenged the jurisdiction of the Senate Public Lands Committee and had refused to testify before it) and contempt of court (he had hired detectives to spy on his jury), and Fall was convicted of receiving a bribe from Doheny and was sentenced to a year in jail and a $100,000 fine (the first cabinet member in American history ever to receive a jail sentence). Doheny, on the other hand, was acquitted of bribing Fall.[49] The verdicts caused Senator George W. Norris to comment that it is "very difficult, if not impossible, to convict one hundred million dollars."[50]

Reverberations of Teapot Dome continued to be felt through the period (including a disclosure that the Republican party had accepted a contribution of $260,000 from Harry Sinclair, some of which was then "washed" by such prominent Republicans as Treasury Secretary Andrew Mellon) and were not wholly ended until President Hoover substantially altered both the personnel and the policy dealing with oil shortly after his coming to office in 1929.[51] It is interesting to note, incidentally, that on July 24, 1975, almost half a century later, the House of Representatives approved legislation that, among other things, would transfer control over oil production at the Elk Hills, Buena Vista Hills, and Teapot Dome Naval Reserves from the Navy Department to the Interior Department.[52]

Warren G. Harding died in Los Angeles on August 2, 1923, while returning to Washington from a successful political tour of Alaska and the West. And while there is some evidence that he was becoming aware of the misdeeds that were being performed in his name, it is unlikely that he really suspected the breadth of the scandals for which his administration ultimately would be remembered. Nor, for that matter, did the nation. His passing was mourned openly and emotionally throughout the land, and he was eulogized in the Senate as "among the most worthy of those who have occupied the Presidency." "His views," Senator Walsh of Massachusetts proclaimed, "were statesmanlike and the honor of our Nation was safe and secure in his hands."[53] And though his reputation was subsequently tarnished, it was, as it had been in the case of President Grant, Harding's guidance and judgment of men rather than his personal honesty that came to be the issue.

A Third-Rate Burglary: The Nixon Scandals

There were, of course, subsequent ripples of scandal that touched upon the executive branch in the succeeding years. Franklin D. Roosevelt was frequently accused of abusing his powers of patronage, Harry Truman was scored for supposedly tolerating widespread corruption and influence peddling—most notably in the Reconstruction Finance Corporation—and even Dwight D. Eisenhower was criticized for the willingness of his aide Sherman Adams to accept gifts from those who had dealings with the government.[54] But fifty years passed before another major scandal, perhaps the most centralized and most pernicious of all, shook the nation to its very foundations and forced the de facto impeachment of a president of the United States. That scandal was Watergate, and the president was Richard Milhous Nixon.

It is difficult at this point in time to present a cogent and comprehensive account of the Watergate Affair, the so-called White House Horrors, and the accompanying corruption of the political process, for in a sense both too much and too little are known about the events that led to the resignation of Richard Nixon. It is true that, as a result of extensive congressional hearings and court proceedings, an unparalleled wealth of detail is available on the inner workings of the Nixon administration and on the planning and carrying out of certain deeds that gave rise to scandal. At the same time, however, the larger organizing loci that could help one interpret and employ these data, the overall patterns of political activity during the Nixon years, are not yet sufficiently remote in time to permit one to clearly discern their outlines. And for much the same reason, the roles of various individuals in the scandals have not yet been clarified. Nevertheless, certain individuals and events do stand out, and there is something to be gained by briefly discussing them here.

Although the corruption of the Nixon years seems, as we shall see, to have been rather more widespread than the name would indicate, it will no doubt go down in history as the "Watergate Affair," much as the Grant scandals are remembered as Crédit Mobilier or the Harding scandals as Teapot Dome. The name Watergate derives from the location of the headquarters of the Democratic National Committee in the Watergate office and apartment complex in Washington, D.C. In the early morning hours of June 17, 1972, five men were arrested inside that headquarters bearing cameras, electronic bugging devices, and several crisp new $100 bills in sequential order. A subsequent investigation revealed additional stacks of fresh hundreds and two notebooks containing, among others, the name of one E. Howard Hunt, with indications that Hunt was somehow associated with the White House. Some days later, the trail led as well to George Gordon Liddy, who happened to be counsel to the Committee to Re-Elect the President, the Nixon campaign organization, popularly known by the acronym CREEP. Questions were thus raised as to what connections the White House and the election committee might have with the Watergate burglars.

On June 19, two days after the break-in and before many details were known, White House press secretary Ron Ziegler responded to inquiries on the matter by terming the affair "a third-rate burglary attempt." As subsequent revelations appeared to implicate still further various persons with close ties to the White House and CREEP, the administration continued its effort to downplay the episode and to dissociate itself from the perpetrators. Then on July 1, John Mitchell, who had only recently resigned as attorney general to head the president's reelection effort, stepped down as director of CREEP, citing personal reasons. Mitchell, later evidence was to show, knew a good deal more of the bugging and espionage attempt than he chose to let on.

Had the matter rested there and had the president given an honest public accounting at that time, the Watergate Affair would have probably caused little more than a ripple. But an alternative course was chosen and followed to the end. There ensued almost from the outset a pervasive attempt to cover up any connection between the president and his closest aides and the Watergate burglary. Elements of the coverup included the payment of thousands of dollars in "hush money" to the burglars, frequent misstatements of fact by the president and his spokesmen (press secretary Ziegler at one point late in the affair announced that all his previous statements were "inoperative"), misuse of the Justice Department and control of its investigation, and even attempts to manipulate the Central Intelligence Agency to block a Federal Bureau of Investigation inquiry into the sources of funds used to support the burglars.

In itself, the Watergate break-in hardly rated such herculean efforts, but as events developed it became clear that much more was at stake. Both the White House and the reelection committee, it seems, had been engaged in certain illicit activities that could have been (and ultimately were) brought to light by an investigation of the Watergate perpetrators. This was true of the White House in that some of the same individuals (most notably Hunt and Liddy) had undertaken a number of clandestine activities, later dubbed the "White House Horrors" by Mitchell, including spiriting a witness in a corruption investigation out of Washington, falsifying diplomatic cables to implicate the Kennedy administration in the assassination of South Vietnamese President Ngo Dinh Diem in 1963, and breaking and entering a doctor's office to obtain confidential records regarding Daniel Ellsberg, a defendant in a politically important espionage trial. And it was true of CREEP in that the money spent on the burglary and coverup was part of a much larger cache that had been raised and expended secretly and illegally. Discovery of these connections could have proven devastating both to the president's chances for reelection in 1972 and to his second administration.

Much of this was not known, however, until well after November 1972, when President Nixon won an overwhelming victory over Democratic contender George McGovern. Indeed, most of it was not discovered until the summer of 1973, when a special committee of the Senate, chaired by Senator Sam Ervin of North Carolina, began delving into the matter in a lengthy series of nationally televised hearings. The hearings got off to a sensational start as John W. Dean, who had served as counsel to the president, charged that Nixon and all those around him not only knew of the coverup but were still actively engaging in it. Dean's testimony was refuted by H. R. Haldeman and John Ehrlichman, two of Nixon's closest aides, and by a series of other White House spokesmen. With the star witness standing virtually alone as the accuser of the president, and with only a series of lesser, though occasionally colorful, figures left to appear, the inquiry seemed to be running out of steam when a little-known White House assistant, Alexander P. Butterfield, shocked the country by announcing the existence of a tape-recording system in the president's office that had probably captured most of the conversations at issue in the hearings. Immediately, both the senators and special prosecutor Archibald Cox, who had earlier been appointed by Nixon to handle Watergate-related prosecutions, attempted to gain access to a whole series of relevant tapes. The White House refused on the grounds of executive privilege, an unwritten doctrine of constitutional law by which the president claims the right to maintain the confidentiality of certain communications internal to the executive branch of government, and a lengthy legal and political battle was joined. This was climaxed on the night of Saturday, October 20, 1973, with the firing of Cox and the resignations of Attorney General Elliot Richardson and Deputy Attorney General William Ruckelshaus, each of whom had refused a presidential order to dismiss Cox. This event, which came to be known as the Saturday Night Massacre, was probably the single most important incident in stirring up the public outcry that ultimately led to impeachment proceedings and the resignation of Nixon.

At that point, events began to move inexorably toward a conclusion. On October 30, the House Judiciary Committee began to consider a presidential impeachment. The following week a Gallup public opinion poll showed that only 27 percent of Americans surveyed approved of President Nixon's performance in office. And in December, Nixon revealed that he had become a millionaire while in office but had paid less than $1,000 in taxes in 1970 and 1971. (He was later billed for an additional $465,000 by the Internal Revenue Service, and those who had helped prepare his tax returns were charged with fraud.) In the meantime, the White House agreed to release tapes that had been subpoenaed by Cox, then announced that two critical tapes were missing and that another had a lengthy gap (later purported to have resulted from a series of purposeful erasures) where a presidential discussion of Watergate should have been. In March 1974, seven of the president's closest aides and election officials were indicted by a grand jury for their role in the Watergate coverup, and seven for the Ellsberg break-in. And in April the White House released more than a thousand pages of edited transcripts of the presidential tapes and announced that no more such evidence would be forthcoming. In July the Supreme Court ordered the tapes upon which these transcripts were based released by the White House, and the discrepancies that immediately became obvious in the president's transcripts added to his difficulties. During the last week in July, in a series of votes that approached party-line tallies, the House Judiciary Committee voted out three articles of impeachment charging the president with obstruction of justice, misuse of power, and defying committee subpoenas, the latter charge having probably been added to help to clarify certain issues in any future impeachment proceedings.

Even with the momentum swinging toward impeachment, however, there was serious question as to whether a successful conviction of the president would have followed in the Senate. Then, on August 5, 1974, the White House released, though only at the insistence of presidential aides and attorneys, three more transcripts that clearly showed Richard Nixon's complicity in the Watergate coverup. His remaining congressional support immediately collapsed, and on August 9, 1974, Richard M. Nixon became the first President of the United States ever to resign his office. Had he not done so, there can be little doubt that he would have been the first ever to be impeached by the House of Representatives *and* convicted by the Senate.[55]

The break-in and coverup, however, and even the White House Horrors, do not constitute the whole story of the Nixon scandals, for there were other seeming misdeeds committed by those around the president. Two of the most noteworthy involved apparent cases of influence peddling by cabinet members and others and perhaps, though the evidence is clouded, by the president himself. The first of these revolved around a Justice Department settlement of an antitrust case against International Telephone and Telegraph Corporation (ITT), which had been brought to account for its acquisition of the Hartford Insurance Company on terms favorable to the company at roughly the same time that ITT had pledged some $400,000 to help underwrite the 1972 Republican Convention in San Diego, California. Following disclosure of this arrangement by newspaper columnist Jack Anderson, the convention, which was to have been headquartered at an ITT-owned Sheraton Hotel, was moved to Miami, Florida. Subsequently, on May 16, 1974, Richard G. Kleindienst became the first attorney general in American history to plead guilty to a criminal offense, admitting that he had failed to disclose at his Senate confirmation hearing in 1972 that President

Nixon had ordered him to see that the Justice Department investigation of ITT was halted.[56]

A second such case centered around the attempts of the Associated Milk Producers (AMPI), a dairy industry lobby, to obtain an increase in government milk price supports in the spring of 1971. In March of that year, Secretary of Agriculture Clifford Hardin had determined after a policy review that price supports for milk would not be raised above the levels prevailing at that time, since raising the supports might well prompt overproduction and lead to unwanted surpluses. Following this decision, on March 22, the Trust for Agricultural Political Education, an industry political fund, donated some $10,000 to Republican campaign coffers. On March 23, the president and Secretary Hardin met with industry leaders, who urged them to reconsider their policy, and on March 24 yet another industry fund, the Trust for Special Political Agricultural Community Education, contributed an additional $25,000. On March 25, Hardin raised milk price supports almost 6 percent, and, by election day 1972, the dairymen had reciprocated to the tune of more than $400,000. Indeed, though at this writing all the evidence is not yet in, it appears that this process of political bartering was not limited to AMPI and ITT. American Airlines early admitted that it had contributed $55,000 to the Nixon reelection campaign in an attempt to influence approval of its proposed merger with Western Airlines, and a number of officers of other corporations have subsequently pleaded guilty to making substantial illegal donations of corporate funds to the campaign.[57] A number of payments were apparently solicited by Herbert Kalmbach, the president's personal attorney and a major figure in the Watergate "hush money" payments, and by Maurice Stans, former secretary of the treasury and later director of the fund-raising activities of CREEP. Both subsequently pleaded guilty to related charges in federal court.

Also tainted by the milk scandal was another former treasury secretary, John Connally, who was indicted by a federal grand jury in July 1974 for accepting a $10,000 payoff to recommend to President Nixon an increase in milk price supports and for perjuring himself in order to cover his tracks.[58] Although an old friend, Jake Jacobs, pleaded guilty to bribery charges and admitted having given the money to Connally for the stated purpose, Connally was acquitted of all charges in the spring of 1975. Subsequent to the trial, however, the court released a transcript of a tape recording of March 23, 1971, in which Connally recommended to Nixon the raising of price supports and was further quoted as telling the president, "It's on my honor to make sure that, that there's a very substantial allocation of oil in Texas that you, that will be at your, at your discretion," to which Nixon responds, "Fine" and then, three sentences later, "This is a cold political deal." The tape, which was difficult to understand, had been played for the jury, but, on a motion from the defense, the transcript had been withheld. For his part, Connally said he was speaking of "taxes," not "Texas."[59]

Then there was the case of financier Robert Vesco, then under investigation by the Securities and Exchange Commission (SEC) and subsequently indicted for fraud and conspiracy, who, on April 10, 1972, gave Maurice Stans a cash contribution for the Nixon campaign of $200,000, which he followed up with a check for $50,000. As the investigation of Vesco moved toward indictment, Stans approached the counsel to the SEC, Bradford Cook, and asked him to delete any reference to the campaign contributions from the pending indictment. Cook, according to his own testimony, was in effect offered the chairmanship of the SEC should he comply. The Vesco indictment was returned in late November 1972, devoid of any reference to the $250,000, and on February 17, 1973, after the way had been cleared by the appointment of the previous SEC chairman, William Casey, to a position in the State Department, Cook was appointed by President Nixon to head the Securities and Exchange Commission. Stans and John Mitchell were later indicted on charges of perjury and conspiracy in connection with the Vesco case, but they were acquitted.[60]

And, too, there was the question of the influence that a close friend of the president, Charles "Bebe" Rebozo, exercised within the administration. Among other things, Rebozo was charged by the chairman of the House Banking and Currency Committee, Wright Patman, with having received several favors from the Small Business Administration, including an $80,000 loan that was approved despite staff objections. Rebozo's most mysterious role, however, was as holder of a $100,000 cash fund paid to Nixon by multimillionaire Howard Hughes in 1969 and 1970, at a time when Hughes was having antitrust difficulties with the Justice Department. The significance of this fund was never clearly established, but one theory held that one purpose of the bugging of the Democratic headquarters in 1972 was to determine whether Lawrence O'Brien, the party's national chairman, was aware of the money. O'Brien, it seems, had been working for Hughes interests at the time of the contribution. A second theory about the money was that Nixon had used it for certain real estate transactions, for the president had acquired during his term in office two expensive vacation homes, one in Key Biscayne, Florida (next door to Rebozo), and the other in San Clemente, California, both with the assistance of Rebozo and another millionaire friend, Robert Abplanalp.[61] These acquisitions were viewed with increasing suspicion, particularly after it was revealed that more than $1 million of public funds had been spent, some quite improperly, to improve these properties.[62] As matters came to a head in the impeachment proceedings, however, the Rebozo connection and the president's real estate dealings faded from the public eye and became lost in the quagmire that was Watergate.

This completes our overview of the Nixon scandals per se. However, no account of corruption in the Nixon years could be complete without mention of one more event, the resignation of Spiro T. Agnew, the thirty-ninth vice-president of the United States, on October 10, 1973. For when Nixon himself stepped down almost a year later, it was not his two-time running mate who took over the reins of government but rather a man who had, under the terms of the Twenty-Fifth Amendment to the Constitution, been appointed vice-president by Nixon and approved by the Congress, Gerald R. Ford. Agnew, it seems, had maintained a kickback scheme with certain contractors during his years in Maryland state and local government, payments from which extended into his years as vice-president. And when an investigation of corruption in Maryland led to discovery of his complicity, Agnew resigned his office under pressure and, in exchange, was permitted to plead no contest to a single charge of tax evasion, for which he received a $10,000 fine and a suspended jail sentence.[63] By voluntarily relinquishing his office in the face of charges of wrongdoing, Agnew established both a realization among the American people that such things actually could occur (much as Colfax's resignation had established such a realization during the Grant years), and a precedent soon to be followed by the chief executive himself.

The degree of Richard Nixon's culpability in the scandals that bear his name is not yet perfectly clear, though there are indications that his involvement was somewhat more direct than had been that of either Grant or Harding. Still, although relatively little of what was done was done by the president himself, much was done in the president's name and in his presumed interest. Nixon's guilt, like that of Grant and Harding, thus appears to lie more in the atmosphere of government and politics that he engendered and in his general disrespect for law and due process than in his specific misdeeds.

Sources of Political Corruption: Some Lessons of History

If one looks closely, one can discern a number of interesting parallels among the three eras of scandal centered in the oval office of the president, and most particularly between the most recent two. In each instance, for example, the seemingly reflexive response of the president was to deny scandal and/or to cover it up and protect his associates. This is most clearly the case in the Nixon scandals, where the coverup was complex and itself became a central issue, but it is true as well in the earlier episodes. Grant, it will be recalled, protected his close associates even to the point of serving as a character witness for a man who had betrayed his trust, and he took steps to purge his cabinet (Bristow) and other agencies (Custer, the St. Louis prosecutor of the Whiskey Ring) of those who would stand as accusers. At one point, as we noted, he even instructed government prosecutors in the Babcock prosecution to deny immunity to those who might testify against his aide, a step also taken a century later by Richard Nixon. And like Nixon, Grant took as personal attacks any efforts to clear the government of his corrupt friends. Harding, too, in the few opportunities he had before his death, displayed this defensive reflex, most notably in his continuing defense of Daugherty and in his offer of an overseas position to Forbes. Even Calvin Coolidge, who inherited the Teapot Dome scandal but was not himself involved, apparently sought to intervene in the congressional inquiry when Edward McLean was falsely named by Fall as the source of a $100,000 payment. It was this intervention that was evidenced in the coded telegrams described earlier. Yet of all these presidents, Nixon was perhaps most cognizant of the danger here, having once commented, "I can categorically state that [the] investigation indicates that no one in the White House staff, no one in this administration, presently employed, was involved in this very bizarre incident [the break-in]. *What really hurts is if you try to cover it up.*"[64] (Emphasis added.)

Similarly, many of the cases in each period were brought to the fore by a combination of congressional hearings and a legal process outside the regular Justice Department channels (thus seeming to reaffirm the importance of the doctrine of separation of powers among the three branches of the government). The Whiskey Ring, for example, was broken and prosecuted under the auspices of the Treasury Department (still, of course, within the executive branch), while bipartisan or nonpartisan special prosecutors were employed in both Teapot Dome and Watergate. In all three instances, the Justice Department was so little trusted or was itself so implicated that any actions it might take were not likely to be viewed as satisfactory. And interestingly enough, the congressional hearings into both Teapot Dome and Watergate were rescued from obscurity first by the chance discovery of a key witness—Carl C. Magee, a newspaper editor who revealed some questionable real estate transactions by Albert Fall that led to the breaking of the Teapot Dome Scandal in the first instance, and Alexander P. Butterfield, who revealed the existence of the presidential tapes in the latter—and second by unusual evidentiary materials, the coded telegrams and the aforementioned tape recordings, which in each instance stimulated great public interest.

In each instance, too, these twin legislative and judicial processes were encouraged and supported by the press, though in different ways. In the Grant era the press was highly partisan and contributed to the public outrage more by editorializing than by informing. Two notable exceptions to this general rule may be found in the Belknap case, the details of which were revealed by the *Washington Herald* and the *New York Herald* prior to congressional hearings on the matter, and in the Crédit Mobilier Scandal, which was first brought to light by the *New York Sun*, but even in these cases the press soon reverted to partisan rhetoric.[65] During the Harding era, however, the press played a more active role, as in the cases of Magee, whose *New Mexico State Tribune* reports on Fall stimulated close scrutiny of the congressional hearings by other newspapers, and, in a rather different way, of McLean of the *Washington Post*, who was himself embroiled in the controversy.[66] Of still more importance was the role of Paul Anderson, a reporter for the *St. Louis Post-Dispatch* whose reporting in 1927 forced the reluctant Coolidge administration to pursue the Teapot Dome conspiracy to its conclusion.[67] But it was not until the Nixon years that the press became a full partner in the investigative process through the activities of such reporters as Jack Anderson, whom we have mentioned above, and Carl Bernstein and Bob Woodward, whose reports on the Watergate Affair in the *Washington Post* continually developed new and fruitful lines of inquiry.[68]

These and other similarities appear relatively minor, however, in the context of three additional considerations. For one thing, all three crises in the presidency followed more or less directly on extended periods of national disarray, and all three were associated with the aftermath of relatively unpopular wars. Grant, of course, came to office shortly after the Civil War and in the midst of a raging controversy over the terms of Reconstruction. He followed into the presidency the unpopular and widely distrusted Andrew Johnson, in whose carriage he himself had refused to ride on inauguration day. Harding took office in 1921, hard upon the heels of not only the Great War but also the period of economic, racial, and political upheaval that we have discussed earlier and to which we shall return in chapter 7, and he did so pledging a return to "normalcy." And Nixon inherited and ultimately claimed as his own an Asian policy war that gave rise throughout his term to vituperative rhetoric and to a violent clash of points of view. Each of these periods was characterized by a redefinition of basic national identities: unification in the first instance, international responsibility in the second, and the limits of power and right in the third. During such periods, popular expectations may be easily calloused and popular judgments distorted as crisis criteria are applied to noncrisis or postcrisis situations, thereby easing the transition from honest to corrupt government and leading to the confusion of just ends with self-interest. Thus, in some circumstances such corruption may be all but unavoidable.

If that is true, however, it is probably no more attributable to the demeanor of the times than to the personal style of the president in office, for it is also true that each of the periods of scandal we have discussed followed hard upon an expansion of the powers of the presidency (arising to a great extent in each instance from the circumstances of the proximate wartime experience). If there were personal differences among the three leaders in question, though Grant and Harding displayed remarkable similarities of personality and style, there are also strong indications that the style of each was reflected in the actions of his subordinates. Grant and Harding were trusting, relaxed, and relatively inefficient administrators, and their underlings and acquaintances took advantage of them for personal gain. Nixon was distrustful, tense, and—through H. R. Haldeman—an efficient organizer, and he became, in effect, the willing victim of his own sycophantic organization, in most cases for collective political gain rather than for personal financial advantage. In each instance, the style of the president effectively helped structure the style of the corruption.

And finally, each period of corruption seems to have resulted in a breakdown in the relationship of trust between the American people and their government and, some would argue, in the moral fortitude of the people themselves. Thus, of the Grant era, historian Allan Nevins has written,

> The festering corruptions of the post-war period sprang up in every part of America and in almost every department of national life. . . . Beyond doubt the reasons for this pervasive malady were numerous, deep-rooted, and complex. . . . The war explained much: its terrible strain upon all ten commandments; the moral exhaustion which it produced. . . . Everywhere tested standards, restraints of public opinion, the cake of custom, were broken down.[69]

Of the Harding era, G. T. Patrick, a student of social questions at the time, wrote in *The Psychology of Social Reconstruction* (in tones echoed half a century later in the antipermissivist rhetoric of the Nixon administration):

> There is a danger even greater than war which threatens our modern civilization and that is decadence—physical, mental, and moral. . . . There is danger that physical degeneracy will follow upon our sedentary manner of living, upon the increase of wealth, ease and luxury. There is danger that mental degeneracy will follow upon the reversal of the law of survival which in the past has eliminated the mentally unfit. There is a danger of moral degeneracy in the period of readjustment from religious to purely ethical sanctions of conduct.[70]

And of the Nixon years, Thomas Griffith has written in *Time* magazine that

> in the present atmosphere no one seems good enough to be President. Perhaps one difficulty comes from a public confusion about what kind of crisis, or combination of crises, the country faces and therefore the kind of qualities it seeks in the man. The romantic longing to rally behind bold leadership, as if this were a wartime emergency with a simple, patriotically accepted goal to be personified in one man, is too simplistic a remedy for that messy complexity of economic, moral, and social problems we all struggle with. The time has come to de-emphasize not the office of the presidency but the myth of the omnipotent President, reigning from the Oval Office, glorified for being lonely in his ordeals when he should be judged by whether he can inspire independent men around him, can listen to divergent advice and make clear choices, and can then involve the strengths of the nation as a whole.[71]

Perhaps former President William Howard Taft put his finger on the popular pulse best when he was asked by Calvin Coolidge, who had recently succeeded to the presidency, what he, Coolidge, ought to do as president. "Do nothing," Taft advised him and then went on to say that he believed that "the public were glad to have him in the White House doing nothing. . . . in the returning prosperity people were glad to have a rest from watching Washington, and that . . . his wisest course was to be quiet."[72]

Conclusion

It is undoubtedly true that some level of scandalous or corrupt behavior takes place in the administration of every president, and those instances that we have selected for analysis here are probably made unique only by the scale on which they transpired. There is, of course, a disturbing regularity about these incidents, which seem to come at the rate of approximately one every fifty years, but it is less the regularity of scandal than its contributing elements on which we should focus our attention. For if we once understand the various sources of such political malfeasance at the highest levels, we may in the process take a significant step toward reducing its regularity.

NOTES

1. Frank R. Kent, "Fat Cats and Free Rides," *American Mercury* 14 (June 1928): 129.
2. From a letter to William G. McAdoo, quoted in Burl Noggle, *Teapot Dome: Oil and Politics in the 1920's* (Baton Rouge: Louisiana State University Press, 1962), p. 111.
3. Quoted in Staff of the *Washington Post,* comps., *The Fall of a President* (New York: Dell, 1974), p. 192.
4. Grayson L. Kirk, "Crédit Mobilier Scandal," *American Mercury* 32 (July 1934): 352.
5. Ibid., pp. 351–59.
6. Ibid.; Esther Strachey, "Godfather to American Corruption," *American Mercury* 32 (June 1934): pp. 170–79; Arthur Warner, "Scandals of the 70's," *Nation,* 16 April 1924, p. 418.
7. Kirk, "Crédit Mobilier Scandal"; Strachey, "Godfather."
8. Kirk, "Crédit Mobilier Scandal," p. 359.
9. Strachey, "Godfather."
10. Kirk, "Crédit Mobilier Scandal."
11. William B. Hesseltine, *Ulysses S. Grant: Politician* (New York: Ungar, 1935), p. 312.
12. Strachey, "Godfather"; W. E. Woodward, *Meet General Grant* (Literary Guild of America, 1928), pp. 411–16; Hesseltine, *Grant,* pp. 169–79.
13. Allan Nevins, *Hamilton Fish: The Inner History of the Grant Administration* (New York: Dodd, Mead, 1937), p. 286.

14. Hesseltine, *Grant*, pp. 380–88; and Nevins, *Fish*, pp. 762–804.
15. Nevins, *Fish*, p. 804.
16. Hesseltine, *Grant*, pp. 363-64.
17. Warner, "Scandals," p. 418.
18. Nevins, *Fish*, pp. 804–09; and Warner, "Scandals," pp. 418-19.
19. Nevins, *Fish*, p. 821.
20. Ibid., pp. 593–95, 657.
21. Ibid., pp. 646–49.
22. Ibid., p. 814.
23. Ibid., pp. 662 64, 771.
24. Ibid., pp. 773–78.
25. Ibid., pp. 815-16.
26. Hesseltine, *Grant*, pp. 321–22, 366–67.
27. Nevins, *Fish*, p. 641.
28. Bruce Bliven, "Ohio Gang," *New Republic*, 7 May 1924, pp. 9-11; Robert K. Murray, *The Harding Era: Warren G. Harding and His Administration* (Minneapolis: University of Minnesota Press, 1969), pp. 429, 459-61; Samuel Hopkins Adams, *Incredible Era: The Life and Times of Warren Gamaliel Harding* (Boston: Houghton Mifflin, 1939), pp. 284-93.
29. Adams, *Incredible Era*, p. 294; Carl C. Dickey, "Plundering the Wounded Men," *World's Work* 48 (June 1924): 167–74.
30. Adams, *Incredible Era*, pp. 296-97.
31. Ibid., pp. 301-02; Murray, *Harding Era*, p. 461.
32. Bruce Bliven, "Ohio Gang Again," *New Republic*, 31 March 1926, pp. 164–67; Blair Bolles, *Men of Good Intentions: Crisis of the American Presidency* (Garden City, N.Y.: Doubleday, 1960), p. 43; Murray, *Harding Era*, p. 481; Edgar Mels, "Alien Property Scandal," *Nation* 14 and 21 April 1926, pp. 391-93, 445–46.
33. Murray, *Harding Era*, pp. 432–36.
34. Bruce Bliven, "Ohio Gang," *New Republic*, 4 June 1924, pp. 40–42; Sherman Blanchard, "President Harding: A Reappraisal," *Current History* 35 (October 1931): 41–47 and Adams, *Incredible Era*, p. 317.
35. Murray, *Harding Era*, pp. 478–79.
36. Adams, *Incredible Era*, pp. 273-83.
37. Ibid., p. 429.
38. Burl Noggle, "Origins of the Teapot Dome Investigation," *Mississippi Valley Historical Review* 44 (September 1957): pp. 237-66; Noggle, *Teapot Dome*, p. 16; J. Leonard Bates, *Origins of Teapot Dome* (Urbana: University of Illinois Press, 1963), p. 118.
39. David Howard Davis, *Energy Politics* (New York: St. Martin's, 1974), p. 46; and Bates, *Origins*, pp. 99-100.
40. Quoted in Bates, *Origins*, p. 100.

41. Ibid., p. 103; Davis, *Energy Politics*, pp. 46–48.
42. Bates, *Origins*, p. 200.
43. Adams, *Incredible Era*, pp. 346–48.
44. Noggle, *Teapot Dome*, pp. 35–36.
45. Ibid., p. 65.
46. Adams, *Incredible Era*, pp. 396–400.
47. Bruce Bliven, "Oil Driven Politics," *New Republic*, 13 February 1924, p. 302.
48. Noggle, *Teapot Dome*, pp. 91–92 reports the text of the president's statement on the appointment of the special prosecutors.
49. Adams, *Incredible Era*, p. 407; Murray, *Harding Era*, p. 472.
50. Murray, *Harding Era*, p. 472.
51. Noggle, *Teapot Dome*, pp. 192–93, 209.
52. "Measure to Let Navy Pump Elk Hills Oil Clears Senate Unit," *Wall Street Journal*, 25 July 1975, p. 5, col. 2.
53. "President Harding and His Administration," *Outlook*, 15 August 1923, p. 577.
54. See for example "WPA Scandals of 1938," *New Republic*, 18 January 1939, pp. 300–01; Jules Abels, *The Truman Scandals* (Chicago: Regnery, 1956), passim; and Bolles, *Men of Good Intentions*, pp. 100–135.
55. For more extensive discussions of Watergate-related events, see Staff of the *Washington Post*, comps., *Fall;* Barry Sussman, *The Great Cover-Up: Nixon and the Scandal of Watergate* (New York: Signet, 1974); Carl Bernstein and Bob Woodward, *All The President's Men* (New York: Warner, 1974); *Watergate: Chronology of a Crisis* (Washington, D.C.: Congressional Quarterly, 1974); J. Anthony Lukas, "The Story So Far," *New York Times Magazine*, 22 July 1973, passim; idem, "The Story Continued," *New York Times Magazine*, 13 January 1974, passim. Our own analysis is based in part on material contained in these sources.
56. "Square Scourge of Washington," *Time*, 3 April 1972, pp. 40–42; Staff of the *Washington Post*, comps., *Fall*, p. 194; and Sussman, *Great Cover-Up*, p. 226.
57. Lukas, "The Story So Far," p. 17.
58. Staff of the *Washington Post*, comps., *Fall*, p. 195.
59. "Oil Allocation Deal Revealed in Tapes," *Roanoke* (Va.) *Times*, 15 June 1975, p. A-9.
60. Sussman, *Great Cover-Up*, p. 153.
61. Lukas, "The Story Continued," pp. 17–19; and Staff of the Washington Post, comps., *Fall*, p. 170.
62. Lukas, pp. 12–16.
63. Richard M. Cohen, ". . . I Have Been Paying Off the Vice President," in Staff of the *Washington Post*, comps., *Fall*, pp. 88–98.

64. Staff of the *Washington Post*, comps., *Fall*, p. 185.

65. Nevins, *Fish*, pp. 804–06; Kirk, "Crédit Mobilier Scandal," p. 351.

66. On the first of these see Murray, *Harding Era*, pp. 467–68.

67. Noggle, *Teapot Dome*, pp. 186–89.

68. "Square Scourge," passim; Sussman, *Great Cover-Up*, passim; Bernstein and Woodward, *President's Men*, passim. For a discussion of the role of the White House press corps in breaking the Watergate story, see Jules Witcover, "How Well Does the White House Press Perform?" *Columbia Journalism Review* 12 (November-December 1973): 39–43.

69. Nevins, *Fish*, pp. 638–39.

70. Quoted in Bliven, "Ohio Gang," (as in note 34 above), p. 42.

71. Thomas Griffith, "In Defense of Politicians: Do We Ask Too Much?" *Time*, 27 January 1975, pp. 32–33.

72. Quoted in Noggle, *Teapot Dome*, p. 62.

5

Political Movements I: Women's Rights and Constitutional Change

When the right to vote at any election for the choice of electors for President and Vice President of the United States, Representatives in Congress, the Executive and Judicial officers of a State, or the members of the Legislature thereof, is denied to any of the male inhabitants of such State, being twenty-one years of age, and citizens of the United States, or in any way abridged except for participation in rebellion, or other crime, the basis of representation therein shall be reduced in the proportion which the number of such male citizens shall bear to the whole number of male citizens twenty-one years of age in such State.

From Section 2 of the Fourteenth Amendment (Adopted 1868)

The right of citizens of the United States to vote shall not be denied or abridged by the United States or by any State on account of race, color, or previous condition of servitude.

Section 1 of the Fifteenth Amendment (Adopted 1870)

The solution of this strange problem [that women are excluded from politics] *may be discovered in two words—Constitutional law! There are forty-two strong reasons why women cannot vote in the United States. The first and greatest lies in the National Constitution, the other forty-one are found in the Constitutions of the different states. In these revered documents one little word of four letters, "male," is all that stands between 15,000,000 women and the suffrage.*

Ida Husted Harper, 1904[1]

For the safety of the nation to
Women give the vote
For the hand that rocks the cradle
Will never rock the boat

Suffrage Banner, 1915[2]

The right of citizens of the United States to vote shall not be denied or abridged by the United States or by any State on account of sex.

From the Nineteenth Amendment (Adopted 1920)

Equality of rights under the law shall not be denied or abridged by the United States or by any State on account of sex.

From the pending Equal Rights Amendment
(Approved by Congress, March 1972)

Over the past two decades a number of significant social and political movements have vied with one another for some share of the public consciousness. Among these have been the civil rights movement of the late 1950s and early to mid-1960s, the antiwar movement of the mid-1960s to the early 1970s, the environmental protection movement, the consumer protection movement, and the drive for full political equality for women. For the most part, these various crusades have been relatively independent of one another, each with its own leadership and primary substantive concerns, each with its own goals. Still, and probably more important, each has had in common with the others its desire to hasten fundamental social change, its reliance upon a predominantly middle-class constituency to support that change, its reliance upon certain strategies and tactics to mobilize support, and even its occurrence during a period of marked domestic uncertainty (to which each no doubt itself contributed). Indeed, in many ways the most interesting point about the political movements of the last twenty years or so may be the fact that they have been so contemporaneous with and so similar to one another that they have fostered the widely held impression that American society has been in the midst of a broadly based, multifaceted, and portentous upheaval.

In the present chapter and the one that follows, we shall explore two of these movements, those pertaining to the rights of women and the protection of consumers, in some depth. Although this selection is admittedly arbitrary, we do find operating in these two movements many of the same forces and historical trends that have been apparent in other sociopolitical movements throughout American history. In each instance some injustice or inequity has been noted within the political system; a resulting public outcry has been continuous though not constant; eventual recourse has been taken through the formal mechanisms of the political system (primarily through the process of constitutional amendment in the case of the women's movement, and primarily through the legislative and administrative processes in that of the consumers' movement); change, albeit slow and incremental, has come in response to these pressures; this change has proven in the long run to be insufficient to deflect the various dissatisfactions to which it was intended to respond; and the proponents of each movement have taken still further recourse to political action. Although every movement has its unique elements, and although each has met with varying degrees of success or failure through time, this continuing dialectic process of irresistible political force meeting immovable political structure is generally typical of all and thus not only offers a useful organizing premise for an investigation of these particular movements but provides an indication that our findings in such an investigation may have still broader applicability.

Woman Suffrage: The Doubling of Democracy

Although it is common to date the women's rights movement from the first quarter of the present century, and more particularly from the successful drive for woman suffrage that culminated in final adoption of the Nineteenth Amendment in August 1920, the true origins of the movement in the United States may actually be traced to a period at least a full century earlier. It was in the 1820s that activists such as Emma Willard began to press for equal educational opportunities for women (Oberlin College became the first to accept both men and women in 1833) and for other social and political rights. And it was in the 1830s and 1840s that the movement received its first real impetus through the participation of women in the organized effort to abolish slavery.

We shall not review the details of the abolitionist movement here, for it falls well before the period on which we are focusing and should, in any event, be generally familiar to many readers. What is of interest to the present inquiry is that, from their participation in antislavery activities, American women learned three political lessons that were later to be of some consequence to the women's rights movement. The first of these, and perhaps the most difficult for these early activists to accept, was that they truly did not possess the political equality that they were striving to extend to others. For all the preachments of American democrats, and for all the righteous indignation the women themselves could muster, they found themselves largely excluded from the political process. Even among their fellow abolitionists, undoubtedly the most socially radical men of the era, women were regularly accorded second-class status, refused membership in certain organizations, and often denied the right to speak in public. This must have been a bitter realization indeed, but it was only one element in a growing awareness of the special status of women in the American polity.

The second lesson of the abolitionist experience was closely related and could in fact be said to have arisen from the first. Largely as a result of their own exclusion and of the unwillingness of men to recognize the justice of their cause, these women came to see a close connection between their own social and political condition and the more formalized servitude toward whose abolition they were so vigorously working. Indeed, given the fact that the cause that had brought them together in the first place was an antislavery movement and that this movement was principally characterized by accusatory rhetoric and public exhortation, it was probably inevitable that the analogy to slavery would occur to the women activists and would subsequently color their verbal assaults on the male-dominated political system. Thus, in a sense the perceptions held by women of their own plight came increasingly to be structured by the very movement that had given rise to them in the first place.[3]

Finally, and in a more practical vein, these early women activists learned through their apprenticeship in the abolitionist movement how, in effect, to be political activists. That is, they learned the complementary arts of public speaking and persuasion, they learned to prepare and circulate petitions, and more generally they acquired political skills that could be used to force freedom and equality not only for black slaves but for themselves as well.[4] Their participation in the abolitionist crusade, then, became for many women a consciousness-raising experience and a training exercise of the first magnitude.

Five women in particular gained fame as leaders of the women's rights movement both during this early period of struggle and into succeeding years. They were Lucy Stone, who served first as a prominent speaker in the cause of women's rights and later as organizer of an important prosuffrage association; Elizabeth Cady Stanton, who is remembered as the "mother" of the women's rights movement for her role in organizing the first women's rights convention in 1848; Lucretia Mott, who met Stanton at the 1840 World Anti-Slavery Convention (the recently married Stanton was spending her honeymoon at the convention) where both were denied full participation, and who later aided her in her organizing activities; Susan B. Anthony, one of the youngest of the original leaders of the movement and one of its hardest-working members; and Amelia Bloomer, publisher of *The Lily*, a protemperance journal that, at the urging of Elizabeth Cady Stanton, became the first women's rights newspaper, and principal defender of the "revolutionary" style of dress for which she is best remembered today, the "bloomer."[5]

The adoption of bloomers as an acceptable form of dress, incidentally, was an issue of some symbolic importance in the 1850s. It was the belief of women's rights advocates at the time that women could never really be emancipated until they had been freed from the uncomfortable and impractical, yet predominant, style of the day, which included tight corsets, multiple petticoats, and lengthy skirts. As an alternative they advocated shorter and looser-fitting dresses, with matching pants to cover those portions of their legs that remained exposed. This style of dress had been common at Robert Owen's utopian community in

Indiana for some time and was in evidence as well at certain New York State health spas, but when Elizabeth Cady Stanton appeared publicly in the outfit in 1851, she caused a nationwide sensation. And when Amelia Bloomer defended the wearing of the costume in editorials in *The Lily* and announced that she, too, was wearing it, the style came immediately to be known as the bloomer. Special bloomer balls were held, theatrical productions featuring bloomers were quite the rage, and lecturers wearing bloomers drew large audiences. Indeed, by July 1851 even the *Courier* of Ottumwa, Iowa, announced that the town was "waiting with anxious solicitude the appearance in public of the first young lady who would have the moral courage to put on the new apparel," though as late as October of that year the editor of the *Fort Des Moines Journal* wrote that "the people of this section are eminently practical and while they deplore the pernicious effects of the present female costume, they fail to see any valuable improvement in the Bloomer." Though the fashion faded as quickly as it had arrived, the women's rights movement had found in the bloomer its first symbol of resistance.[6]

If the bloomers of 1851 were the first organizing symbol of the movement, the first attempts at organization per se predated them by some three years, for it was on July 19, 1848, that the first "Women's Rights Convention" was called to order in Seneca Falls, New York. Under the leadership of Stanton and Mott, some 300 persons gathered on that day and the next to approve a Declaration of Sentiments (a document patterned after the Declaration of Independence) and a series of resolutions that included a demand for the franchise.[7] More than the vote, however, the women who attended this meeting were interested in what they saw as the much more fundamental issues of control of property and earnings, access to employment opportunities, guardianship of children, and rights to divorce, all of which demands have a particularly modern ring and all of which were reflected in the declaration, which stated in part:

> He [mankind] has never permitted her to exercise her inalienable right to the elective franchise.
>
> He has compelled her to submit to laws, in the formation of which she had no voice.
>
> He has withheld from her rights which are given to the most ignorant and degraded men—both natives and foreigners. . . .

> He has made her, if married, in the eye of the law, civilly dead.
>
> He has taken from her all right in property, even to the wages she earns. . . .
>
> In the covenant of marriage, she is compelled to promise obedience to her husband, he becoming, to all intents and purposes, her master—the law giving him power to deprive her of her liberty, and to administer chastisement.
>
> He has so framed the laws of divorce . . . as to be wholly regardless of the happiness of women—the law, in all cases, going upon a false supposition of the supremacy of man, and giving all power into his hands. . . .
>
> He has monopolized nearly all the profitable employments, and from those she is permitted to follow, she receives but a scanty remuneration. He closes against her all the avenues to wealth and distinction which he considers most honorable to himself. . . .
>
> He has endeavored in every way that he could, to destroy her confidence in her own powers, to lessen her self-respect, and to make her willing to lead a dependent and abject life.[8]

In retrospect, it seems clear that so broad a set of demands could hardly have been met successfully simply through the extension of suffrage to women, but the leaders of the women's rights movement believed that the right to vote constituted a clearly defined and easily defensible primary demand and that, once the right to vote had been obtained, many additional demands would be met as a natural consequence. Thus, through a series of women's rights conventions held in various cities almost every year until the Civil War began, woman suffrage became the focal point of rhetorical attention and political action. Commenting on one such meeting in Worcester, Massachusetts, in 1850, the *New York Herald* wondered editorially, "What do the leaders of the women's conventions want? They want to vote and hustle with rowdies at the polls. They want to become members of Congress, and in the heat of debate subject themselves to coarse jests and indecent language."[9]

Still, it was not until the war had begun that the first formal organization of activist women, the Women's National Loyalty League, was formed with the primary goal of supporting the Union effort. (This was a natural direction for organizing efforts to follow since all these women had been active as abolitionists.) And it was not until 1865, after the war had ended, that a man,

Theodore Tilton, proposed formation of the American Equal Rights Association, a group that came into existence the following year under the guidance of Stanton, Anthony, and Stone. A primary goal of the Equal Rights Association was to have been inclusion of women under the provisions of the Fourteenth Amendment, which was under consideration at the time, but, by the time the group became functional, Congress had already passed the amendment and had sent it to the states for ratification with the word "male" included in its phrasing. Then, when the women sought to influence the wording of the Fifteenth Amendment, which dealt more specifically with individual suffrage, most of those men who still supported them deserted the cause claiming that attempts to gain woman suffrage at that particular moment would detract from the need of Negroes to obtain their rights.

Faced with these pressures and with a notable lack of success, the American Equal Rights Association fell victim to a factional dispute early in 1869. In January of that year, Elizabeth Cady Stanton, Susan B. Anthony, and others formed the National Woman Suffrage Association (NWSA), which opposed ratification of the Fifteenth Amendment; which concerned itself not only with suffrage issues but with questions of divorce, economic change, and even free love; and which as a consequence attracted a number of extremists to its cause. Then, some ten months later, in November 1869, at a women's convention in Cleveland, Ohio, Lucy Stone and Julia Ward Howe (an active reformer who is best remembered today as the composer of *The Battle Hymn of the Republic*) announced formation of a rival organization, the American Woman Suffrage Association (AWSA), which supported the Fifteenth Amendment, restricted its focus to the suffrage issue alone, and was generally a more conservative spokesman for the cause.[10] Both organizations turned their attentions primarily to changing state laws with regard to suffrage, though the National Association also pushed for a federal suffrage amendment.[11]

One of the more interesting activities of the National Woman Suffrage Association, by the way, was undertaken in the centennial year of 1876. In that year the group opened an office in Philadelphia, where the official celebration was to be held, and asked General Hawley, chairman of the Centennial Commission, for permission to present a Declaration of Rights of Women to the celebrants on July 4. Hawley not only refused the women's request but even went so far as to refuse them admission to the hall where the principal meeting was to be held. Later, and undoubtedly to his ultimate regret, Hawley relented and sent five tickets to the NWSA. Armed with these tickets, a parchment proclamation, and copies of their declaration, five representatives of the group, including Susan B. Anthony, attended the celebration, and, when the crowd rose to welcome the emperor of Brazil, who was for some undetermined reason the guest of honor, they walked onto the stage and presented their scroll to the master of ceremonies, Senator (and woman suffrage advocate) Thomas W. Ferry. The women then walked wordlessly off stage and, while Hawley shouted for a restoration of order, distributed copies of their declaration to the crowd. Finally, they proceeded to Independence Square, where Anthony read a copy of the declaration to a large crowd.[12]

Though both the NWSA and the AWSA focused their attentions on gaining the vote at the state level, the right of women to vote under state law was almost as slow in developing as it was under the federal constitution. In 1838 women were given the right to vote on school trustees in Kentucky, but the next major steps were long in coming. Municipal elections were finally opened to women voters in Kansas in 1887, bond-issue elections in Montana in 1889, and the selection of presidential electors in Illinois in 1913. Wyoming granted full suffrage to women in 1869 when it was still a territory and, since no full states had followed suit in the interim, became the first state with full suffrage when, after some debate on the issue, it joined the Union in 1890. At about that time, however, the pace of change quickened, and by 1919, when the Nineteenth Amendment passed the Congress, the majority of states had already begun to permit full woman suffrage.[13]

The first real attempt to establish woman suffrage at the federal level came in 1866, when the Fourteenth Amendment was pending. The suffragists claimed that the language of that amendment recognized the citizenship of both men and women and that the framers' intent was that all citizens should be allowed to vote. This rather dubious assertion was finally put to the test in 1872 when Susan B. Anthony and several other women voted in a congressional election in New York. Anthony was promptly arrested (at the behest of President Grant), tried (she was ruled incompetent to testify in her own behalf), and fined $100.[14] The Supreme Court subsequently held that the right to vote was not necessarily protected by the Fourteenth Amendment and that, even though women were indeed citizens, they still might be denied the vote.[15]

In the wake of this Supreme Court decision, Representative George W. Julian of Indiana submitted to the Congress on January 10, 1878, a proposal to amend the United States Constitution to provide for an extension of the franchise to women. This initial resolution met with no support and was never even brought to a vote, but four years later, in 1882, both houses of Congress set up committees on woman suffrage. (The House committee was discontinued after two years and was not reinstated until 1918.) The first vote on a suffrage amendment came in the Senate in 1887, at which time it was soundly defeated.[16] In 1890 the two rival suffrage associations agreed to merge into the National American Woman Suffrage Association, which took on the more conservative goals and philosophy of Lucy Stone—but which elected as its first two presidents Elizabeth Cady Stanton and Susan B. Anthony.[17] Even this reunified group, however, was unable to force a further congressional vote on a suffrage amendment for almost a quarter of a century (the Senate voted down such a measure in 1914, the House in 1915) despite its regular introduction in each Congress.[18] The predominant mood of the day seems to have been amply summed up by Lyman Abbott, who wrote in 1901 in an article entitled "The Rights of Man,"

> Ought women to vote. . . ? Women do not vote; nor aliens; nor non-residents, although they may be taxed in the district; nor men under twenty-one years of age. . . . There is no natural right of suffrage. The question is not, therefore, Has a woman the right to vote as she has a right to the protection of her person, her property, her family, and her reputation? The real question is two-fold: Is it necessary for the protection of her rights that she should vote? if not, is it for the interest of the community that the suffrage should be multiplied by two. . . ? History shows us that the personal and property rights of women can safely be intrusted [*sic*] to the rest of the community.[19]

For a decade or so after Abbott's writing, things remained rather quiet on the woman suffrage front. Little was attempted during these years and even less accomplished. But in 1913 the movement was given renewed impetus when two women, Lucy Burns and Alice Paul, the latter a veteran of hunger strikes and jailings in the British suffrage movement, organized a suffragist march in Washington the day before Woodrow Wilson's inauguration as president. Five thousand women marched up Pennsylvania Avenue that day, where they were attacked by throngs of angry bystanders who overwhelmed the local police. Indeed, so violent was the women's reception that it proved necessary to call in the cavalry to restore order and permit the women to conclude their demonstration. And in the wake of the violence, the activist women were the objects of great sympathy, and their cause was once again a focal point of public attention.[20]

An important ally of the suffragists during these years was the Women's Christian Temperance Union (WCTU), which had been formally established in 1874 and which, with some 200,000 members across the country, had grown into the largest women's organization of the time. Under the leadership of its second president, Francis Willard, the WCTU took the position that prohibition could be brought about only when women had obtained that political power that could come only with the vote. Thus, many local chapters of the WCTU became active in the suffragist movement, and it was hardly a coincidence that the Eighteenth Amendment (prohibition) and the Nineteenth were both passed during the same session of Congress.[21]

Nor was it accidental that both amendments were passed in a year that was also eventful in other ways, the postwar year of 1919. Indeed, it was the wartime experience that finally served to muster sufficient public support for each amendment. More specifically, it was the increasing incidences of drunkenness and alcoholism among veterans that encouraged the passage of prohibition and the popularity of the rhetoric of democracy that lent force to the movement for woman suffrage. As the *Washington Herald* commented editorially, "Any vision of human liberty which excludes freedom of women is indecently camouflaged. Any war policy which demands of women their all and denies them equal partnership is inconsistent, tyrannical and vicious, anything but democratic. Our democracy comes into the court of the Almighty with unclean hands; the best part of our democracy is not free and equal."[22]

More than the rhetoric to which it gave rise, however, the wartime experience furthered the cause of political equality for women because it gave them an opportunity to participate in both government and industry on an unprecedented scale, an opportunity of which they quickly availed themselves. Working under the guidance of the Woman's Committee of the US Council of National Defense, American women registered for various forms of war service (such as sewing together the thousands of pairs of pajamas subsequently disposed of by Charles Forbes), worked to conserve food supplies, replaced men in arsenals and other critical manufacturing facilities, advanced their status in law, medicine, and other professions, and formed the voluntary Woman's Land Army to assure that American agriculture continued to function. One woman even went so far as to offer to form a cavalry regiment for women, though her offer was, of course, declined.[23] Looking back on the period a little over a decade later, one observer commented, "It was a great war, and the women in this country had a fine time; it is this joy of women in wartime which must be taken into account in any scheme for universal peace, for women will not cease to run to the bugle's calling until something more interesting appears in their lives."[24]

Perhaps it was in an attempt to offer this "something more interesting," or perhaps it was simply in recognition of the contribution that women had made to the war effort, that Woodrow Wilson finally turned the tide in favor of woman suffrage by himself changing his opposition to support and by urging members of his party in Congress to pass such a measure without delay. So it was that the Nineteenth Amendment was approved by the House on May 21, 1919, and by the Senate on June 4. A week later, Wisconsin became the first state to ratify the suffrage amendment, and, with approval by the Tennessee legislature on August 18, 1920, constitutional change came in time for women to participate in the election of Warren G. Harding.[25] Looking back over the years of struggle, Carrie Chapman Catt, then president of the National American Woman Suffrage Association, observed:

> In order to get the word "male" . . . out of the Constitution cost the women of the country 52 years of pauseless campaign. . . . During that

time they were forced to conduct 56 campaigns of referenda to male voters; 480 campaigns to get Legislatures to submit suffrage amendments to voters; 47 campaigns to get state constitutional conventions to write woman suffrage into state constitutions; 277 campaigns to get state party conventions to include woman suffrage planks; 30 campaigns to get presidential party conventions to adopt woman suffrage planks in party platforms; and 19 campaigns with 19 successive Congresses.[26]

Not everyone, nor even every woman, of course, welcomed the new order harbingered by woman suffrage. The American Constitutional League, for example, engaged in several legal actions to delay implementation of the suffrage amendment, most notably in Maryland, where it argued without success that the amendment was invalid in that state because it imposed unwanted rules upon the electorate.[27] And the antisuffragist paper *The Woman Patriot* declared that "the suffragists are bringing us to the culmination of a decadence which has been steadily indicated by race suicide, divorce, break up of the home, and federalism, all of which conditions are found chiefly in primitive society."[28] Suffragists were labeled Bolsheviks and "red sisters," and such diverse groups as the League of Women Voters, the American Association of University Women, the YWCA, and the WCTU were denounced as Communists and malcontents. The Daughters of the American Revolution even went so far as to blacklist such "radicals" and advocates of woman suffrage as Roscoe Pound, Felix Frankfurter, Clarence Darrow, and Jane Addams.[29] Such actions notwithstanding, women at last possessed the franchise, and the nation somehow survived.

Women's Rights: Votes Were Not Enough

Though some saw adoption of the suffrage amendment as an end in itself, many leaders of the women's rights movement saw it only as a beginning, as a means to a larger end. And indeed, during the decade or so following ratification, women expanded their economic and political roles in a number of ways. In addition to the League of Women Voters, which was formed in 1919 upon completion of congressional action on the Nineteenth

Amendment, and the Women's Joint Congressional Committee, an issue-oriented women's lobby, such organizations as the National Federation of Business and Professional Women's Clubs, the National Association of Bank Women, the National Association of Women Lawyers, and even the Society of Women Geographers were founded and flourished during this period.[30] In addition, increasing numbers of women attained positions of responsibility in government. Helen H. Gardener, vice-president of the National American Woman Suffrage Association, for example, was appointed by Woodrow Wilson to the Civil Service Commission, and Wilson placed other women on the District of Columbia Commission, the D. C. Rent Commission, and the Employee's Compensation Commission. President Harding, too, appointed a few women to significant positions and also supported certain of their other aims while withstanding pressures to take government jobs away from married women as an economy move. Even Calvin Coolidge maintained the trend, as evidenced by his appointment of Jessie Dell to fill a vacancy on the Civil Service Commission created by the death of Helen Gardener. In the 1920s increasing numbers of women became commission members or even chairmen, state and federal judges, and assistants to United States attorneys.[31] Discrimination in both jobs and compensation was still apparent, but conditions were improving.

In addition, it was during the 1920s that American women sought to reestablish their right to individual citizenship, a right that had been taken from many of them by earlier congressional action. In 1855, faced with increasing waves of immigrants, the United States had adopted the rule that women who married American men automatically became American citizens, but the Congress had made no parallel provision for American women who married aliens. This omission was corrected in 1907, when a second rule was adopted that automatically withdrew American citizenship from such women for the duration of their marriage. Since various states and the federal government had laws at the time that prohibited aliens from inheriting property, buying real estate, engaging in such professions as medicine, teaching, or the law, taking any state or federal civil service examination, or holding any elective or appointive government position, this involuntary surrender of citizenship could, and in many cases did, create a serious hardship. In fact, during World War I many American women who had married resident aliens from Germany or its allies, no matter how long before, were themselves classified as enemy aliens, and their property was seized and held by the Alien Property Custodian. Finally, after a lengthy legislative struggle spearheaded by the Association of Women Lawyers, the League of Women Voters, and the Women's Joint Congressional Committee, the Cable Act was passed by Congress in the summer of 1922 and signed into law by President Harding. The bill did respond to many of the needs of women who married aliens, but it reflected as well the racism and nativism of the times in its removal of citizenship from any woman who married a foreigner who was himself ineligible for naturalized citizenship because of his race, and in its provision changing the status of an American woman married to any alien to that of naturalized citizen. Proponents of full citizenship rights for all women were thus forced to settle for the proverbial half a loaf, at least until 1930, when the Cable Act was amended and many of its inequities removed. Women also discovered during this period, incidentally, that, even for those whose birthright could not be questioned, suffrage did not bring with it all the privileges of citizenship. Women continued to be routinely excluded from jury duty and public office in many states throughout the decade, a fact that helped maintain some momentum for the women's rights movement.[32]

That momentum notwithstanding, however, the onset of the Great Depression in 1929 brought a temporary end to the effectiveness of the organized drive for women's rights, for the nation moved at that point into two decades of economic dislocation and total war in which such issues were regarded as secondary at best. It is true, of course, that women continued during these years to expand their participation in government and public service, and, particularly during the war, in industry and commerce. It is also true that women achieved economic and political gains that many had long sought. Moreover, a newly independent American woman, perhaps best symbolized by Eleanor Roosevelt, had begun to emerge. But it is true, too, that both economic and political discrimination continued largely unabated throughout the period and that women found themselves with far less organization and sense of political purpose at the end of World War II than they had possessed twenty years earlier. Largely as a result of this loss of direction, the late 1940s and the 1950s passed with an absolute minimum of related political activity and probably marked the nadir of the women's rights movement.[33]

All that was to change, however, in the turbulent decade that followed. The first significant impetus to a renewal of the movement came in December of 1961 when President John F. Kennedy established the President's Commission on the Status of Women and charged the group with recommending ways to overcome all barriers to full equality for women. The report of this commission, which was issued in October 1963, was generally quite moderate in tone (the commission rejected the outright barring of sex discrimination in hiring, for example, and opposed a constitutional amendment to provide women with equal rights) and thus could hardly have served as the rallying point for a radical social movement, but its issuance did serve to call attention to, and, importantly, to legitimize a concern with the economic, social, and political disadvantages of women.[34]

If *American Women*, as the commission's report was titled, was insufficiently radical to arouse the slumbering women's rights movement, however, two books that came out on the subject were rather more pointed in their attacks. The first of these, and probably the more influential, was Betty Friedan's *The Feminine Mystique*, published in 1963. Basing her analysis on interviews with upper-middle-class, college-educated women, Friedan argued that American women were not well served by the social roles into which their energies were channeled, most notably those pertaining to home and family. *The Feminine Mystique* substantially raised the level of dissatisfaction with the status quo among many women, heightened their political awareness, and led to new calls for a national women's rights organization. A second and much more radical book, Kate Millet's *Sexual Politics*, which was published some seven years later, offered American women a relatively revolutionary conceptualization of their problems and served to clarify and update the political dimensions of Friedan's earlier arguments.[35]

There were as well during the decade of the 1960s a number of important legislative and administrative advances for the women's rights movement. Most notable among these were the Equal Pay Act of 1963, which for the first time required that men and women receive equal pay for equal work performed; the inclusion of "sex" among the categories where discrimination was disallowed in the equal employment opportunity provisions (Title VII) of the 1964 Civil Rights Act; and a similar inclusion in Executive Order 11375, in which Lyndon Johnson outlawed discriminatory hiring by federal contractors and by the federal government itself.[36] The case of Title VII is particularly interesting (and revealing) in that Herman Edelsberg, the first executive director of the Equal Employment Opportunities Commission, and hence the official charged with the initial implementation of the antidiscrimination regulations, gave public notice that he regarded the inclusion of "sex" as a "fluke" that had been "conceived out of wedlock," that in his view "men were entitled to female secretaries," and that he could not, therefore, be counted upon to enforce these provisions.[37] Mr. Edelsberg's comments notwithstanding, these policy changes did constitute significant advances.

One cannot overemphasize the importance of the more general civil rights movement, which itself was in full force during this period, in furthering the cause of women's rights; it affected both the timing and the substance of the women's movement. Many of the legislative advances of the women's movement in the 1960s came either in connection with or on the heels of equivalent advances against racial discrimination, and patterns and perceptions developed in the one area were frequently generalized to the other. Moreover, much as the abolitionist and prohibitionist movements had given impetus, focus, and organization to earlier drives for women's rights, the civil rights movement of the 1960s, together with the burgeoning sentiment against the war in Vietnam, provided similar stimulation for that of more recent years.[38] Indeed, it would seem that the existence at a given point in time of *any* one effective social movement serves to legitimize, reinforce, and make more viable other movements of the same period, a mutual reinforcement that may, in effect, be yet another manifestation of the so-called contagion theory that was discussed in a different context in chapter 2. (We should hasten to add that this interactive effect is not always intended or even welcomed by members of the various movements involved, a condition that is perhaps suggested most clearly in the comments of Stokely Carmichael, leader of the civil-rights-oriented Student Non-Violent Coordinating Committee (SNCC), who, when confronted in 1964 with a paper on the position of women in the organization, is said to have rejoined that "the only position for women in SNCC is prone."[39])

As one might expect under such circumstances, there arose in response to an increasingly widely felt need a variety of new and relatively militant women's rights organizations, most prominent among which has been the National Organization for Women (NOW). NOW originated at a meeting of the National Conference of State Commissions on the Status of Women in June 1966 and formally began operations in October of that year under the leadership of Betty Friedan. At a conference in Washington a little over a year later, the organization adopted a "Bill of Rights" (note the continuing constitutional analogy) that called, among other things, for enforcement of laws banning sex discrimination, for equal employment and educational opportunities, and for an equal rights amendment to the Constitution. NOW has subsequently been active in publicizing and bringing pressure on the government in each of these areas of concern, but it has been the final demand for a constitutional amendment that has captured the public's imagination and become the focus for most women's rights activities in recent years.[40]

Before we detail those activities, however, we ought to look at one additional event of the 1960s, the appointment by President Richard M. Nixon in September 1969, of a Task Force on Women's Rights and Responsibilities, whose function was to develop ideas that might be included in the president's forthcoming State of the Union Message and that might provide as well the basis for governmental action in the 1970s. The group's report, entitled *A Matter of Simple Justice,* was completed by mid-December 1969, though none of its recommendations nor even any reference to women appeared in the president's subsequent address. The contents of the report were made public some six months later, however, and included a call for passage of a women's rights amendment as well as for a number of lesser administrative and legislative changes. The report apparently helped sensitize members of both Congress and the administration to the needs of women, for there followed in relatively short order a spate of antidiscrimination legislation and, ultimately, the Equal Rights Amendment (ERA).[41]

The idea of an Equal Rights Amendment is not a particularly new one. As a matter of fact, the first ERA was introduced in Congress in 1923, only three years after the suffrage amendment had been finally adopted, by Senator Charles Curtis and Representative Daniel Anthony, a nephew of suffragist Susan B. Anthony. But the amendment was to languish in Congress for years. Hearings were held from time to time, and twice in the 1950s the Senate actually voted favorably on an ERA, though in each instance the measure included a floor amendment introduced by Senator Carl Hayden of Arizona that substantially weakened its potential impact. The Judiciary Committee of the House held hearings on an ERA in 1948, but the committee's perennial chairman, Emanuel Celler of New York, prevented all subsequent consideration for more than two decades. And in every presidential campaign from 1944 to 1960 both the Republican and Democratic platforms endorsed the amendment proposal. Still, it was not until the 1970s that ERA's time seemed to have come.

The final congressional debate over ERA was heated but relatively brief as such things go. It commenced in February 1970, when several women from NOW disrupted a hearing of the Subcommittee on Constitutional Amendments of the Senate Judiciary Committee, which was considering what has since become the Twenty-Sixth Amendment, that extending the vote to eighteen-year-olds. Yielding to the women's demands, Chairman Birch Bayh of Indiana scheduled hearings on an ERA for the following May, and his subcommittee reported out an amendment at the end of July. In the House of Representatives, meanwhile, on June 11 Representative Martha Griffiths of Michigan introduced a discharge petition to force the ERA out of its traditional resting place in the Judiciary Committee, and she was able to force a floor vote on the issue on August 10. Much to her surprise and delight, the amendment was approved after but an hour's debate by the overwhelming margin of 352 to 15.

This House action placed the ball squarely in the Senate's court, where Senator Sam Ervin of North Carolina, who later played an important role in the Senate Watergate investigation, strove to delay action. Taking a lesson from Senator Hayden's tactics in the 1950s, Ervin introduced a substitute amendment that read in part, "This article shall not impair the validity of any law . . . which is reasonably designed to promote the health, safety, privacy, education, or economic welfare of women, *or to enable them to perform their duties as homemakers or mothers.*" (Emphasis added.) The Senate, unable as ever to oppose motherhood, refused to approve the House version of the ERA.

The forces supporting the amendment were not this time to be denied, however, and when the measure was reintroduced in the Ninety-second Congress in January 1971, it was endorsed not only by the traditional supporters of such causes but even by the conservative Nixon administration as well.[42] The Equal Rights Amendment was approved by Congress in March 1972, and is, at the time of this writing, the object of a ratification drive whose success is still in doubt. In the first rush to approve, twenty-two of the necessary thirty-eight states had ratified the Twenty-Seventh Amendment by the end of 1972, but since that time the pace has slowed considerably, and two states, Nebraska and Tennessee, have rescinded previous ratification, a step of doubtful legality.[43] Opposition to the amendment has been abundant and has in many cases been stated, not by men or corporations who might be accused of seeking to continue the repression of women, but rather by women themselves, many of whom fear that ERA is more an amendment of equal responsibilities (or at least of reduced privileges) than of equal rights.[44] Led by women such as Phyllis Schlafly, many of these opponents fear that should the ERA be added to the Constitution, American women would lose, among other things, their immunity from military conscription and the protection of special labor laws the attainment of which was itself a very lengthy and difficult process.[45] Reflecting the conservative orientation of many ERA opponents in a statement to the Citizens' Advisory Council on the status of women in May 1975, and not incidentally echoing sentiments expressed under similar circumstances some fifty years earlier, Andrea S. Fordham declared that

> The ideas of the feminists are not new; they were tried with disastrous effects in Soviet Russia in the 1920's and early 1930's. Just as the feminist ideologists in the United States today are pushing for open

marriage, easy divorce, sexual license, easy abortion, devaluation of the family, abolition of sex roles, group living, sharing of housework, and universal child care by the state, the early Soviet Communists tried to incorporate these same ideas (every one of them). . . .

I hope we do not have to repeat the experiment in America. . . .

Women in this country are the most advantaged group in the world, and . . . radical feminism is against the best interests of women, men, and children.[46]

Conclusion

Whatever the eventual outcome of the ratification drive for the Equal Rights Amendment, certain points become clear as we consider the history of the women's rights movement. One, of course, is that fundamental social and political change is a painfully slow and grudging process that is as likely to move backward as forward, for not everyone in a society benefits from or is willing to tolerate deviation from the status quo. When change does come, however, it tends to come in response, not to isolated demands, but to large clusters of demands. Thus, both the ERA and the earlier suffrage amendment were approved at times of general social upheaval that helped place what had earlier been perceived as especially radical demands into a context that made them appear either more reasonable or more moderate. Closely related to this is the fact that effective action on behalf of women's rights has tended in each instance to be derivative in nature, from abolitionist and prohibitionist activities in the earlier case, from civil rights and antiwar agitation in the latter. And finally, in each instance action on women's rights has tended to focus on a process of constitutional change, of progress through formal codification, which has given direction to a variety of organizations and individuals, helped structure a century's worth of legislative, administrative, and political activity, and given to the women's rights movement a substantial degree of continuity through time.

Before concluding, however, we ought to point out that women's rights as we have defined them really constitute only half the objectives of the contemporary women's movement, for today, as they have for many years, activist American women continue to struggle as well for what they term "liberation," the equality not only of political privilege but of social role and cultural identification as well. The earliest feminists were concerned, as we have seen, not only with voting, but with education, marriage contracts, employment opportunities, and a host of related issues, and this concern has carried forward to the present day. Indeed, if activist women today are troubled by what they see as the willing (or at least uninformed) subjugation of women, by "sexist" portrayals of women in educational materials and in the media, by unequal job opportunities and pay, and by other legal or extralegal restrictions on their freedom of action, the focus of their concern reflects less a new element in their drive for equality than a new sophistication in the perception of their dilemma. And if, in this chapter, we have not duly emphasized this second dimension of the women's movement, the striving for social advancement, our purpose has most assuredly not been to discount its importance. To the contrary, the significance of women's liberation and its bearing on questions of women's rights cannot be denied.

At the same time, though, it should be recognized that women's liberation is primarily a social movement, while the drive for women's rights is primarily political in character. And though the two are certainly closely related, they are nevertheless analytically distinct. Moreover, we have noted that, throughout the period in question, political action, and more particularly constitutional action, has been viewed by the feminists not only as a means to obtain their broader social goals but also as the most effective device for mobilizing support for their movement. This was as true of Elizabeth Cady Stanton as it is of Betty Friedan. Thus, not only the political emphasis of our own analysis but also the dynamics of the women's movement itself would seem to suggest the value of limiting our present attentions to the struggle for political rights. Having said that, it must nevertheless be recognized that underlying and giving impetus to the political actions of women activists both past and present are a number of social dissatisfactions the awareness of which is vital to an understanding of the continuities of the women's movement. Only in the context of those larger but often more diffuse discontents can the role of women in the American political system, and the limitations that are placed upon that role, be properly appreciated.

NOTES

1. Ida Husted Harper, "Why Women Cannot Vote in the U.S.," *North American Review* 179 (July 1904): 31.
2. Quoted in Gerda Lerner, "The Feminists: A Second Look," *Columbia Forum* 13 (Fall 1970): 25.
3. Judith Hole and Ellen Levine, *Rebirth of Feminism* (New York: Quadrangle, 1971), pp. 2–4.
4. June Sochen, *Herstory: A Woman's View of American History* (New York: Alfred Publishing, 1974), pp. 122–23.
5. Louise R. Noun, *Strong Minded Women: The Emergence of the Woman-Suffrage Movement in Iowa* (Ames: Iowa State University Press, 1969), pp. 4–16.
6. Ibid., pp. 16–20.
7. Hole and Levine, *Rebirth*, pp. 5–7; Eleanor Flexner, *Century of Struggle: The Women's Rights Movement in the United States* (New York: Atheneum, 1971), pp. 74–77. William H. Chafe provides an interesting analysis of this gathering in "Feminism in the 1970's," *Dissent* 21 (Fall 1974): 508.
8. Quoted in Hole and Levine, *Rebirth*, pp. 432–33.
9. Quoted in Flexner, *Struggle*, p. 81.
10. Robert E. Riegel, "Split of the Feminist Movement in 1869," *Mississippi Valley Historical Review* 49 (December 1962): 485–96; and Sochen, *Herstory*, pp. 174–77.
11. Hole and Levine, *Rebirth*, p. 11.
12. Flexner, *Struggle*, p. 172.
13. Ibid., p. 178; Nathan G. Goodman, "Extension of the Franchise to Women," *Historical Outlook* 18 (April 1927): 157–59. For information on suffrage campaigns in the various states, see, for example, James J. Kenneally, "Woman Suffrage and the Massachusetts Referendum of 1895," *Historian* 30 (August 1968): 617–33; "Eastern Suffrage Campaigns," *Review of Reviews* 52 (November 1915): 518–20; "Suffragists Take New York State," *Literary Digest*, 17 November 1917, pp. 14–15; Pearl Tyer, "Idaho's 20 Years of Woman Suffrage," *Outlook*, 6 September 1916, pp. 55–59; Elsie W. Moore, "Suffrage Question in the Far West," *Arena* 41 (July 1909): 414–24; Mrs. Barclay Hazard, "New York Anti-Suffrage Association," *Harper's Bazaar*, July 1909, p. 730; Florence Kelley, "Campaign for the Enfranchisement of Women in Oregon," *Outlook*, 21 July 1906, pp. 675–76; Estelline Bennett, "How Woman Suffrage Came to Wyoming," *Harper's Weekly*, 21 August 1909, p. 28.
14. Goodman, "Extension," p. 159; and Flexner, *Struggle*, p. 167.
15. *Minor* v. *Happersett*, 21 Wall. 162, 22 L.Ed. 627 (1875).

16. Goodman, "Extension," p. 159.

17. Hole and Levine, *Rebirth,* p. 12.

18. Goodman, "Extension."

19. Lyman Abbott, "The Rights of Man," *Outlook,* 8 June 1901, pp. 353–54.

20. Flexner, *Struggle,* p. 264.

21. Sochen, *Herstory,* p. 180; "War Breaking Down the Barriers to Prohibition and Woman Suffrage," *Current Opinion,* February 1918, p. 82.

22. "War Breaking Down," p. 84.

23. J. Stanley Lemons, *The Woman Citizen: Social Feminism in the 1920's* (Urbana: University of Illinois Press, 1973), pp. 14–21.

24. Lorine Pruette, "Why Women Fail," in *Woman's Coming of Age: A Symposium,* ed. Samuel D. Schmalhausen and V. F. Calverton (New York: Horace Liveright, 1931), p. 247, as cited in Lemons, *Woman Citizen,* p. 15.

25. "American Woman Voter Arrives," *Literary Digest,* 28 August 1920, p. 9; Lemons, *Woman Citizen,* p. 13.

26. Carrie Chapman Catt and Nettie Rogers Shuler, *Woman Suffrage and Politics* (New York: 1923), p. 107 as cited in Flexner, *Struggle,* p. 173.

27. Lemons, *Woman Citizen,* pp. 13–14.

28. "American Woman Voter Arrives," p. 10.

29. Lemons, *Woman Citizen,* pp. 209–25.

30. Ibid., pp. 41–59.

31. Ibid., pp. 73–77.

32. Ibid., pp. 61–69.

33. Shulamith Firestone, "On American Feminism," in *Woman in Sexist Society: Studies in Power and Powerlessness,* ed. Vivian Gornick and Barbara K. Moran (New York: Basic Books, 1971), pp. 491–92; Chafe, "Feminism," p. 509. Alice S. Rossi, in "Women—Terms of Liberation," *Dissent* 21 (Spring 1974): 320, sees in these years the laying of the foundation for the advances of the 1960s.

34. Hole and Levine, *Rebirth,* pp. 18–24.

35. Sochen, *Herstory,* pp. 390–91; Jo Freeman, *The Politics of Women's Liberation* (New York: McKay, 1975), p. 53.

36. Hole and Levine, *Rebirth,* pp. 28–48.

37. Freeman, *Politics,* pp. 53–54.

38. Ibid., p. 28; and Lerner, "The Feminists," p. 28.

39. Hole and Levine, *Rebirth,* p. 403.

40. Ibid., pp. 81–95; Freeman, *Politics,* pp. 71–102; Sochen, *Herstory,* pp. 435–36.

41. Hole and Levine, *Rebirth,* pp. 48–51.

42. Ibid., pp. 54–57.

43. "Equal Rights for Women—Is '75 the Year?" *U.S. News and World Report*, 17 February 1975, pp. 49-50.

44. Margaret I. Miller and Helene Linker, "Equal Rights Amendment Campaigns in California and Utah," *Society* 11 (May-June 1974): 53. For a related analysis of the ERA campaign in Connecticut, see Susan Tolchin and Martin Tolchin, *Clout: Womanpower and Politics* (New York: Coward, McCann & Geoghegan, 1973), pp. 105–34.

45. "Women's Rights: Some Like It Not," *Newsweek*, 15 January 1973, pp. 17–18.

46. Andrea S. Fordham, "Status of Women: A Dissent," *Roanoke* (Va.) *Times*, 2 August 1975, p. 4.

6

Political Movements II: Consumer Protection and the Legislative/Administrative Process

Consumption is the sole end and purpose of all production: and the interest of the producer ought to be attended to only so far as it may be necessary for promoting that of the consumer. The maxim is so perfectly self-evident that it would be absurd to attempt to prove it. But in the mercantile system, the interest of the consumer is almost constantly sacrificed to that of the producer; and it seems to consider production, and not consumption, as the ultimate end and object of all industry and commerce.

Adam Smith, *The Wealth of Nations*

The consumer's future can be read not in tea leaves but in corn flakes and crispies of all kinds.

William Robbins, *The American Food Scandal*

Regulatory bodies, like the people who comprise them, have a marked life cycle. In youth, they are vigorous, aggressive, evangelistic and even intolerant. Later they mellow, and in old age—after a matter of ten or 15 years—they become, with some exceptions, either an arm of the industry they are regulating or senile.

John Kenneth Galbraith[1]

If, as we have argued, the main emphasis of the women's rights movement through the years has been on forcing fundamental social and political change through a process of constitutional amendment, the thrust of the second political movement that we shall consider, the consumer protection movement, has been rather different. Where the suffragists, and later the proponents of the Equal Rights Amendment, sought to extend the very meaning of American democracy to a disadvantaged political outgroup, American women, through reliance on self-actualization as codified through the constitutional process, proponents of consumer protection have sought, in effect, to restrict the freedom of action of an advantaged political ingroup, American businessmen (and most particularly, in many cases, large corporations), through a more limited but still potentially effective reliance on the legislative and administrative processes. And where the women's rights advocates have fought, at least in part, for the relatively abstract goals of liberty and equality, the consumer protectionists have struggled almost exclusively for a relatively narrower but in many ways more concrete notion of the public safety. In the present chapter we shall chronicle that struggle.

Trains, Trade, and Tampering: The Origins of Government Regulation

The consumer protection movement of the 1970s had its beginnings during the period of rapid industrial expansion that followed the Civil War, when the abuse of corporate privilege was commonplace. The movement's development is clearly evidenced by the formation and growth of a lengthy list of government agencies, most notable among which are the Interstate Commerce Commission, the Federal Trade Commission, and the Food and Drug Administration. Throughout the past century, those who would safeguard the interests of the consumer have seen in the countervailing power of governmental bureaucracy a force to stay the greed and perfidy of big business. As a result, the story of the consumer movement is in large measure the story of those government agencies through which its occasional public appeal has been institutionalized.

The first of these agencies, the Interstate Commerce Commission, was created by an act of Congress on February 4, 1887, less out of a concern for the welfare of the consumer (who, as the words of Adam Smith suggest, was not granted any claim to economic or political consideration) than in response to a protracted political battle between the competing interests of farmers and shippers, on the one hand, and the nation's railroads, on the other. As was clearly illustrated in our discussion of the Crédit Mobilier Scandal in chapter 4, government policy through the first four decades of the railroad industry was basically designed to encourage the development of new rail lines (through large grants of public lands and public monies) and protect them when built (through the granting of particularly liberal charters). Railroads were valued not only as technological advances of the first order but also as the best available means to advance and consolidate both the spread of American civilization and the expansion of the new industrial order. The extension of the railroad was seen as analogous to the growth of the nation.

In business, as in government, however, the attainment of power in the absence of accountability offers the potential for corruption, and the combination of land, money, and freedom of action available to the railroad barons proved an irresistible temptation. Rates were fixed at exorbitant levels in areas under the monopolistic control of one or another railroad, prices were applied on a discriminatory basis so that favored shippers were placed at a competitive advantage over others, and, in areas where two or more roads traversed the same route, agreements were reached for the pooling of traffic and revenues and for the equalization of rates. The power of the railroads, both economic and political, was at its peak. Almost paradoxically, however, the very strength of the railroads also gave rise to their greatest weakness. Despite the mutual advantages of their cartel arrangements, each sought to compete aggressively with the others for relative advantage within the consortium. Since traffic that originated in areas of single-railroad monopoly but traveled over cartel-controlled track was not subject to revenue-pooling arrangements, for example, many roads tended to overbuild track in economically marginal areas so as to extend their hegemony, to stake a claim as it were, with the net effect that their own economic viability was weakened rather than strengthened. Similarly, although rate wars were common in areas where two or more roads competed with one another in the absence of a cartel, rates were increased to artificially high levels in areas of monopoly to offset any losses. It was, you will recall, just such an inequitable pricing practice that helped foster public support for the Pittsburgh railroad strike-riot of 1877. Moreover, it was the continuation of such practices that gave rise to a more general public resentment of the railroads throughout the post-Civil War years. This resentment, in turn, led to the first efforts in American history to regulate private enterprise through government action.[2]

As has often been the case in consumer-related actions, movement came first, not at the federal level, but in various of the states, particularly in those with large and politically important farm populations. The farmers, who lived in precisely the types of areas that were most likely to be monopolistically controlled by one or another railroad, felt that they had suffered greatly from discriminatory freight rates, and, through the Granger movement of the 1870s and 1880s, they made their feelings known to governors and state legislators. State officials responded—especially in such midwestern states as Illinois, Iowa, Michigan, Minnesota, Missouri, and Wisconsin—with laws that set maximum legal rates that railroads might charge and established administrative commissions empowered to assure that all charges were just and reasonable. These early commissions, which were, as one might expect, bitterly opposed by railroad and industrial interests as threats to private enterprise, effectively controlled much rail traffic and, far more importantly, clearly established the right of the states to regulate the carriers.

In 1886, however, the limitations of these commissions and the need for federal action became clear when the Supreme Court handed down the so-called *Wabash* decision in which it held that an individual state did not have the right to regulate commerce whose origin or destination lay beyond the boundaries of that state. Since some 75 percent of all rail tonnage was in fact interstate in character, and therefore under the *Wabash* decision beyond the jurisdiction of state regulators, the pressure on Congress to pass federal regulatory legislation mounted rapidly. The Act to Regulate Commerce, which forbade railroad price discrimination and created the Interstate Commerce Commission (ICC) to enforce this prohibition, followed soon thereafter.[3]

Like the state commissions that had preceded it, the Interstate Commerce Commission was, in its early years, actively supported by farmers and commercial shipping interests but fervently opposed by the railroads, which began at once and with considerable success to challenge its powers and actions in the courts. Before long, in fact, the commission found its regulatory abilities severely limited and its influence on the wane. For the ICC had been born of congressional compromise in an era when its function seemed illegitimate to many and contrary to the commonly accepted American economic myth, and the combination of weak enabling legislation and potential illegitimacy left the commission in an unenviable political position. Indeed, until 1906, when its powers and jurisdiction were significantly expanded through legislation known as the Hepburn Act, the effectiveness of the ICC was severely hampered.[4] As one scholar later described the situation, "the Act's provisions had been reduced to utter debility and the railroads were evading them with serene immunity."[5]

The Hepburn Act is particularly interesting, incidentally, because it resulted in part from pressures brought by a group of individuals who were, from that time forward, to be influential in the passage of virtually all subsequent consumer-oriented legislation, the so-called muckrakers. The muckrakers were journalists, novelists, and other writers who took it upon themselves to expose the unseemly aspects of American social, economic, and political life and to foster a widespread public indignation that would, in turn, force the correction of abuses. As a political force, they were just coming into their own about the turn of the century, and the fight to bolster government control over the railroads was one of their earliest crusades. Through such widely read journals as *The Arena, Review of Reviews,* and *The Nation,* various journalists made the public aware of corruption in the railroad industry and the lack of concern within the industry for the safety of employees and passengers alike. Most effective of these was Ellery Sedgwick, whose articles in *Leslie's* stressing high accident rates and the need for rail safety legislation gave the issue sufficient momentum and drama to force congressional action. Without the pressure of public opinion generated by

Sedgwick, Ray Stannard Baker, Charles E. Russell, and others, the Interstate Commerce Commission would have remained an empty administrative shell.[6]

The years from 1906 until the end of World War I marked the high point of power and prestige for the ICC. By 1920, in fact, the commission controlled entry into and exit from the railroad industry, regulated capital formation (issuing of stocks and bonds), and had the power to set minimum rates for freight and passenger service. And throughout these years the commission retained the political support of those groups who had been instrumental in its creation, the farmers and the shippers.

But the war brought many changes to American society, and the Interstate Commerce Commission was by no means immune to them. If anything, the ICC was particularly susceptible to change, in part because of the degree of its own success and in part because those who had applauded that success were themselves losing influence. For one thing, vigorous ICC actions had, by 1920, already eliminated the worst practices of the railroad industry and had convinced the railroads themselves that government regulation must be accepted. As a result, consumers and shippers were losing interest in railroad regulation (because the threat to their well-being had been substantially reduced), and, at the same time, the railroads were starting to seek ways to adjust to regulation and mitigate its effects. Moreover, the increasing urbanization that we noted in chapter 2 was reducing not only the number but the political importance of farmers, who had to that time served as the commission's principal constituency. In effect, then, the conditions under which the ICC operated had, within a relatively short period of time, undergone fundamental and irreversible change, and the need of the commission to adjust to the new circumstances was becoming apparent.[7]

Then, in 1920, Congress voted its approval of the Transportation Act, which brought a basic change in the nature of the ICC's duties and responsibilities. Where the commission had earlier been charged with setting minimum freight rates to end devastating rate wars, for example, it was required under the Transportation Act to *fix* rates so as to permit a "fair return" on investment (and it was empowered to determine what constituted a fair return). Where the commission earlier had opposed pooling of traffic and revenues as a monopolistic practice, it was now instructed by the Congress to allow pooling. And where the commission had earlier sought to foster competition and efficiency, it was mandated under the Transportation Act to prepare a rail consolidation plan and support weak railroads by elevating its rate scale. With passage of the Transportation Act of 1920, in other words, not only had the conditions of regulation changed, but the balance in the terms of that regulation had been substantially altered as well. Indeed, the change was even greater than one might at first suspect, for in order to carry out its required activities under the new law, the Interstate Commerce Commission was forced to rely more and more on industry sources for the information on which to base its policies. Fixing rates was a more complex process than establishing minimum fees, and planning for consolidation required substantial knowledge of route structures, corporate structures, and other decision-making materials, all of which information was, of course, available from only one source. The Transportation Act of 1920, then, marked the first success of the railroads in capturing the agency that the government had set up to regulate them. Since those efforts happened to correspond with a loss in interest and a decline in influence of its traditional primary clientele, the agency succumbed with noticeable rapidity.[8]

Something else changed during this period as well. At the same time that rail freight rates were being allowed by the ICC to rise to levels that would permit a "fair return," that is to say greater profit, for the railroads, competition was developing on another front with the growth of automobile technology, and more particularly with the rise of the trucking industry. In fact, at the same time that railroad rates were rising under the watchful eye of the by-then-captive Interstate Commerce Commission, freight trucks were becoming more versatile and more cost-efficient than trains, a fact that did not escape the notice of commercial shippers. As a result, just as the railroads reached a new plateau in their political power, their economic base began to erode, and they found themselves in a major decline that contributed in no small measure to the Great Depression of the 1930s. In 1935 Congress responded by bringing truck traffic under the control of the ICC, and in 1940 it extended this action to include certain river barge shipping as well.[9] As the reason for their inclusion suggests, however, these nonrailroad interests were brought under the ICC umbrella less for their own protection than for that of the railroads, and in relative terms they have never been able to compete effectively with railroad interests within the commission structure. Even to the present, the Interstate Commerce Commission remains a creature of the railroads it was meant to govern, and the railroads have acted to protect not only their own interests before the commission but the commission's interests before Congress, and they have even lobbied to have its powers extended.[10] For this reason, an agency that was set up to serve consumer as well as other related interests has itself become one of the institutional targets of recent consumer-protection activities.

Its ultimate shortcomings notwithstanding, however, the ICC was in its early years a model of action for those who sought to serve the consumer. Thus, the second protectionist bureaucracy that was set up by the government during these years, the Federal Trade Commission, created in September 1914 to prevent unfair competition or deceptive practices in commerce, was in fact consciously patterned after the Interstate Commerce Commission. Like that of the ICC, the history of the Federal Trade Commission (FTC) is illustrative of both the problems that plague American consumers and the powers that hold sway in American politics, and its fate has not been dissimilar.

In 1890, responding to increasing public pressure as well as to a specific request by President Benjamin Harrison, Congress passed with only one dissenting vote the Sherman Anti-Trust Act, the purpose of which was to "protect trade and commerce against unlawful restraints and monopolies" by declaring such practices to be federal offenses. This rather straightforward goal was mitigated, however, by three factors that arose in part from the congressional compromises needed to obtain passage of the bill and that contributed in the aggregate to its fundamental weakness. The first of these was that, although Congress chose to outlaw certain business practices, it provided no adequate means for enforcement of its prohibitions, no agency to carry out its mandate. Thus, for all its outward appearances of vigorous confrontation with business monopolies, the Sherman Anti-Trust

Act had very few teeth. On top of that, the scope of the law was so ambiguous that the courts were given great latitude in its interpretation. Since the judges of the day tended to restrict the application of the law to the narrowest of circumstances (as in the ruling by the Supreme Court that the American Sugar Refining Company, which controlled 98 percent of the American sugar industry, could not be forced to divest itself of four previously independent sugar refineries because sugar refining was a manufacturing process and the Sherman Act referred only to "trade and commerce"), its impact was further weakened. And finally, the Sherman Act was passed just before an unprecedented wave of mergers that saw some 5,000 independent concerns gathered in by about 300 corporations by 1904 as well as the beginnings of consolidation of the larger trusts themselves. Thus, the sheer size of the problem made enforcement of even the strongest law under the most supportive of conditions a virtual impossibility. The need for additional government action was apparent.

So it was that in 1903 Congress established the Bureau of Corporations within the Department of Commerce and Labor to gather information on American corporations. Yet even here effective power was withheld. The Bureau of Corporations could, it is true, investigate corporations and publish its findings, but it had no regulatory powers and no independence of action, and, located as it was within the executive branch, it was subject to political interference and policy directives. The bureau lacked even the power to compel the cooperation of business in its inquiries. It is little wonder, then, that the Bureau of Corporations failed to respond effectively to the spreading concern over increasing economic concentration.[11]

Then, in 1911, the Supreme Court handed down its ruling in the case of *Standard Oil Company of New Jersey* v. *United States*, and in the process it gave renewed vigor to the antimonopoly forces in the Congress and among the public at large. John D. Rockefeller had begun to piece together the Standard Oil Company in 1862 and by the turn of the century owned or controlled fully 87 percent of American crude oil supplies, 82 percent of refining capacity, and 85 percent of all the kerosene, fuel oil, and gasoline sold in or by this country. His companies owned everything from oil leases to pipelines, from drilling rigs to service stations. But in 1904, Rockefeller and his cartel became the objects of a classic case of investigative journalism when Ida Tarbell published *The History of the Standard Oil Company*, which was highly critical of the business practices of both the man and the corporation, and which was serialized in the popular and actively muckraking magazine *McClure's*. Almost overnight, Tarbell's name became a household word, and Rockefeller a pariah. In the wake of this assault, Standard Oil became an obvious target for investigation by the Bureau of Corporations. The investigation concluded that Rockefeller interests were guilty of discriminatory pricing, improper distribution practices, and other presumably illegal activities. The evidence gathered by the bureau provided the basis for legal action under the Sherman Act that resulted in 1911 in an order to break up the Standard Oil Trust.[12] Although the government seemed to have won the battle, however, the outcome of the larger war was put in jeopardy by the phrasing of the Supreme Court's decision, which, though finding fault with the particulars of Standard Oil practices, at the same time promised wide latitude for similar abuses if only the motives of their perpetrators were less questionable. In essence, the Court ruled that only *unreasonable* contracts in restraint of trade were unlawful under terms of the Sherman Act.

Almost immediately, Senator Francis J. Newlands of Nevada proposed creation of an "Interstate Trade Commission" modeled after the ICC so that corporations might be faced, not with occasional legal action, but with continuing administrative scrutiny. His proposal was picked up by Woodrow Wilson during the presidential campaign of 1912 and was the subject of a speech before Congress in January 1914. Later in that year, two bills dealing with antitrust questions were passed and signed into law by the president, the first being the Clayton Act, which outlawed several specific practices in restraint of trade, the second being the Federal Trade Commission Act, which established the Federal Trade Commission and gave it relatively broad powers to define and enforce acceptable standards of competition. The first FTC commissioners were sworn into office in March 1915.[13]

From that point forward, the pattern of growth and development of the FTC is suggested by a lengthy list of supplemental legislative acts that generally served to broaden its mandate and direct its attention to particular problem areas. These included such items as the Webb-Pomerene Export Trade Act of 1918, which directed the commission to take steps to promote American exports; the Miller-Tydings Act of 1934, which prohibited conspiracies in restraint of trade; the Robinson-Patman Antidiscrimination Act of 1938, which resulted from what was, in effect, internecine warfare between small businessmen and large corporations and which supplemented existing laws on restraint of trade; and the Wheeler-Lea Amendment of the same year, which for the first time put consumers on a par with competitors in the eyes of the FTC by declaring unlawful "deceptive acts or practices" rather than simply "unfair methods of competition in commerce," and which also gave to the FTC specific jurisdiction over false advertising. For a time, it must have seemed that every member of the Congress wanted his name on a trade-regulation bill. There followed, however, a series of more specifically product-oriented bills such as the Wool Products Labelling Act of 1939, whose purpose was to protect the public (and reputable wool merchants) from substitutes and mixtures; the Insurance Act of 1945, which clarified the intent of Congress with regard to the insurance industry; the Lanham Trade Mark Act of 1946, which provided for registration and protection of trademarks; the Fur Products Labelling Act of 1951, which prohibited misbranding, false advertising, and falsification of invoices; and the Flammable Fabrics Act of 1953, which outlawed the shipment of highly flammable wearing apparel in interstate commerce.[14]

The last of these is fairly typical of both the impetus for and the effectiveness of trade-related legislation. The act came about after two highly publicized incidents, the first in 1945 when several small boys were burned to death while wearing cowboy suits with highly flammable chaps made of rayon pile, and the second several years later when severe burns and several deaths were caused by so-called exploding sweaters of brushed rayon. Finally, in 1953, Congress responded with legislative action, but it was action designed for maximal show and minimal effect. The Flammable Fabrics Act did outlaw interstate transportation of flammable clothing, but it made no such prohibition regarding flammable fabrics in general, so that flammable materials could be shipped across state lines and then sewn into garments without incurring the wrath of the federal government. This "oversight" was not corrected until December 1967, when the original law was amended to include all fabrics. More pernicious still, however, was the procedure established by Congress for enforcement of the Flammable Fabrics Act. Rather than providing for a centralized and therefore effective administration of its provisions, Congress chose instead to divide that responsibility among three agencies. Thus, the Department of Health, Education, and Welfare was ordered to gather clothing-related burn statistics, the Department of Commerce to promulgate regulations based on these statistics, and the Federal Trade Commission to administer and enforce these regulations. This particularly cumbersome procedure, which relies on notoriously inefficient channels of interagency communication and cooperation, and which was not fundamentally altered even by the 1967 amendments, has stymied effective protection under the 1953 legislation.[15]

For its part, the Federal Trade Commission has over the years gone through alternating periods of intense activity and equally intense inactivity. In the 1920s, for example, the operating premise of the FTC (as of the government in general) seems to have been that it was the sole duty of consumers to continue "to absorb the output of industry."[16] William E. Humphrey, who became FTC chairman in 1925, regarded the commission as "an instrument of oppression and disturbance instead of a help to business," and he worked to correct this "problem." And the Supreme Court, which in 1924 instructed the FTC not to go on "fishing expeditions" into private corporate papers on the chance that it might find something actionable, contributed to the decline as well. During the early 1930s, and particularly during the years of the National Recovery Act, the FTC became an object of political patronage and cronyism and lost any political importance that might have survived Humphrey. But then, during the last half of the decade and into the 1940s, renewed interest in antitrust activities and in the prohibition of deceptive advertising led to a renaissance of sorts for the commission—which saw its appropriations as well as its popularity and its success rate in the courts rising—and to an expansion of its powers with passage of the Wheeler-Lea Amendment. Between the late 1930s and the early 1950s, the powers of the FTC were regularly expanded, and its actions met with widespread approbation. In the late 1950s and early 1960s, however, the commission made a tactical judgment that has opened it to a wave of criticism in recent years: the decision to rely more heavily on industry guidance and voluntary compliance with FTC orders than on confrontation and litigation, that is, to be less hostile to business.[17] Reflecting this shift in policy, 216 voluntary compliance agreements (in which firms essentially state that they are not guilty of any regulatory violation but will not do it again) were signed in 1061, and by 1967 the number had risen above 600 annually.[18] It is this practice, more than any of its other actions or inactions, that has left the FTC vulnerable to charges of coddling those it was intended to regulate and that has fueled an attack on the commission that we shall discuss shortly.

The third and final consumer-oriented government bureaucracy that we shall consider, the Food and Drug Administration (FDA), may be seen to have much in common with those we have already discussed, particularly with the Federal Trade Commission. For like the FTC, the FDA was created as an enforcement agency several years after regulatory legislation had been enacted and had proven ineffective. Like those of the FTC and the ICC, its powers were repeatedly extended during the years after its creation. And like both of the earlier agencies, the FDA has been subject to criticism in recent years for having developed too cozy a relationship with those it was intended to regulate. Although the FDA was like its precursors in these important aspects, however, the origins of the agency and its intended functions were unique in two significant ways. First, though certain writers and other individuals had, as we have seen, been of some importance in the creation of both the ICC and the FTC, the Food and Drug Administration (or at least the legislation that it was later created to enforce) to a much greater extent owed its existence to the combined efforts of muckraking writers and a single-minded consumer crusader without whom no such legislation or agency would have become reality. Second, and consistent with its origins, the FDA, more than either of the earlier commissions, was primarily intended to serve, not some notion of the proper distribution of economic power, and thus indirectly the interests of the consuming public, but rather the personal health, safety, and well-being of the ultimate consumer. In that sense, then, the Food and Drug Administration was the first real consumer protection agency of the federal government.

By 1906, when the Pure Food and Drug Act became law, food and drug legislation in the United States was really nothing new, dating to passage of the first general food law in Massachusetts in 1784. In 1848 Congress had passed the so-called Edwards Law, which prohibited the importation of adulterated drugs, and in 1879 the Department of Agriculture had begun an investigation of food and drug adulteration that led the next year to a call by chief chemist Peter Collier for a national food and drug law to regulate imports and exports. In 1890 several such laws were passed, particularly relating to the export of diseased meat, which was being excluded from European markets at some cost to American exporters in lost trade. In 1902 Congress approved the Sherman Act (not that of antitrust fame), which prohibited the false labeling of food and dairy products. In fact, between 1897 and 1906, more than 100 food and drug bills were introduced into Congress.[19] None of these, however, constituted legislation of any major importance, and it remained the task of three men, operating more or less independently of one another, to force meaningful congressional action.

The first of these men was Dr. Harvey Wiley, who had parlayed an interest in the chemistry of sugar developed while he served on the first faculty of Purdue University into an appointment in 1883 as chief chemist for the Department of Agriculture (succeeding Collier). From that position, Wiley opened a multipronged and life-long attack on the adulteration of food and drugs and was instrumental in securing passage of the 1906 act and subsequent legislation. Wiley's real strength was that he knew how to mobilize public opinion and use to advantage the pressure that it could exert on congressmen. He testified before congressional committees, stimulated the introduction of pure food and drug bills, and issued press releases geared to arouse the interest of the public. In perhaps his most effective action, Wiley formed a group of volunteers, popularly known as the "Poison Squad," who were placed on experimental diets to test the effects of various food additives, including borax, sulphurous acid, and formaldehyde. These experiments captured the public imagination as had no earlier campaigns against impurities in foods. They even became the subject of songs in minstrel shows, and, when a fallacious newspaper article stated that borax had been found to produce a beautiful pink and white complexion in one who consumed it, several women actually wrote for additional information. When the official results of Wiley's experiments were finally published in a series of reports issued from 1904 to 1906, they gave rise to a widespread clamor for protective action and made Dr. Wiley a much sought-after public speaker, a status he used to great advantage.[20] Wiley, however, was much more than a simple publicist. As chief chemist, he instituted the systematic investigation of foods and food additives. He was instrumental in the development of new analytic techniques and tested the effects of chemical preservatives on human beings. He helped organize pure food conferences and recruited others to assist in his cause. An although he did not draft the law that Congress finally approved in 1906, the Pure Food and Drug Act was in many ways a product of his effort and his influence.[21]

But although Wiley was extremely influential in the pure food and drug effort, probably because of his position within the government, his was by no means the only significant voice raised in the struggle. There were as well a number of journalists who saw in the attack on adulteration not only a chance for public service but a potentially lucrative and easily dramatized subject matter as well. Chief among these was Samuel Hopkins Adams, whose series of twelve articles entitled "The Great American Fraud," which began in *Collier's Weekly* in October 1905, did for patent medicines and popular remedies what Wiley had done for food adulterants, that is to say, made them objects of popular reprobation. By describing the manufacture and sale of various products such as Peruna, a popular home remedy for catarrh (defined by the manufacturer of Peruna to include virtually every ailment known to man) that turned out to contain 28 percent alcohol and was cited as leading to drunkenness, and Liquozone, a curative that was found to contain .9 percent sulphuric acid, .3 percent sulphurous acid, and 98.8 percent water, Adams discredited patent medicines and debunked their advertising with accurate chemical analyses that were later substantiated in a series of actual and threatened libel suits.[22]

In one of the most interesting legal cases arising from the Adams series, *Collier's* editorialized against Post Cereals for advertising its Grape-Nuts as a cure for appendicitis. Post's countercharge that *Collier's* was simply peeved because the cereal company refused to advertise in its pages was deflected when *Collier's* produced letters from Post requesting placement of advertisements, which *Collier's* had refused. *Collier's* sued for libel and received a judgment of $50,000, which was later reversed on a technicality. While this suit was in progress, however, Adams noticed a Post advertisement that told of three individuals who had been dying from drinking coffee but who were saved by consuming Postum. Adams traced the "doctor" who had documented these astounding cases and found him to be, in fact, a printer who sold pills as a sideline and had assumed a medical title. This gentleman told of having corresponded with Mr. Post regarding his "findings" and of having been offered a sum of money if he could get those findings published in a medical journal from which advertisements might then quote. He had found a medical journal of dubious repute that agreed to accept his article (but that had since ceased publication). When the good "doctor" was summoned as a witness in the libel suit, the result was assured.[23]

Finally, there was added to the voices of Wiley and Adams that of novelist Upton Sinclair. In September 1904, Sinclair, who was twenty-six at the time, arrived in Chicago to research conditions at the stockyards for a book he hoped to write. He stayed there for some seven weeks observing, studying meat inspection laws, and interviewing workers. For the better part of a year thereafter, he struggled with the manuscript and with a series of publishing houses unwilling to bring it into print. Sinclair's book, *The Jungle*, was finally published in 1906, in the wake of the work of the Poison Squad and the disclosures of the "Great American Fraud." But where Sinclair, an ardent socialist, had intended the book as an exposé of working conditions in the stockyards, the public, sensitized by the continuing assault on adulteration and deception, focused instead on a few pages in which the author described rather graphically certain details of meat production.[24] "There was never the least attention paid to what was cut up for sausage," Sinclair wrote.

There would come all the way back from Europe old sausage that had been rejected, and that was moldy and white—it would be dosed with borax and glycerine, and dumped into hoppers, and made over again for home consumption. There would be meat that had tumbled out on the floor, in the dirt and sawdust, where the workers had tramped and spit uncounted billions of consumption germs. There would be meat stored in great piles in rooms; and the water from leaky roofs would drip over it, and thousands of rats would race about on it. It was too dark in these storage places to see well, but a man could run his hand over these piles of meat and sweep off handfuls of the dried dung of rats. These rats were nuisances, and the packers would put poisoned bread out for them; they would die, and then rats, bread, and meat would go into the hoppers together. . . . The meat would be shoveled into carts, and the man who did the shoveling would not trouble to lift out a rat even if he saw one—there were things that went into the sausage in comparison with which a poisoned rat was a tidbit.[25]

If Wiley and Adams had set the stage, Sinclair carried the day. *The Jungle* was an instant sensation, and the public outcry to which it gave rise was not to be denied. Sales of meat and meat products dropped by half, and the loss of European markets loomed as a distinct possibility. Additional journalists took up the battle, the American Medical Association joined in the attack on patent medicines, and President Theodore Roosevelt urged prompt congressional action. (As Sinclair himself described the impact of his book at the time, "I aimed at the public's heart and by accident I hit it in the stomach.") So it was that in June 1906 two pieces of legislation, the Pure Food and Drug Act and the Meat Inspection Act, which together gave federal officials the authority to prohibit much, though not all, adulteration of food and drugs and ban hazardous preservatives, were passed into law. There followed a series of broadening amendments such as the Sherley Amendment of 1912, which prohibited false labeling of therapeutic claims for medicines (the fact that, under the 1906 legislation, contents of patent medicines had to be truthfully stated but their efficacy and uses could be falsified had been the subject of a later Adams muckraking series), the Gould Amendment of 1913, which required package labels to include the quantity of the contents, and the Kenyon Amendment of 1919, which required net weight labels on packaged meats. But it was not until 1927 that Congress saw fit to create an agency to enforce these various provisions. It was in that year that the Food, Drug, and Insecticide Administration, which four years later became the Food and Drug Administration, first opened its doors.[26]

Thanks once again to the muckrakers and other interested parties both within and outside the government, however, the public soon learned that its protection was not as effective as it might have been. As early as 1925, the conservative National Civil Service Reform League had concluded, after an investigation of meat inspection procedures:

> The trusting confidence of the American public in the efficiency of laws was never more clearly shown nor more grossly betrayed than in the matter of food inspection. We have enacted "pure food" laws and ordinances, therefore, presumably we have "pure food." But between the law and the "pure food" lies a most important factor—the human element charged with the interpretation and the administration of these laws and ordinances. This element—given great powers of discretion; power to make "rules and regulations" to an extent practically nullifying the intent of the law; subject to overwhelming commercial and political pressure—is the weak link in the chain, and practically the end of the effect of the law. . . .[27]

Then, in the 1930s, books such as Ruth deForest Lamb's *American Chamber of Horrors* and Arthur Kallet and F. J. Schlink's *100,000,000 Guinea Pigs* demonstrated that the Pure Food and Drug Act of 1906 had been so weakened by court decisions and had become so technologically outdated that new legislation was necessary.

A case in point was that of "Marmola," a purported cure for obesity that consisted of thyroid extract and bladderwrack (a seaweed rich in iodine). When ingested, this compound would supplement thyroid secretions and stimulate the gland itself to greater activity, thereby enabling fat to be burned at a higher rate than normal. Thus, if a person's thyroid activity were normal, use of Marmola would abnormally increase the amounts of its potentially dangerous components in his system; but if one's thyroid were already overactive, ingestion of Marmola might result in increased nervousness, irregularities of the heart, headaches, delirium, fever, collapse, coma, or even death. Although complaints against the drug reached the Bureau of Chemistry as early as 1909, Marmola continued to be sold by mail order until 1926, when the manufacturer was threatened with charges of mail fraud. At that point, the Marmola Company suddenly became the Raladam Company and continued to market the drug until 1928, when the Federal Trade Commission filed a complaint against the company and ordered it to stop advertising Marmola as safe, effective, and dependable. Legal challenges to this order followed, and, when the case eventually reached the Supreme Court, that august body ruled that, since the question at issue was not one of promoting competition in commerce, the FTC had exceeded its jurisdiction and its powers in bringing the action. Nor, it would seem, could the newly created Food, Drug, and Insecticide Administration take action, for Marmola was neither a food nor a drug within the meaning of the Pure Food and Drug Act of 1906 (largely because the Court did not consider obesity to be a disease) and thus was not subject to regulation.[28]

For its own part, the FDA in its early years dramatized the need for updating and strengthening the food and drug laws with an exhibition of useless and dangerous home remedies, unsafe cosmetics, and adulterated foods that came to be known (after Lamb's book) as the "Chamber of Horrors." The exhibit included posters showing horrible disfigurement, blindness, poisoning, and death that ostensibly resulted from use of these products, and it was documented by bottles, labels, advertising, and even death certificates. Still, the impetus for final passage of a strengthened food and drug law had to be provided by more immediate tragedy, the deaths of some 100 persons who had taken a new wonder drug, elixir sulfanilamide, that had been marketed without any tests for its safety. When the public learned that the FDA could act in this instance only after the fact, and even then only because the drug had been improperly labeled as an "elixir," which was merely a technical violation of the law, it was incensed. A new and tougher (though still limited) law was passed within a matter of months.[29]

This new law, the Food, Drug, and Cosmetic Act of 1938 (also known as the Copeland Act) retained many of the provisions of the 1906 legislation but also extended coverage to cosmetics. It required predistribution clearance on the safety of drugs; provided tolerance levels for unavoidable or required poisonous substances; authorized standards of identity, quality, and fill for food containers; mandated informative and truthful labeling; authorized factory inspections; and added the remedy of court injunctions to the powers of seizure and prosecution already held by the FDA. The Copeland Act has been amended a number of times since, but it remains the principal enabling legislation for the Food and Drug Administration.[30]

From this point on, the FDA, like its sister agencies, entered an extended period of decline traceable in large measure to the closeness of its ties with the food and drug industries. Indeed, so friendly were industry-agency relations that, at one point in the 1950s, the Pharmaceutical Manufacturers Association, a major trade group, presented FDA Chairman George Larrick with its award for "devoted service to the public welfare" and for "understanding [of] our mutual problems," and a trade journal described Larrick's stewardship of the FDA as "sweetness and light, togetherness, [and] loving one's neighbor."[31]

Before leaving the 1930s, we should point out that those years were for two related sets of events of great import to the consumer protection movement. The first of these was the formation during this period of several consumer-oriented organizations, including the so-called magazine institutes (such as the *Good Housekeeping* Institute and the consumer services bureaus of the *Ladies' Home Journal* and the *Woman's Home Companion*), which, as a means of increasing their respective magazines' circulations and advertising revenues, tested products and issued recommendations (e.g., the *Good Housekeeping* Seal of Approval), and Consumers' Research, considered at the time to be quite radical, which, financed only by its user-subscribers, tested the functions and efficiency of a wide range of products. In addition, such other groups as the American Medical Association, the American Home Economics Institute (the professional society of home economics teachers), the Better Business Bureau, and Underwriters Laboratories worked to raise the standards of production. Although none of these organizations save Consumers' Research would be considered "activist" by recent standards, their value at the time as loci of consumer protection activity should not be underestimated.[32]

The second event of interest to consumers during these years, and especially during the years of the National Recovery Administration (NRA), was the establishment within the NRA of the Consumers Advisory Board (CAB). The CAB, whose function was to defend the interests of the consumer in the drafting and administration of NRA industrial codes, was variously criticized at the time as ineffective (by the chairman of Consumers' Research), as weak and of tenuous status (by its own chairman), and as "a kind of conscience-saving appendage" of the NRA (by a contemporary scholar).[33] And it suffered throughout its brief existence, which ended when the NRA was declared unconstitutional by the Supreme Court in 1935, from a controversy over whether the consuming public must be specifically represented before an agency (the NRA) that presumably existed solely to serve the interests of that public.[34] But the CAB did take the lead in a drive to promulgate product standards and did, for a short time, obtain for the public a voice in the making of wage and price decisions during the New Deal.[35] Most important of all, however, much as the FDA had pioneered the serving of consumer interests per se, the CAB became the first agency of government in the United States to recognize that the concerns of consumers might be somehow distinct from the so-called public interest, and it attempted to give to those concerns representation similar to that granted by the government to other special interests.

Bandits and Raiders: The Rebirth of Consumer Protection

The successes of the 1930s, limited though they were, marked a high point for a time in consumer protection activities, for much like the women's rights movement, the drive for product safety and consumer protection went into a protracted period of inactivity and ineffectiveness at the outset of World War II that lasted some two decades until the movement emerged once again, as did the women's movement, during the turbulent 1960s. There were undoubtedly many factors that contributed to the rebirth of consumerism, ranging from muckraking books such as John G. Fuller's exposé of the remaining dangers in food, drugs, and cosmetics, which, in recognition of Kallet and Schlink's earlier work as well as the growth of the American population, he titled *200,000,000 Guinea Pigs,* to continuing product-related tragedies such as the thalidomide scandal of 1962 (in which numerous birth deformities were attributed to the use of a new sedative by pregnant women), and even to renewed government action, of which we shall have more to say below. Yet the most important contributing element of all, as it had been earlier, was undoubtedly the emergence of a few dedicated, publicity-oriented individuals who took it upon themselves to become advocates for the consumer's cause.

One such individual was a professor of law at George Washington University named John Banzhaf III, who may be best remembered for having begun the legal action that resulted in the placing of antismoking commercials on television and, indirectly, in the later removal of all cigarette advertising from the broadcast media. Acting through such acronymic groups as ASH (Action on Smoking and Health, his first group, formed in 1968), LASH (Legislative Action on Smoking and Health), CAP (Collection Agency Practices), TUBE (Termination of Unfair Broadcasting Excesses), PUMP (Protesting Unfair Marketing Practices), and even SOUP (Students Opposed to Unfair Practices), Banzhaf's law students, dubbed by the press "Banzhaf's Bandits," worked to pressure the Federal Communications Commission and the FTC, to lobby the Congress, and to investigate credit and sales abuses. Through these groups, Banzhaf, whose motto, "Sue the Bastards," became a rallying cry of the consumer movement, attempted to use existing legal processes to force both the government and private corporations to act in the best interests of the consumer. In the process, he became a model for a generation of "public interest" lawyers whose goal has been protection of the public through use of the law.[36]

Better known than Banzhaf, however, probably because of the wider scope of his activities, has been a second consumer advocate, the seemingly ubiquitous Ralph Nader. Nader first came to the attention of the public when his book *Unsafe at Any Speed,* in which he argued that automobiles in general and one General Motors model in particular were, in effect, designed to be dangerous, was published in 1965. In the controversy that followed its publication, General Motors admitted that it had hired a detective to investigate Nader in the hopes of either silencing or discrediting him. This admission gave added credibility to Nader's charges and propelled him to the forefront of a newly renascent movement. It was a position of leadership that Nader was not to relinquish.

During the decade since his rise to prominence, Nader, while cultivating an image of spartan living, demanding leadership, and single-minded devotion to duty, has acted on two fronts to serve the consumer and, in the process, to institutionalize his own position of influence. On the one hand, several pieces of legislation—most notably the National Traffic and Motor Vehicle Safety and the Highway Safety acts of 1966 (which made the design of motor vehicles subject to federal regulation and which followed closely on the publication of *Unsafe at Any Speed*); the Wholesome Meat Act of 1967; the Natural Gas Pipeline Safety Act, the Radiation Control for Health and Safety Act, and the Wholesome Poultry Act, all of 1968; and the Comprehensive Occupational Health and Safety Act of 1970, all of which had been advocated and/or actively supported by Nader—passed into law during this period. It is doubtful whether, in the absence of Nader or some advocate of equal stature, such measures could have won approval.[37]

At the same time that he was lobbying in Congress for these various measures, Nader was active as well in the formation of several consumer-oriented organizations. These include the Center for the Study of Responsive Law, a tax exempt agency formed in 1968 with an annual budget of some $300,000 in foundation grants that has produced several in-depth studies of government regulatory agencies; the Center for Auto Safety, also opened in 1968, whose staff of attorneys, engineers, and researchers, funded principally by another consumer group, Consumers' Union, deals with automobile-related problems; the Public Interest Research Group, formed in 1970 and funded by Nader himself out of proceeds from a suit against General Motors, whose staff of thirteen (including eleven lawyers) conducts investigations with the intention of taking later legislative, administrative, or legal action, and which has recently begun organizing affiliates in a number of states; and Public Citizen, Inc., established in 1971 to raise funds and generate public support for Nader's activities.[38] Through these and other similar organizations, Nader has been able to mobilize a cadre of students and other activists who, calling themselves "Nader's Raiders," have delved into almost every corner of American industry and government in pursuit of the muckraking tradition.

Among their other activities, the Raiders have conducted investigations of the three major consumer protection agencies that we discussed earlier, and in each case they have issued scathing denunciations based on their findings. In January 1969, for example, a Nader task force headed by Edward F. Cox, who later married the daughter of President Richard Nixon, conducted a study of the Federal Trade Commission in which it noted "alcoholism, spectacular lassitude and office absenteeism, incompetence by the most modest standards, and lack of commitment"; such "typical" events as the suppression of a report on automobile warranties until after the 1968 election so as not to anger contributors to the Humphrey campaign; and its own experience of finding an assistant general counsel asleep at his desk with the sports page of the *Washington Post* covering his face. The task force, which based much of its analysis on a Civil Service Commission study that itself charged the FTC with duplicative and conflicting assignments and inadequate leadership, concluded that the commission had failed to detect violations of its rules, establish efficient priorities for its enforcement policy, use its powers adequately, and seek sufficient statutory authority to increase its effectiveness.[39]

When Richard Nixon took office shortly after the Nader report was issued, he requested that the American Bar Association (ABA) conduct an investigation of its own to assess the charges against the FTC. The ABA confirmed the findings of the Raiders and added some charges of its own, and Nixon brought pressure on the commission, whose slow investigative pace and obsession with trivia had long since earned it the sobriquet "Little Old Lady of Pennsylvania Avenue," to mend its ways. He eventually appointed Miles Kirkpatrick, the lawyer who had headed the ABA investigation, to chair the FTC. Under Kirkpatrick, the commission was reorganized into two bureaus (from four), including a Bureau of Consumer Protection headed by Robert

Pitofsky, who had served as counsel to the ABA inquiry, and more than 100 consumer protection specialists were hired and dispatched to the FTC's eleven regional offices to conduct investigations and provide liaison with local consumer groups. Enforcement procedures as well as the commission's regulations were tightened, and a number of actions were begun against tire manufacturers, credit card companies, and others. For all this show of activity, however, the $25 million budget of the FTC and its limited staff continue to be outmatched by the resources available to private industry.[40] Indeed, it was not until August 1975 that the FTC, for the first time in its history, found itself able (or perhaps willing) to form a task force to determine whether its orders against deceptive trade practices dating back to the 1920s were in fact being complied with by the business community.[41]

In March 1970, Nader followed his attack on the FTC with a similar assault on the Interstate Commerce Commission. In this case, seven law students headed by Robert C. Fellmeth charged that rather than regulating the 17,000 rail, truck, shipping, and pipeline companies under their jurisdiction, the members of the ICC in effect operated a cartel in their behalf, a cartel that protected monopoly and inefficiency and permitted discrimination in rates. The Naderites documented a close relationship between the commissioners and the industry that included industry funding of luncheons and junkets and even, on one occasion, a hairdresser for Chairman Virginia Mae Brown. They noted that eleven of the twelve commissioners who had most recently retired from the ICC either took high positions in ICC-regulated industries after leaving or appeared as lawyers arguing cases before the commission. The report, entitled *The Interstate Commerce Omission,* concluded that "the ICC has become an extension of the industry it regulates. In a very real sense, the industry regulates the ICC."[42]

Nor did the Food and Drug Administration escape the attention of Nader's Raiders. Indeed, in April 1970, only a month after the exposé of the ICC was published, yet another Nader report, *The Chemical Feast,* charged the FDA with distorting scientific data and harassing scientists within the agency who disagreed with its findings, charges that were substantiated in subsequent congressional hearings. The FDA was pictured as having succumbed to political pressures, responded to special industry interests, been unwilling to protect consumers, and deliberately misled both the public and the Congress. The report suggested that the Food and Drug Administration underused its authority and misused its staff with the net effect that the public interest was not served.[43]

Banzhaf and Nader, of course, were not the only ones interested in the protection of the consumer during the 1960s and 1970s, nor were they the only ones with effective organizations. Other important groups active during these years have included Consumers' Union (an offshoot of Consumers' Research), a nonprofit product testing organization founded in 1936 and financed by grants and subscriptions; the Consumers Federation of America, an association of interested groups (local consumer organizations, unions, and the like) formed in 1968 to serve as a clearinghouse for consumer information and as a legislative lobby in Washington; the National Consumers League, a membership organization founded in the 1890s to assure fair labor conditions and acting more recently as a national lobby in favor of increased minimum wages, no-fault insurance, and the establishment of an independent consumer protection agency; and a number of state and local consumer groups. The activities of these organizations are further augmented by an increasing number of ombudsman-like consumer advocates in the employ of various of the news media in such cities as New York, San Francisco, Los Angeles, Chicago, Detroit, Houston, and Atlanta.[44] Indeed, it is largely because of the breadth and vigor of the consumer movement in recent years that governments on various levels have once more been moved to action in the area of consumer protection.

Regulation, Part II: The Government Responds

Taking the lead in the official response to consumer demands, much as they had in each of the earlier periods of consumer activism, have been several of the state governments. In 1966 alone, for example, just as the consumer protection movement was gathering momentum, Massachusetts enacted legislation mandating full disclosure in lending and installment sales; Michigan updated its usury laws and empowered the state attorney general to halt deceptive advertising without prior (and time-consuming) court action; Washington banned referral sales schemes; and Pennsylvania and ten other states outlawed various credit abuses. California, Illinois, Nevada, Delaware, New Mexico, and Oregon strengthened their laws relating to misleading advertising, while Massachusetts, California, Montana, and Pennsylvania took action on packaging or weights and measures. By 1972, twenty-three states had set up consumer protection offices or consumer departments (Connecticut had established the first cabinet-level consumers' department with full powers in 1959), and thirty-nine had consumer fraud agencies (the New York Consumer Frauds and Protection Bureau was handling about 85,000 cases per year), while some fifty cities and twenty counties also had consumer protection agencies. And by 1974, forty-eight of the fifty states as well as eighty-six counties and 166 cities were organized for consumer protection.[45] Clearly, the movement to reverse the doctrine of *caveat emptor* (let the buyer beware) was national in scope.

But if the movement to protect the consumer was nationwide, so, too, was the threat to his well-being, and therein lay a serious problem. Just as state action had proven insufficient to end rail monopolies, restraint of trade, and adulteration of food and drugs in an earlier era, it was once again proving unequal to the task of ensuring the safety and integrity of the consumer products of more recent years, and for essentially the same reason. Even the best and most well intentioned state action, after all, can be effective only within the boundaries of that state and can have at best a limited impact on interstate commerce and the national welfare. Just as water flows downhill and corporations flock to Delaware (which has the least stringent laws of incorporation of all the states), consumer fraud, dangerous products, and deceptive practices tend to center in those areas of least restriction. Given such tendencies, the conclusion once again seems to have been that only a nationwide law with nationwide jurisdiction could provide nationwide enforcement. As a result, pressure for federal action has mounted once again.

The federal government has responded to both the need and the pressure in two principal ways, the first legislative and the second organizational. On the legislative front, Congress has passed into law not only various amendments to food and drug legislation designed to improve drug safety requirements (following the thalidomide scare) and restrict distribution of amphetamines and barbiturates but also the Fair Packaging and Labelling Act of 1966, which set new standards to be administered by the FTC; the 1968 Truth in Lending Act, which required full disclosure of costs of financing (and which was modeled after the earlier legislation in Massachusetts); a bill to curb land-sale frauds; two bills that required printing of health warnings on cigarette packages and prohibited broadcast advertising of the product; and the various "Nader bills" mentioned earlier.[46] In many ways, these actions have simply continued a long series of product- or problem-specific attempts by the Congress to respond to particular public dissatisfactions.

More interesting, but in many ways no less an extension of past practice, has been the second governmental response to consumer demands, the organizational response. This began early in the 1960s, when President John F. Kennedy appointed a Consumer Advisory Council whose functions were to advise the president on consumer affairs, issue statements and proposals on consumer problems, and contribute to the making of economic policy within the executive branch. In 1964 Lyndon Johnson reorganized this council as the President's Committee for Consumer Interest, appointed Esther Peterson as special assistant for consumer affairs (with cabinet rank), and named public representatives and executive branch personnel to the committee. At about the same time, Johnson created a second Consumer Advisory Council consisting of twelve private citizens appointed by the president for terms of one or two years. The President's Committee, under the stewardship of Betty Furness, who soon succeeded Peterson, was in charge of consumer education, providing support for state and private consumer assistance programs, working with the business community in a liaison capacity, getting consumer information to the public, studying federal consumer programs, and serving as a clearinghouse for consumer complaints. The Advisory Council, also under the direction of the special assistant, investigated consumer problems but lacked real powers. When Richard Nixon became president, he first appointed Willie Mae Rogers to the consumer post and, upon her resignation shortly afterward, then appointed Virginia Knauer. In 1971 the President's Committee for Consumer Interest was again reorganized, this time as the Office of Consumer Affairs (with a staff of about fifty and Ms. Knauer as director), and in 1973 it was transferred from the White House to the Department of Health, Education, and Welfare.[47]

Nor was this the only organizational response at the federal level. In addition to expansion of the federal role in consumer protection, there was a move toward consolidation that may, in the long run, prove more important. In 1967 the responsibility for consumer protection was divided among at least thirty-six government agencies ranging from the Department of Defense (which set minimum standards for products sold to military personnel) to the Post Office Department (which was charged with protecting the public from dangerous articles, contraband, fraudulent promotional materials, and pornography). In a preliminary move toward centralizing some of these functions, President Johnson recommended to Congress that a National Commission on Product Safety (NCPS) be established to study consumer problems.[48] Congress approved, and the commission began what was to prove a brief existence in 1968. From the outset, the NCPS acted more as a regulatory agency than as a fact-finding group and proved relatively effective in using its only weapon, adverse publicity or the threat of adverse publicity, to induce manufacturers to alter the designs of their products so as to incorporate various safety features. The independence of the commission displeased Johnson's successor, however, who wanted all consumer protection activities to be located in the more easily controlled Department of Health, Education, and Welfare, and Nixon terminated the NCPS in 1970, refusing even to meet with its chairman, Arnold Elkind, who was forced to turn over his final report to an employee at the White House gate.[49]

There matters stood until November 1972, when Congress passed, and the president reluctantly signed, the Consumer Product Safety Act, the first consumer protection act ever to threaten meaningful penalties for violators (including fines of up to $50,000 and as much as a year in jail for the executives of offending corporations). The act established a five-member Consumer Product Safety Commission (CPSC) with a broad mandate to gather product safety data and the power to order recall, repair, or replacement of any dangerous product, or even to seize it or ban it from the marketplace. The commission, which was directly responsible to Congress rather than to the executive branch, began operations under Chairman Richard O. Simpson in May 1973 with a staff of 750 lawyers, technicians, and administrators, fourteen field offices and product-testing laboratories, and an annual budget of over $30 million. Charged with developing uniform product safety standards, helping consumers evaluate the safety of products, gathering statistics and conducting research on product-related injuries, and helping harmonize federal, state, and local product safety laws and enforcement, the CPSC was criticized almost from its inception by members of Congress and the White House (President Nixon tried unsuccessfully to sack Chairman Simpson) for being too aggressive, and by industry for its preference for public announcements rather than privately negotiated settlements (a sharp contrast to the FTC). Commission estimates that shortcomings in product safety account for injuries requiring medical attention to 20,000,000 Americans, the permanent disabling of 110,000 persons, 30,000 deaths, and $5.5 billion in economic losses *each year* suggest the need for a potent and independent consumer protection agency.[50]

Finally, the organizational response to the problems of the consumer has included moves toward establishing a cabinet-level Department of Consumer Affairs. This is not really a new idea, having been proposed as early as 1934 by Frederick Schlink of Consumers' Research, and it has rattled around in Congress at least since Senator Estes Kefauver introduced such a measure in 1961.[51] In 1968 Congressman Benjamin Rosenthal of New York introduced a measure in the House to establish such a department to take over food grading and classification from the Consumer and Marketing Service of the Department of Agriculture, home economics and nutrition research from the Agricultural Research Service, price and cost-of-living reporting from the Bureau of Labor Statistics, and packaging and labeling enforcement and setting of food safety standards from the Department of Health, Education, and Welfare. The agency envisioned by Rosenthal would also represent the consumer in court and before regulatory agencies, handle consumer complaints, establish an Office of

Consumer Information to disseminate information, establish a National Consumer Information Foundation to encourage voluntary product testing, establish an Office of Consumer Safety to check product safety, and conduct a variety of economic surveys.[52] A variation of this bill, which would effectively centralize much of the consumer protection activity of the federal government, has been introduced in each subsequent Congress. Such a measure passed the house in 1974 on a vote of 293 to 94 but was filibustered to death in the Senate.[53] Typical of the opposition to the bill are the sentiments expressed by Senator James Buckley of New York, who observed that

> The American people have had their fill of "cure-all" solutions to problems that are both more difficult to solve and less pervasive than the advocates of such solutions would have us believe. This bill would create one more costly agency, hamstring other agencies and bring the American business-man under even more red tape.[54]

Conclusion

Recent events in the drive for consumer protection, then, may be viewed as something of a repetition of similar activities in the past. Muckrakers and concerned citizens have raised the cry that the consumer is threatened by widespread abusive business practices, and they have organized to force governmental action. Laws have been passed to protect the consumer but have proven ineffective because of the lack of meaningful enforcement. Specialized federal agencies have been formed to enforce the laws, but they have been limited either by political disagreements in the short run or by industrial pressure in the long run. In each instance, the government has responded with the minimal amount of change needed to calm a disquieted citizenry, and in each instance save the present, where the process is still in mid-cycle, that public has indeed been quieted to the point of losing interest in the battle.

Whether or not this pattern of concern, response, and quiescence repeats itself in the future, one point does stand out rather consistently with regard to the consumer protection movement, especially in comparison to the women's rights movement. Where the women's rightists have traditionally sought fundamental change and an expansion of social roles, consumerists have invariably been satisfied with incremental change directed toward a restriction of corporate freedom. Inherent in the consumer protection movement since its very inception has been a reliance on the passing and implementation of *specific* laws—on the twin processes of legislation and administration—which sets it quite apart from the women's rights movement, with its consistent reliance on constitutional mandate. In a very real sense, the history of the consumer protection movement is written in law and revised daily in the actions of a multitude of federal agencies. It is codified, rationalized, and institutionalized. There appears every reason to expect that, in this regard, the established strategy of the movement will continue to predominate.

If the consumer protection and women's rights movements differ in this regard, however, they do have in common, not only with one another but with almost all political movements in the United States, one feature that is undoubtedly more important still. Underlying all these struggles for protection, representation, and influence is the common assumption that, given sufficient pressure, the political system will respond to the legitimate interests of its citizens. This assumption says more about the fundamental character of American politics than anything else that comes to mind. Political movements come and go, only to come once more. The government gives what it must and withholds what it can, only to be forced to give once more. But even the participants in political movements, undoubtedly the least-satisfied citizens of any given era, are almost always willing to play the political game by the rules and are seldom moved to question seriously the validity of those rules. That basic, largely unchallenged consensus is the source of both stability and change in the United States, and it provides a necessary setting for understanding virtually all American political movements. Thus, even in change, there is stability.

NOTES

1. Quoted in "Nader's Raiders Strike Again," *Time*, 30 March 1970, p. 88.

2. I. L. Sharfman. *The Interstate Commerce Commission: A Study in Administrative Law and Procedure*, pt. 1 (New York: Harper and Row, 1931)., pp. 11–14; Dan Cordtz, "It's Time to Unload the Regulators," *Fortune*, July 1971, pp. 64–67, 143–45.

3. Sharfman, *ICC*, pp. 15–19.

4. Samuel P. Huntington, "The Marasmus of the ICC: The Commission, the Railroads, and the Public Interest," *Yale Law Journal* 61 (April 1952): 470–72.

5. Louis Filler, *The Muckrakers: Crusaders for American Liberalism* (Chicago: Regnery, 1950, 1968), p. 203

6. Ibid., pp. 203–216.

7. Huntington, "The Marasmus," pp. 470–72.

8. Ibid.

9. Cordtz, "It's Time," passim.

10. Huntington, "The Marasmus," pp. 473–81.

11. Susan Wagner, *The Federal Trade Commission* (New York: Praeger, 1971), pp. 4–11.

12. David Howard Davis, *Energy Politics* (New York: St. Martin's, 1974), p. 43; Filler, *Muckrakers*, pp. 102–109.

13. Wagner, *FTC*, pp. 11–21; and Donald F. Rothschild and David W. Carroll, *Consumer Protection Reporting Service* (Cincinnati: W. H. Anderson, 1973, 1974, 1975), pp. 58–60.

14. "Congress and Consumer Protection Moves," *Congressional Digest* 45 (June 1966): 165, 192; Rothschild and Carroll, *Consumer Protection*, p. 59.

15. Wagner, *FTC*, pp. 167–68; Rothschild and Carroll, *Consumer Protection*, pp. 223–26.

16. Robert S. Lynd, "The Consumer Becomes a 'Problem,'" *Annals* 173 (May 1934): 5.

17. Wagner, *FTC*, pp. 24–32.

18. "A Little Old Lady With a Tough New Look," *Newsweek*, 23 October 1967, pp. 82–83.

19. Lynd, "The Consumer," p. 2; and Rothschild and Carroll, *Consumer Protection*, pp. 164–65.

20. Oscar E. Anderson, Jr., *The Health of a Nation: Harvey W. Wiley and the Fight for Pure Food* (Chicago: University of Chicago Press, 1958), pp. 128–52.

21. Ibid. p. 195.

22. C. C. Regier, *The Era of the Muckrakers* (Chapel Hill, N.C.: University of North Carolina Press, 1932), pp. 180–82; and Filler, *Muckrakers*, pp. 153-55.

23. Regier, *Era*, pp. 183–85.

24. Filler, *Muckrakers*, pp. 163–65.

25. Upton Sinclair, *The Jungle* (Cambridge, Mass.: Robert Bentley 1906, 1972), p. 135.

26. "Congress and Consumer Protection Moves," pp. 164-65: Regier, *Era*, p. 182; Robert O. Herrman, "The Consumer Movement in Historical Perspective," in *Consumerism: Search for the Consumer Interest*, 2d ed., ed. David A. Aaker and George S. Day (New York: Free Press, 1974), p. 11.

27. Arthur Kallet, "Foods and Drugs for the Consumer," *Annals* 173 (May 1934): 27.

28. Ruth de Forest Lamb, *The American Chamber of Horrors* (New York: Ferrar and Rinehart, 1936), pp. 5-9.

29. Mark V. Nadel, *The Politics of Consumer Protection* (Indianapolis: Bobbs-Merrill, 1971), pp. 17-18; and Herrman, "Consumer Movement," p. 13.

30. "Congress and Consumer Protection Moves," pp. 164-65.

31. Milton Silverman and Philip R. Lee, *Pills, Profits and Politics* (Berkeley: University of California Press, 1974), p. 237.

32. Edith Ayres, "Private Organizations Working for the Consumer," *Annals* 173 (May 1934): 158-65.

33. Frederick J. Schlink, "Safeguarding the Consumer's Interest—An Essential Element in National Recovery," *Annals* 172 (March 1934): 113-22; Lynd, "The Consumer," p. 5; and Ben W. Lewis, "The 'Consumer' and 'Public' Interests Under Public Regulation," *Journal of Political Economy* 46 (February 1938): 97-107.

34. Lewis, "'Consumer' and 'Public' Interests," pp. 98-100. See also, Gardiner C. Means, "The Consumer and the New Deal," *Annals* 173 (May 1934): 14-15.

35. Paul H. Douglas, "The Role of the Consumer in the New Deal," *Annals* 172 (March 1934): 88-97; Paul G. Agnew, "The Movement for Standards for Consumer Goods," *Annals* 173 (May 1934): 62-63.

36. "Banzhaf's Bandits," *Time*, 2 March 1970, pp. 15-16; A. Lee Fritschler, *Smoking and Politics: Policymaking and the Federal Bureaucracy*, 2d ed. (Englewood Cliffs, N.J.: Prentice-Hall, 1975), pp. 145-47; Joseph A. Page, "The Law Professor Behind Ash, Soup, Pump and Crash," in *Styles of Political Action in America*, ed. Robert Paul Wolff (New York: Random House, 1972), pp. 124-34.

37. Charles McCarry, *Citizen Nader* (New York: Saturday Review Press, 1972), pp. xii-xiv, passim. For two contradictory biographical views of Nader, see Robert F. Buckhorn, *Nader: The People's Lawyer* (Englewood Cliffs, N.J.: Prentice-Hall, 1972) and Ralph De Toledano, *Hit and Run: The Rise—And Fall?—of Ralph Nader* (New Rochelle, N.Y.: Arlington House, 1975).

38. Julius Duscha, "Stop! In the Public Interest," *New York Times*,

21 March 1971, p. VI-4; McCarry, *Citizen Nader*, pp. xiii-xiv; Rothschild and Carroll, *Consumer Protection*, pp. 750–51.

39. "FTC Gets Nader Needling," *Business Week*, 11 January 1969, pp. 34, 36; Edward F. Cox, Robert C. Fellmeth, and John E. Schulz, *'The Nader Report' On the Federal Trade Commission* (New York: Richard W. Baron, 1969), pp. 39, 170.

40. "The FTC Gets Tough," *Changing Times*, July 1972, pp. 17–20; "An Old Lady's New Kick," *Newsweek*, 14 December 1970, pp. 87, 89; "Critique of the FTC," *New Republic*, 18 October 1969, pp. 8–9; John Osborne, "Reform at the FTC," *New Republic*, 2 October 1971, pp. 13–15.

41. "FTC Sets Compliance Check on Trade Rules," *Wall Street Journal*, 22 August 1975, p. 26, col. 3.

42. "Nader's Raiders Strike Again," *Time*, 30 March 1970, p. 88; "An Entrenched ICC Fights Off the Reformers," *Business Week*, 9 October 1971, pp. 48–49.

43. Anita Johnson, "Greasing the Skids for Approval," *Nation*, 2 November 1974, pp. 435–36; Philip M. Boffey, "Nader's Raiders on the FDA: Science and Scientists 'Misused,'" *Science*, 17 April 1970, pp. 349–52; James S. Turner, *The Chemical Feast* (New York: Grossman, 1970), passim.

44. Rothschild and Carroll, *Consumer Protection*, pp. 736–58; "Consumer Galahads," *Newsweek*, 15 September 1975, pp. 69–70.

45. "Consumers Battle at the Grass Roots," *Business Week*, 26 February 1972, pp. 86, 88; "The New Look in 'Consumer Protection,'" *Changing Times*, November 1966, pp. 43–46; "Controversy Over Proposals to Establish a U.S. Consumer Protection Agency," *Congressional Digest* 53 (Novemer 1974): 259–88.

46. "Congress and a Consumer Protection Agency," *Congressional Digest* 50 (February 1971): 33–64.

47. Rothschild and Carroll, *Consumer Protection*, pp. 212–13.

48. "Congress and Consumer Proposals," *Congressional Digest* 47 (March 1968): 67–96.

49. Michael Lemov, "Whatever Happened to Product Safety?" *New Republic*, 3 April 1971, pp. 12–13.

50. "Semi-Tough," *Newsweek*, 13 November 1972, pp. 86–88; "Dictating Product Safety," *Business Week*, 18 May 1974, pp. 56–62.

51. Schlink, "Safeguarding," pp. 121–22; "Controversy Over Proposals," p. 263.

52. "Cabinet Rank for U.S. Shoppers?" *Changing Times*, January 1969, pp. 15–16.

53. "Controversy Over Proposals," p. 263.

54. Ibid., p. 277.

7

Pride and Prejudice: The American People and Foreign Affairs

We had built a spiritual haven, a land of justice for all, refuge for the world's oppressed masses. We saw ourselves as a compassionate people who would share our ideals and some of our bounty with less fortunate humans. As our missionaries once fanned out to bring the blessings of Yankee culture to the savages, so would our Government's foreign aid and our businessmen transform the world in our image. As the *power with primary responsibility for mankind, we would chart a course to universal peace, prosperity and social justice.*

Fletcher Knebel[1]

They see the world in strictly American terms. . . . Such things as patriotism, charity, and motherhood are always seen and described as American virtues, as though the rest of the world wouldn't have known the concepts if the U.S. hadn't invented them.

T. J. S. George[2]

I don't see why we need to stand by and watch a country go communist due to the irresponsibility of its own people.

Henry Kissinger[3]

If there's one way to scare an American to death it's mention the word "Communist."

Deirdre O'Doherty in Jimmy Breslin's *World Without End, Amen*

To this point, we have focused our attention principally on questions of domestic politics and policy. We have investigated social, economic, and racial violence, urban development and decay, the occasional moral degeneracy of those holding positions of public trust, and the advances and setbacks of two major political movements. In the process, we have provided a rather broad perspective on the many forces that help shape contemporary American political life.

There remains, however, one major area that we have yet to examine, that of American foreign policy, which also contributes significantly to an understanding of politics today. In the modern world, no nation can hold itself wholly apart from the ebb and flow of world events or from a concern with both its sense of security and its sense of purpose. No internal political system can function effectively without giving due regard to the demands of international relations. A nation of the scale and power of the United States is surely no exception. Indeed, America's domestic policy frequently flows from her perceived opportunities or difficulties overseas, and her foreign policy from the requisites of domestic politics. In the present chapter, therefore, we shall consider certain aspects of the relationship between world and domestic affairs, notably those relating to public opinion, in an effort to suggest the impact of each area of policy upon the other. In so doing, we shall attempt, not to "explain" American foreign policy, but to examine the perceptions that Americans have of the world and of themselves and the ways in which those perceptions are reflected in the course of events.

Most analyses of the historical development of the relationship between public opinion and foreign policy in the United States dwell upon what is generally termed the "internationalist-isolationist" dimension, and they make the argument that the American people tend to fluctuate with some regularity between a preference for a high level of involvement in world affairs and that for an almost total withdrawal from the international arena. Thus, the period of the Spanish-American War and the Panama Canal venture, during which American interests came for the first time to include the domination of foreign lands, might be seen as internationalist in character; that between the two world wars, when the nation rejected participation in the League of Nations and later sought to maintain neutrality in the face of German aggression, can be characterized as isolationist; that following World War II, during which the United States propped up the sagging states of Europe with Marshall Plan aid and took the lead in forming the United Nations and various regional defense alliances, might be viewed as internationalist; that of the present, when the nation shows signs of recoiling from foreign entanglements in the wake of the Vietnam debacle, can be seen as isolationist; and so forth. In this context, the actions of policy makers are generally seen as reflecting (or occasionally resisting) the alternating pressures of contemporary public opinion as foreign policy is formulated.

This author finds this descriptive model rather appealing, since it seems to reflect discernible and consistent patterns of American public opinion and behavior. Discrete periods of involvement and withdrawal may, in fact, be observed with remarkable regularity in both American policy and expressions of the popular will. But at the same time, the internationalist-isolationist argument seems to be of somewhat limited usefulness in that it really suggests no mechanism to account for the frequent reversals in public preference upon which it is predicated. That is to say, the internationalist-isolationist conceptualization tells us what happens, but not why. It tells us much about the results of political decision making, but little of the process. For this reason, we shall attempt in these pages to look behind the internationalist-isolationist dichotomy to some more basic elements of the American political culture that might help explain the behavior we have described. In particular, we shall look at two elements of that culture that have been the subject of frequent intellectual speculation through the years and that play a vital role in linking foreign to domestic affairs.[4]

The first of these elements we shall label "pride," a concept closely akin to what former Senator J. William Fulbright once termed "the arrogance of power," and one that is clearly reflected in Fletcher Knebel's recollections of the 1930s quoted at the outset of this chapter. Pride in American politics has traditionally consisted of a complex admixture of moralism, nationalism, patriotism, humanitarianism, progressivism, and good old American pragmatism, a blend of ethnocentrism and evangelical righteousness, all combined with liberal doses of pure and unequalled power. It is the explosion of a dynamic national character onto the world scene, the proselytization of what is American among all the peoples of the world. And it is, at the same time, a reflection of a powerful sense of national destiny and of the rightness and ultimate success of a seemingly endless social, economic, and political expansion. This "pride" is, in short, the projection into foreign affairs of an enthusiasm and concern for mankind that has been noted by such diverse observers as Charles Dickens, Herbert Spencer, and Margaret Mead and that has been variously attributed to such causes as the absence of a feudal tradition in the American experience and the consistently successful taming of a succession of frontiers from Massachusetts to the moon. In studying it, we shall emphasize the impact of domestic affairs upon American foreign policy.[5]

At the same time, however, there is a second element of the American political culture that bears on the role of the United States in world affairs, an element that is quite different from, and in many ways directly contradictory to, the first. We shall label it "prejudice." Even a cursory examination of American history reveals that, along with the important periods of dynamic and indeed missionary zeal, when the flow of energy, ideas, and resources has been outward and when the American people have manifested almost unbounded confidence in their ability to control events, there have also come other periods when the iniquities of world politics have impinged upon the accustomed domestic tranquility and when the people of the United States have been troubled by fear, insecurity, and self-doubt. There have come times when public opinion has turned inward, when suspicion has outweighed social concern, and when the nation has doubted not only its efficacy but its safety and its likelihood of survival. In such times, the American nation has frequently come to the very brink of paranoia and repression as the faith and optimism of one age have given way to the distrust and pessimism of another. For the realizations that there are, in fact, uncertainties in world politics and that events frequently lie beyond the effective control of any one nation, no matter how powerful, is neither an easy nor a pleasant one for a people accustomed to great wealth and power. And when that people is, as Americans seem to be, inclined toward racism and nativism even in the best of times, the perception of externally imposed adversity can readily give rise to various manifestations of xenophobia, the fear and hatred of foreigners, that have the potential to destroy the very society they are intended to protect. Such xenophobic tendencies have indeed been apparent in American society over much of the past century, most notably in response to the perceived dangers of international communism, and they constitute the principal component of the dimension to which we refer here as prejudice.[6]

These two dimensions, then, pride and prejudice, ethnocentrism and xenophobia, clearly go to the very heart of the matter. They deal at a fundamental level with the motivations and justifications for American actions both at home and abroad. They suggest both the projection of domestic concerns into foreign affairs and the intrusion of foreign problems into domestic politics. For these reasons, we shall employ these two concepts as the basis for the discussion that follows.

Pride and American Foreign Policy

From the very beginning of their national history, Americans have celebrated their governmental experiment in words and deeds. The land was filled with riches and promise, and the times with struggle and hope for the future. It should not be surprising, then, that the birth of the American nation was accompanied by some of the most brilliant and thoughtful writing on the nature and practice of democracy and human rights that the world has yet seen, though not all this literature was produced solely by citizens of the new land. The air was literally ripe with visions of a glorious future. Perhaps the words of Alexis de Tocqueville, a Frenchman who visited the United States in 1831, best captured the mood of the day. Writing in his *Democracy in America* (first published in 1835), Tocqueville noted:

> All other nations seem to have nearly reached their natural limits, and they have only to maintain their power; but [the United States is] still in the act of growth. All the others have stopped, or continue to advance with extreme difficulty; [the United States is] proceeding with

> ease and celerity along a path to which no limit can be perceived . . . [and] seems marked out by the will of Heaven to sway the destinies of half the globe.[7]

Such sentiments, and they were relatively common, were heady intellectual brew indeed for the citizens of an emerging nation, and they helped create an atmosphere in which the national sense of pride and will first manifested itself in a doctrine that came to be known as "manifest destiny." The term "manifest destiny" was once defined by one of its staunchest adherents as "an assured natural tendency of events, more or less subject to influence by man's volitional interference . . . [the use of which] is limited to the political evolution of the United States."[8] It was first used in Congress on January 3, 1846, by Massachusetts Representative Robert C. Winthrop, who, in opposing a resolution for a joint occupation (with Great Britain) of the Oregon Territory, spoke of "that new revelation of right which has been designated as the right of our manifest destiny to spread over the whole continent."[9] Almost at once, Winthrop's phrase became popular as a rationale and justification for the Mexican War, which happened to be raging at the time, and then, after a period of disuse, was revived as a rationale for American involvement in the building of the Panama Canal. The first of these events, the Mexican War, took place long before the period of our own concern, but the latter, which occurred shortly after the turn of the present century, will more than suffice to illustrate the salient points of the notion of manifest destiny. If we are to understand fully the many ramifications of the canal undertaking, however, we must first set the stage with a rather extended analysis of a second, roughly contemporaneous and closely related event, the Spanish-American War.

As we noted in our discussion of American political violence, the latter half of the nineteenth century was a period of rapid and widespread industrialization. Railroad barons and captains of industry were the order of the day, and the national well-being of a previously agrarian society came to be equated with continued commercial success. Economic optimism was widespread. At the same time, however, spurred by an essay written by historian Frederick Jackson Turner, many Americans, and particularly those influential in the making of foreign policy, began to realize that their traditional frontier was rapidly disappearing and that at some point future economic growth might have to center, not on the North American continent, but in foreign markets. The United States, it seemed, was catching up with some of the traditional problems of its European forebears. In this context, it was only natural to expect that so powerful a concept as manifest destiny would be commercialized and externalized, and, indeed, near the turn of the century this took place with the formulation of a closely related doctrine that we can call "mercantilist imperialism" and the accompanying rise of the American imperialist movement.

Although American business interests may have been the principal beneficiaries of mercantilist imperialism, it was less the commercial segment of the society than the intellectuals, principal among whom was a minor naval officer named Alfred Thayer Mahan, who gave rise to the imperialist movement. In the late 1880s, Mahan was asked to give a series of lectures on a topic of his choice at the Naval War College at Newport, Rhode Island. He settled on an analysis of the role of seapower in world history, and in 1890, subsequent to his lectures, he published a book entitled *The Influence of Seapower upon History* in which he argued rather forcefully that navies, a merchant marine, harbors, naval bases, and distant colonies were necessary to provide seaborne commerce and the means to protect that commerce. In the same year, John W. Burgess, a professor of history and political science at Columbia University, published a more obscure but at the time influential treatise entitled *Political Science and Comparative Constitutional Law* in which he set forth the view that only Germanic peoples including Anglo-Saxons were capable of political permanence. The Darwinian influence is evident in Burgess's assertions that "there is no human right to the status of barbarism," and that advanced peoples should organize to educate backward peoples. This call to assume what Rudyard Kipling had termed the "white man's burden" was picked up by American historians such as John Fiske, by ministers such as Josiah Strong, and by journalists such as Albert Shaw, Whitelaw Reid, and Horatio Bridge.[10] Even college students at the turn of the century were flocking to join the ranks of the

Student Volunteers for Foreign Missions, whose motto was "The Evangelization of the World in This Generation."[11]

All these proponents of a new outward-oriented, aggressive foreign policy were influential, but none could match Mahan in terms of well-placed disciples. His writings influenced such luminaries as Theodore Roosevelt (then in the Navy Department), the powerful Senator Henry Cabot Lodge, Secretary of State John Hay, and two successive naval secretaries, Benjamin F. Tracy (1889–1893) and Hilary A. Herbert (1893–1897). Mahan's views represented an attractive blend of industrialism, financialism, Darwinism, and humanitarianism that these men and others found virtually irresistible.

Mahan spoke less of a colonial empire than of a commercial empire, and the difference, particularly in the light of the American self-image, was a significant one. He accepted the white man's burden, but also the importance of the individual. He accepted the need for expansion, but only to obtain service facilities and not for purely political hegemony in any corner of the world. He saw seapower, not as an end in itself, but as a necessary accompaniment to the development of overseas markets into which the increasing surpluses of American industry might be channeled. In other words, Mahan viewed colonies, not as sources of raw materials and outlets for surplus populations, as had earlier mercantilist writers, but as outlets for production and bases for commerce, shipping, and the navy. The American presence today in Guantanamo (Cuba), Manila, the Canal Zone, and even Hawaii bears testimony to Mahan's impact on American foreign policy.[12] And it was in the wake of his writings that the clamor for an American overseas venture, and particularly for a war with Spain, then a colonial power, crystallized.

The Spanish-American War began shortly after February 15, 1898, on which date the United States armored cruiser *Maine* exploded and sank in Havana Harbor under somewhat mysterious circumstances with a loss of 260 lives. But the *Maine* incident was only an excuse for an act of assertion, an organizing symbol of affrontery that gave focus to a widespread though not nearly unanimous public ardor to teach the Spanish a lesson. Beneath that ardor lay all the themes of mercantilist imperialism and American pride.

In February 1895, there had begun in Cuba a moderate-sized insurrection against Spanish colonial rule that captured the imagination of the American people. Despite the fact that the participants in this movement extracted large sums of money from American interests on the island by threats against their property, despite the fact that, when extortion failed, that property was destroyed, and despite the fact that the methods of the rebels were cruel and destructive, the insurrectionists retained American sympathies and were permitted (though not by the government) to launch raids against the Spanish from United States soil. The cry "Cuba Libre!" came, in effect, to be equated with America's own sense of independence and self-perceived revolutionary heritage.[13]

Then, in 1896, General Campos, who had been in charge of all Spanish forces in Cuba, was recalled to Spain and his position filled by General Valeriano Weyler, or, as he was referred to in the American press, "Butcher" Weyler. When Weyler arrived in Cuba in February of that year, he conducted a brief survey of the situation and came to the conclusion that Spain could never triumph over the rebels so long as there existed on the island a rural population willing to offer them assistance. In an action that must have been similar in purpose and effect to the American "strategic hamlet" program in Vietnam in the 1960s, Weyler therefore ordered that all the island's citizens be housed in so-called reconcentration camps located near Spanish military facilities. Travel in Cuba without military authorization was forbidden, and the conduct of all business on the island was made subject to military oversight. Conditions in the camps were deplorable, and many died.[14]

These events received rather intemperate coverage in the American press and caused a political tumult in Washington. President Cleveland tried to calm the situation, but in the spring of 1896 both houses of Congress overwhelmingly passed a resolution in support of the Cuban rebels. The debates that accompanied passage of this measure caused a great outcry in Spain, where in one instance a mob of several thousand stoned the United States consulate in Barcelona, tore up the American flag, and chanted "Down with the American pig killers." In retribution, students and workers in the United States took to the streets to shout their support for the congressional action, and the Chamber of Commerce of Youngstown, Ohio, announced a boycott of the Spanish onion. For his part, Cleveland ignored both the resolution and the clamor, and took no action.[15]

At this point, William Randolph Hearst took charge of events. Hearst was the publisher of several American newspapers, principal among which in 1896 was the *New York Morning Journal.* Together with Joseph Pulitzer, his major competitor, he was in the process of creating a mass circulation, sensationalist medium popularly known as the "yellow press" (the name derived from the use of color comics, which was begun by Hearst) that was described by one observer as having "the keyhole for a point of view, sensationalism for a policy, crime, scandal, and personalities for a specialty, all vested interests for a punching bag, cartoons, illustrations, and comic supplements for embellishment, and circulation for an object." Hearst euphemistically termed his style "the new journalism."[16]

For some time Hearst and Pulitzer had been vying for readership by proclaiming, not always with notable candor or accuracy, the treachery of the Spanish in Cuba, but now Hearst became truly innovative. To begin with, he embellished a dispatch by one of his reporters in Cuba to create an international incident regarding the imprisonment of one Evangelina Cisneros, whose father, one of the *insurrectos*, had been captured by Spanish authorities, and who had herself insisted on accompanying him to jail. Hearst prevailed upon Mrs. Jefferson Davis, widow of the late Confederate president, to appeal for the girl's safety to the Spanish Queen Regent; he also convinced Mrs. Julia Ward Howe, a prominent author and reformer, to appeal to the Pope. He printed a petition bearing the signatures of many prominent American women, and the *Journal* even obtained 200,000 names on a petition that it circulated in London. And through it all, Hearst continued to describe in the most graphic terms the plight of the unfortunate Miss Cisneros.

Finally, when the story had been milked for most of its circulation value, Hearst secretly dispatched an operative, one Karl Decker, to Cuba to help Miss Cisneros escape. Decker found this an easy task, since the supposed Cuban martyr was being held under the most minimal of security, and he quickly secreted

Miss Cisneros to American turf, whereupon the *Journal* modestly proclaimed in banner headlines, "AN AMERICAN NEWSPAPER ACCOMPLISHES AT A SINGLE STROKE WHAT THE RED TAPE OF DIPLOMACY FAILED UTTERLY TO BRING ABOUT IN MANY MONTHS." Evangelina Cisneros was feted at a celebration at Madison Square Garden hosted by Hearst and, of course, covered by his newspaper, was introduced to President McKinley, and was then quickly forgotten.[17]

Meanwhile, sometime in 1896 another of Hearst's operatives in Cuba had filched a letter written by Spanish Ambassador to the United States Dupuy de Lôme in which that gentleman had made some rather disparaging remarks about incoming President William McKinley. The letter was sent to New York, where it was held until February 1898, and then, just two weeks after the cruiser *Maine* had been dispatched to Havana as an act of "courtesy," was printed on the front page of the *Journal* under the headline, "THE WORST INSULT TO THE UNITED STATES IN ITS HISTORY." One week later the *Maine* went down, and, although the cause of the sinking remained a mystery for some time, the American public, encouraged by Hearst and others, generally assumed that the Spanish were responsible and demanded war with Spain. Such a course was opposed by business interests, who feared the uncertainties it might engender, but the political pressures from a public wearied by a recent economic depression and excited at the prospect of flexing its newly developed military muscle proved irresistible, and McKinley reluctantly concurred.[18]

When war finally did erupt some two months after the *Maine* incident, Hearst took an active role that exceeded even today's so-called advocacy journalism. On one occasion, with the Spanish fleet fleeing Santiago harbor under heavy fire, Hearst himself joined the fray with his press boat.

> As sailors from the burning Spanish battleships *Uquendo* and *Teresa* leaped overboard and swam for shore, the Hearst vessel took after them heroically. A boat was dropped, bearing Hearst and reporters. Before the boat reached shore Hearst jumped into the water, his trousers pulled up around his knees. Brandishing a revolver, followed by his armed crew, he called to the Spaniards to halt.

> Dripping, dejected, frightened, the Spaniards weakly held up their hands. They were herded into the Hearst lifeboat and hauled aboard the *Journal*'s ship, where their photographs were taken and they were interviewed. The photographs and stories were quickly rushed to New York, and the *Journal* announced an historic battle *led by the Hearst yacht*.[19]

But if Hearst was the most sensationalist supporter of the war with Spain, he was not by any means the only one. Even the religious press took up the cry. The Presbyterian journal *Evangelist* proclaimed, "If it be the will of Almighty God, that by war the last trace of this inhumanity of man to man shall be swept away from this Western Hemisphere, let it come!" while the Episcopal *Church Standard* argued that history had declared against Spain as a colonial power. *Outlook* saw the war as an act of conscience; the *Baptist Union* found its purpose unselfish and righteous.[20]

In the end, war came two days *after* the Spanish had capitulated to virtually all American demands regarding Cuba,[21] and could only be seen as a concession to the American will to do battle, whether for the cause of manifest destiny and God's will as the religious press suggested, for the cause of national honor and humanitarianism as Hearst rather profitably suggested, or for the cause of mercantilist imperialism as Mahan, Burgess, and others suggested.[22] It was, in any event, a swift and one-sided war in which each point of view could find some victory and from which the United States emerged as a nascent, quasi-colonial world power. The nation felt itself ready for the twentieth century.

It was in this context, then, that the movement to acquire an Isthmian canal took hold in earnest. Indeed, given the new American policy of naval superiority in the Caribbean and the new policy toward land in that area after the Spanish-American War that included the establishment of protectorates (Cuba), the supervision of finances in Latin American nations (Dominican Republic, 1905), the control of all potential canal routes, the acquisition of naval stations (Guantanamo, 1903), and the *requirement* that governments in the area be based upon constitutions and the consent of the governed, the building of such a canal by American interests probably became inevitable.[23] In effect, the much-touted Monroe Doctrine had been converted in a few short years from the defensive pleading of a weak agrarian nation to the terms of hegemony of a newly emergent industrial and naval power.

For many years, men of various nations had envisioned the joining of the Atlantic and Pacific oceans via a Central American canal. As far back as 1850, the United States and Great Britain had signed the Clayton-Bulwer Treaty, which prohibited either from building an Isthmian canal except as a joint venture with the other, but since that time the issue had remained relatively dormant. When the *Maine* was sunk in Havana harbor, however, and the need to mobilize American naval forces in the area became apparent, the importance of such a canal was dramatized in the voyage of the battleship *Oregon*, stationed in San Francisco and dispatched to the scene of the potential conflict in February 1898. The seventy-one-day journey around Cape Horn and up the Atlantic coast, publicized step by step in the American press, highlighted the desirability of developing a shorter passage. As Mark Sullivan described the impact of the voyage in *Our Times*, "By that experience, America's vague ambition for an Isthmian canal became an imperative decision."[24] So it was that in January 1900 a bill was introduced in Congress that would have effectively abrogated the joint-venture provision of the treaty with Britain by providing for the construction of a canal in Nicaragua as an exclusively American undertaking. Convinced that this bill would be approved regardless, and already committed to involvement in the Boer War in South Africa, Britain attempted to salvage what it could from the situation by agreeing in February of that year to renegotiate the canal issue. Thus, the first Hay-Pauncefote Treaty was concluded, an agreement that would have allowed American construction of a canal but would have banned any fortification of the waterway when it was completed. When the Senate took umbrage at this ban, however, perceiving it as an affront to American sovereignty, the British backed down and agreed instead to a second treaty that simply omitted reference to the fortification question. The way was thus cleared for the canal project to move forward on American terms.

The history of the canal from that point on is a familiar one. Plans to build in Nicaragua were scuttled in the wake of some politically timely volcanic activity in the region, negotiations for an alternative route through Colombia snagged over terms of a one-sided treaty that was rejected by the Colombian Senate (in whose establishment the United States itself had been instrumental), and finally, after a revolution which, if not inspired by then-President Theodore Roosevelt was certainly supported by him, construction began in the newly proclaimed Republic of Panama. After a struggle with heat, yellow fever, and some managerial blunders, the Panama Canal opened for business as an American protectorate in 1914.[25] In the Panama Canal the United States had a clear trophy of its newly proclaimed international status. In the highly advantageous treaty with the Republic of Panama that gave the United States virtual sovereignty over nearly 650 square miles of Central American real estate, the Americans had a document that would prove a source of hemispheric disaccord for decades to come.

By 1914, of course, Woodrow Wilson was president of the United States and had begun to put his own stamp on America's foreign policy, a stamp grounded less in the aggressive nationalism of the mercantilist imperialists than in the strict moralism of his own religious upbringing. Indeed, as if to symbolize the difference between himself and Roosevelt, he undertook (without success) to indemnify the government of Colombia in the amount of $25 million to atone for the canal episode. Yet the moralism of Wilson, for all its symbolism of change, proved no less reflective of American pride and arrogance than had the rather more chauvinistic actions of his predecessors, and Wilson's actions, too, help illustrate our point.

Wilson's sense of high moral purpose is apparent in his efforts to remain above the fray in World War I (which erupted at roughly the same time that the canal began operations), and subsequently in his reluctant agreement to become, in effect, the final arbiter in the "war to end all wars," but it is most clearly visible in the so-called Fourteen Points that Wilson perceived as war aims. Among other things, Wilson's Fourteen Points called for open diplomacy, freedom of navigation, removal of barriers to international trade, partial disarmament, adjustment of colonial claims according to the principle that "the interests of the populations concerned must have equal weight with the equitable claims of the government whose title is to be determined," and, of course, formation of the

League of Nations.[26] No reference was made to the traditional themes of retribution, recrimination, and national self-interest. Wilson saw in these points an extension of the American experiment into world affairs, and he presented himself as the voice of democracy and right. He was received in Europe as a political savior and during the peace negotiations wielded great authority, though less than he would have preferred. For Wilson was America, and America was, in his view and that of many others, the way of the future. If Wilson was ultimately dismayed that his own United States in the end rejected the cornerstone of his policy, the League of Nations, perhaps he knew that that rejection may have resulted from the very same American pride and self-righteousness that had led him to propose it in the first place, though these traits were this time reflected in an unwillingness to engage in what was perceived by many to be a surrender of national sovereignty to an international body. Manifest destiny, by whatever name, could, after all, only be served if the chosen nation preserved its independence of action.

The interwar years were to some extent a period of confusion and disarray in American foreign policy. The nation had barely had time to consider itself a world power when it was drawn into the unpopular world war, and no doubt it emerged from the experience somewhat less certain that such status was desirable. Pressure increased for disarmament and withdrawal, and, as was characteristic of American policy, this pressure was translated into the noble language of (1) the Washington Conference of 1921, at which Secretary of State Charles Evans Hughes announced that the way to disarm was to disarm and that the United States would lead the way by reducing its naval strength by nearly one million tons,[27] and (2) the so-called Kellogg-Briand Pact of 1928, which, in effect, outlawed war among the United States and sixty-one other signatory nations. America's position of moral leadership was at its apex.

As things turned out, however, increasing numbers of Americans soon came to realize that the authority they had been wielding since 1919 derived less from their righteousness than from their power. And as the nation became less willing to exercise that power, it found its influence on the wane. Other voices were being heard, and other forces felt. Thus, by 1937, as the approach of a second worldwide conflagration became clear, Franklin D. Roosevelt determined that, in defense of its moral position, the United States must again take an active role in world affairs, a view that he set forth in his now famous "Quarantine Speech" in Chicago on October 5, in which he said in part,

> Those who cherish their freedom and recognize and respect the equal right of their neighbors to be free and live in peace, must work together for the triumph of law and moral principles in order that peace, justice, and confidence may prevail in the world. . . .
>
> There is a solidarity and interdependence about the modern world, both technically and morally, which makes it impossible for any nation completely to isolate itself from economic and political upheavals in the rest of the world. . . . There can be no stability or peace either within nations or between nations except under laws and moral standards adhered to by all. . . . It is, therefore, a matter of vital interest and concern to the people of the United States that the sanctity of international treaties and the maintenance of international morality be restored.[28]

There followed, of course, World War II, the effective annihilation of Europe, the crushing of Germany and Japan, and the rise of the Soviet Union to power. Conditions were at best unstable, and a new world order was, by the mid-1940s, in the process of emerging. It was out of this atmosphere of widespread chaos, fear, and despair that American humanitarianism, mixed as always with ample portions of national self-interest, came to the fore and reclaimed a position of world leadership, this time perhaps more ideological in character than moral, for the United States. Out of the tragedy of World War II and the nascent Cold War came the Marshall Plan for the redevelopment of Europe and the establishment of a network of regional defense alliances, in all of which the United States took a central role.

The Marshall Plan, or as it was more properly known, the European Recovery Plan, was first suggested by Secretary of State George C. Marshall in a speech at Harvard University on June 5, 1947. It represented a willingness on the part of the United States to commit vast sums of money (about $17 billion) to the reconstruction of war-ravaged Europe. These contributions, of course, were not to be made for purely altruistic reasons. Indeed, proponents of the plan argued in Congress that such massive spending would provide a necessary impetus to American industry and would also, by removing the sources of revolution-breeding dissatisfaction, strengthen Western Europe against the further spread of Soviet communism. In the end, it was the latter argument that carried the day, for while Congress was debating the plan there occurred a Communist coup d'état in Czechoslovakia that brought home the reality of the Communist threat. The plan carried the House by a vote of 329 to 74 and the Senate by 69 to 17, and President Truman signed it in April 1948.[29] The Marshall Plan, for all its elements of self-interest, represented a massive commitment of resources that had no precedent, and, in the act of passage, the United States assumed, or perhaps more correctly accepted, a mantle of ideological leadership in world affairs, a leadership based in large measure, as had been earlier entries into foreign affairs, on humanitarianism and a commitment to human rights and on the generally accepted belief that the American people had a unique right, ability, and duty to define and serve the best interests of mankind.

During roughly this same period and against the same background, the United States took a leading role as well in establishing a number of political and military associations, both worldwide and regional, that served to institutionalize its role of ideological leadership. These associations included NATO (North Atlantic Treaty Organization, formed in 1949), SEATO (Southeast Asia Treaty Organization, formed in 1950), and the United Nations, which began operations in January 1946.[30] Each of these organizations derived at least in part from a conscious policy of containment—that is, quarantining international communism by either political or military means—that had first been manifested in the Truman Doctrine for postwar aid to Greece and Turkey and that subsequently became a cornerstone of American policy. And in the end, each served to create a structure of conflict between the United States and the Communist world (as well as of the perception of that conflict by both American and Communist leaders) that survives to the present. Indeed, it is only with the policy of détente with the Soviet Union and the dialogue with the People's Republic of China, both begun in the early 1970s by President Richard Nixon, that any significant shift in American foreign policy has been signaled, and here too the constant byword has been caution. Even today, the need of the American nation occasionally to reassert its potency, its *machismo,* is still felt and, as in the case of the attack on Cambodia in 1975 after that nation had seized the American freighter *Mayaguez* in disputed waters, still elicits a response from America's political leaders that clearly reflects the arrogance of power.

The motives for these various actions have been mixed at best, and the effectiveness of American policy is certainly open to question. But all these undertakings have been based, at least in part, on one common assumption, and it is that assumption in which we must be interested here. In each of these policies and actions, we find an assertion of the belief that the United States of America is a rightful and just determiner of what is moral, what is proper, and what must be done. It is not the substance of that judgment that is at issue, but rather its basis—and the fact that it is made at all. For therein lies the dimension of foreign policy that we have termed "pride."

This pride and positive orientation notwithstanding, however, all in the relationship between the American people and foreign affairs is hardly sweetness and light. And if the United States and the American people have, as we have argued, well served the world in their own image, they have through their leaders performed as well some rather dastardly deeds over the years, ranging from unfortunate inaction in Eastern Europe to unfortunate action in Latin America and Southeast Asia, for which the American nation must recognize and accept its share of culpability. In the ebb and flow of world events, the United States has on more than one occasion played the heavy, and it is often for these misdeeds, some arising from noble purpose and others from misdirected self-interest, that Americans are best remembered. Nowhere, though, is the seamy side of American policy and action, and the impact of the popular mood upon it, more apparent than in the United States itself, a point that should become clear as we consider the second of our twin themes, the impact of foreign affairs on American domestic politics.

Prejudice: A Response to Threat

Just as American foreign policy for the last three decades has centered upon a response to what was perceived as the threat of international communism to the external well-being of the nation, much of American domestic policy for an even longer period has centered upon a response to what has been perceived as the threat of domestic communism, anarchism, and terrorism arising from and supported and encouraged by these same international forces. Indeed, significant (and often violent) political reactions within the United States to the so-called Bolshevist threat date back at least as far as the Russian Revolution, and they have been characterized by rather intense periods of nativist outbursts, economic repression, political fear, and the suppression of individual liberties. In many instances, in fact, the events that we shall describe have arisen in large measure from *domestic* turmoil or instability and are of particular interest in the present context largely because, in each case, the reaction of American society to the pressures with which it was confronted was given direction by *external* considerations.

In each case, political action was channeled, and to some extent stimulated, by the intrusion of outside realities into the American myth of invincibility, and in each case that action took the form of attempts to purge the society of impure (and presumedly alien) elements. Thus, in periods of uncertainty, externalities, especially those that fall under the heading of the "Communist menace," have frequently provided the organizing symbols for intensely patriotic introspection and largely reflexive exercises in collective self-doubt. Their importance in this regard should not be underestimated, for, as the focal points for some very real and politically important fears, these perceptions of threat from the world beyond Fortress America have led to periodic attempts at political self-flagellation, generally termed "red scares," that reflect the importance of xenophobic tendencies in the American political culture, the congruity of those tendencies with other elements of that culture (e.g., racism and nativism), and the impact that they can have on the quality of American political life. In the remainder of the present chapter, therefore, we shall focus on these periods of illiberalism and repression as evidences of the second of our concerns, that which we have termed "prejudice."

In November 1917, the Bolshevik faction of the Russian Communist party seized power from the moderate socialist leaders who had ruled since the abdication of the Czar some eight months earlier. Under the leadership of Vladimir Lenin, the new regime established a "dictatorship of the proletariat," abolished private ownership of land, and instituted a reign of terror against its political foes. By March 1918, the Bolsheviks had, at heavy political cost, withdrawn Russia from participation in the world war by agreeing to the Treaty of Brest Litovsk, and they had begun to extend their authority beyond the European regions of Russia.

Although coming to terms with Germany lessened the burden of the Bolsheviks, it made life considerably more difficult for the Western Allies (the United States among them), who had counted rather heavily on the maintenance of an eastern front to divide German strength. So it was that a combined Allied expeditionary force of tens of thousands of men was dispatched to Siberia, ostensibly to reopen the eastern assault on Germany and protect various stores of war materiel. In point of fact, however, these troops were also intended to counter the spread of the ideology of bolshevism, which was perceived as a serious threat to all the Western powers, and to attempt to restore a more conservative government in Russia. Some 5,000 Americans took part in the Archangel-Murmansk campaign that lasted from September 1918 to May 1919 (by which date the war had long since ended), and 10,000 Americans were involved in a drive into eastern Siberia and Vladivostok that continued until the following April.[31] Those dates take on particular significance if one recalls that 1919 and 1920 were years of domestic racial turmoil and labor violence unprecedented in American history.

Put yourself in the place of a reasonably well-informed American in 1919. Cities were burning across the country, and racial hatred had surfaced in North and South alike. Jobs were tight because of the large number of returning veterans, and those lucky enough to have jobs were refusing in record numbers to perform them. Industrialization and modernization were proceeding apace, but the government had just determined that the nation's supply of oil, which was becoming an increasingly vital fuel, could last only ten more years. The president of the United States (Wilson) had suffered a debilitating stroke, and it appeared that the nation was drifting for lack of leadership. American women had just been given the vote. And American boys were still fighting in an icy wasteland halfway around the world because a year and a half earlier some godless Russians had denounced everything that Americans thought they stood for and everything that the greatest war in the history of mankind had sought to establish. Social and economic expectations had run high with the conclusion of the war, but reality was proving rather more bitter. The American people were tired, nervous, and afraid, and American politics was due for a shaking-out. It came in the first of what has since become a tradition of anti-Communist outbursts, the first red scare.[32]

The red scare of 1919 appears to have begun in Seattle, Washington, in early February with a strike of some 35,000 shipyard workers. When management refused to negotiate with the strikers, the Seattle Central Labor Council and a number of American Federation of Labor locals agreed to walk off their jobs in a sympathy action. This amounted to a threat of a general strike. In the public panic that followed the announcement of this intention, stores in the Seattle area sold out of not only food and other essential supplies but guns as well. Thus, in many ways the strike situation resembled many others that we have discussed earlier.

But then the newspapers went to work. The *Seattle Star* said rather pointedly in an editorial that a general strike might very well be an appropriate labor tactic in Russia, but it was not in the United States; the *Seattle Post Intelligencer* chimed in with a front-page cartoon that depicted a red flag flying above an American flag, both over the caption, "Not in a Thousand Years." Even the distant *Chicago Tribune* raised its voice, proclaiming that "it is only a middling step from Petrograd to Seattle." When the threatened general strike commenced regardless, Seattle mayor Ole Hanson called for federal troops to put the "anarchists" in their place. The strike soon became a memory, but the red scare had just begun.[33]

Sensing either a just cause or an expedient one, Mayor Hanson resigned his office and embarked upon a seven-month nationwide speaking tour in which he warned of the dangers of the red menace—and for which he collected some $38,000 in lecture fees.

In the meantime, March saw 175 labor strikes; May, 248; June, 303; July, 360; and August, 373—virtually all of which were decried by the press as Communist plots. There were also reported a series of bomb plots and radical conspiracies including one to capture the United States arsenal in Pittsburgh and use the arms thus obtained to destroy the city. In April, a series of mail bombs, thirty-six in all, were actually sent to a number of prominent figures, including Senator Thomas Hardwick of Georgia (his wife and servant were injured in the explosion), Mayor Hanson, Attorney General A. Mitchell Palmer, Supreme Court Justice Oliver Wendell Holmes, Judge Kenesaw Mountain Landis, the postmaster general, the secretary of labor, the commissioner of immigration, and prominent industrialists J. P. Morgan and John D. Rockefeller. These bombs were placed in three-by-six-inch packages, wrapped in brown paper as gifts from Gimbels Department Store, and dropped in the mail. Most were recovered after an alert postal clerk, learning of the Hardwick bombing, remembered having set aside a number of such packages to be returned because of insufficient postage. A hasty investigation located the errant missives, and, though their sender was never identified, they were generally assumed to be part of an anarchist-Bolshevist plot.[34] In June another wave of bombings took two lives and demolished the front of the home of the attorney general; on September 16 a bomb blast on Wall Street claimed thirty-four lives and injured more than 200 (Palmer announced that it was clearly part of a plot to sovietize the United States); and in that same month the Communist party of the United States was officially formed with the avowed purpose of stimulating industrial unrest and destroying the capitalist system.[35] This latter event prompted one representative of the Department of Justice to issue a cry that has been heard many times since—and that clearly reflects the xenophobic tendencies of which we have spoken. "The formation of this revolutionary organization," proclaimed James Branch Bocock, special agent, "was planned and carried out by alien radicals aided and abetted by naturalized radical agitators."[36] As we shall see, this outside-agitator theory became the operating assumption behind the government's response.

As one might expect, reaction to these threats and acts of

violence was not long in coming. Americanism became the watchword of the day. America's glorious history and institutions were celebrated vociferously in schools and churches. Patriotic pamphlets and biographies of American heroes were issued in profusion. Immigrants were pressured to speak only English and adopt American customs. And the flag itself took on new meaning. In one incident, a Brooklyn truck driver decided in June 1919 that it was unpatriotic to fly the required red flag from his load of lumber, so he flew the American flag in its place. He was arrested for disorderly conduct, fined, and sternly reprimanded.

Another aspect of the response to the perceived Bolshevik threat, however, was considerably more dangerous. In mid-1919, spurred by the ubiquitous Mayor Hanson and by Massachusetts Governor Calvin Coolidge, General Leonard Wood, and Attorney General Palmer, the country turned to "purifying" its population by deporting nonconformists.[37]

These deportations were carried out under the Deportation Act of 1918, which covered aliens who advocated overthrow of the United States government by force or violence, or who believed in such overthrow, or who belonged to any group that espoused or intended such overthrow. The act set no limit on residence at the time of deportation (i.e., one could have lived in the United States for twenty years and still be subject to its provisions) and established any attempts to return after deportation as felonies. The Deportation Act was particularly deadly because it took the deportation process, not through the courts, which might insure due process, but rather through the Department of Labor, whose secretary had the final word. It was, however, the attorney general and not the secretary of labor who planned and conducted the raids on suspected Communist sympathizers that commenced on the night of January 2, 1920, and it was the Bureau of Investigation of the Justice Department, under the direction of J. Edgar Hoover, that provided central coordination and timing.

Raids took place in Detroit, Boston, Hartford, New York, Philadelphia, Rochester, Cleveland, Chicago, Pittsburgh, Portland, San Francisco, St. Louis, El Paso, and, of course, Seattle. Arrested aliens were taken to local police stations or to Bureau of Investigation offices. Bail for each was initially set at $10,000 but was subsequently reduced to $1,000 or less. The slightest pretext provided grounds for arrest, but those against whom no warrants had been issued and no evidence could be found were released within several days. Those who were released or were able to make bail found themselves without jobs and were objects of suspicion in their communities. In all, 3,289 warrants were issued during the so-called Palmer Raids, of which, 2,709 were served; many persons were arrested without the formality of a warrant. Of those arrested, 390 persons were actually deported. And when Acting Secretary of Labor Louis F. Post attempted to exercise restraint in ordering deportations, a resolution to impeach him was brought in the House of Representatives.[38]

The Palmer Raids were greeted with approbation not just in the Congress but in many quarters. The *New York World*, for example, commented:

> We have as much right to exclude or deport aliens as for ordinary crimes, eye disease, prostitution, or idiocy. For various causes we have excluded 290,000 intending immigrants in twenty-seven years. In ten years we deported 27,000 persons who had been actually admitted to the country, some of them without time limit. A few Communists may as well join these unfortunates on their way home.[39]

Newspapers in such disparate places as New York, Rochester, Utica, Philadelphia, Pittsburgh, Washington, Mobile, Dayton, Oshkosh, Kansas City, and Los Angeles echoed these sentiments.[40] And labor, too, generally supported the deportations. *Literary Digest* reported on a survey of 526 labor leaders in March 1920, of whom 293 fully approved of Palmer's actions, twelve approved conditionally, 132 disapproved, forty-five disapproved conditionally, twenty-two were undecided, six were indifferent, and sixteen wanted to know what a "red agitator" was. Their motives, however, may have been somewhat mixed, as suggested by the comment of a labor federation president from Mississippi who noted with some irony that "labor has always fought the importation of cheap foreign labor. Organized American capital has always insisted upon the importation of cheap foreign labor. Is Labor or Capital, then, responsible when cheap foreign labor causes trouble?"[41]

The Palmer Raids continued until about May Day, 1920, when a Communist demonstration, which the government predicted would be massive, failed to materialize, and from that point on they faded out rather quickly. In late May, a sixty-seven-page report issued by a group calling itself the National Popular Government League and signed by such luminaries as Roscoe Pound (dean of the Harvard University Law School), Felix Frankfurter (later a Supreme Court Justice), and Francis Kane (a former United States attorney who had resigned his position in protest over the raids) accused the Department of Justice and the attorney general of using agents provocateurs to infiltrate radical groups and incite them to violence and instigating widespread arrest and imprisonment without warrants, illegal search and seizure, forgery to create evidence, theft of valuables from those arrested, cruel and unusual punishment, brutal and indecent treatment of women in custody, and use of government funds for purposes of propaganda. These charges were supported by various case studies and led the authors to conclude that the attorney general had probably done more to undermine American institutions than any of the radicals he had arrested.[42] Still, it was probably less this expression of outrage that led to the cessation of the red scare by mid-1920 than the removal of its more fundamental causes. For by mid-year, the various worrisome European revolutions had been put down (save that in Russia itself), the bombings had stopped, prices were on the way down, labor strife had declined, and in general prosperity was at hand.[43] In short, the psychological need for a red scare had dissipated.

That need to find a red under every bed was revived, however, with the fear and insecurity that accompanied the onset of the Great Depression. Again it became convenient to place the blame for events not only on the bankers but also on the labor movement and its supposed friends in Moscow and in the American Communist party.

In the first months of 1930 there were a number of ugly incidents. On January 25, for example, some 400 Communists and Communist sympathizers, most of them teenagers and all apparently unarmed, met in front of City Hall in New York to protest the killing of one Steve Katovis, a striking market worker, by police in the Bronx. They were surrounded by 100 patrolmen, ten sergeants, twenty-five mounted police, and thirty-five plainclothes detectives, all armed with guns, nightsticks, and blackjacks. Beyond the police perimeter were several hundred onlookers. In an action that must have been similar to the Chicago violence of 1968, the police suddenly went on a rampage. They slugged men and women and beat them indiscriminately, knocked people down and kicked them, chased others up Broadway, and spurred their horses into the crowd. Most of the injured had simply been bystanders; one, for example, was slugged for reading a handbill, and another was beaten with a nightstick for trying to get the shield number of a policeman who was kicking an old man.[44] Later in the year in Newark, a Communist party candidate for the Senate, Dozier W. Graham, was convicted under the sedition laws for speaking at a party meeting to organize the unemployed. An atheist witness was not allowed to testify in his behalf because the judge decided the man could not take an oath. In Chester, Pennsylvania, two young Communists were arrested outside a mill for distributing leaflets that protested unemployment. The court in this instance cast doubts upon the sanity of anyone who believed in the overthrow of the capitalist system and almost sent one of the defendants to an insane asylum. The other got one-to-twenty years and a $5,000 fine. In Imperial Valley, California, growers infiltrated the Communist-run Agricultural Workers Industrial League, which was organizing migrant workers, and succeeded in having nine leaders charged with conspiracy to overthrow the government *and to spoil the cantaloupe crop.* All were convicted, with sentences running as high as forty-two years. And in Atlanta, Communist party organizers were arrested and charged with inciting to insurrection after police used tear gas to break up a peaceful meeting.[45]

By May 22, then, things were going hot and heavy. And on that date the House of Representatives, ever mindful of the needs of the nation, passed House Resolution 220, which established a special committee headed by Congressman Hamilton Fish, Jr., of New York to investigate Communist activity in the United States. It was the first of many such committees.

The Fish Committee took its task seriously, visiting and hearing witnesses in major cities across the country, and on January 17, 1931, it filed a 100-page final report supported by twenty-two volumes of evidence that found that, in general, there were some half million American Communists planning for the overthrow of the United States government on orders from Moscow—*and that most Communist activity was led by resident aliens*. The American Civil Liberties Union, which had aided in the defense of many arrested radicals, was singled out for special condemnation.[46] The report went on to recommend amendment of the immigration laws to facilitate the deportation of alien communists, amendment of the postal laws to make Communist publications nonmailable, passage of a law providing for the prosecution of Communists or other persons, organizations, or publications for spreading false rumors that might cause runs on banks (thereby establishing quite clearly the depression-based nature of the committee), declaration of the Communist party of the United States and other similar organizations as illegal, and, finally:

> that the Treasury Department request of the Soviet Government that Treasury agents be permitted to inspect Russian lumber camps and report back whether Russian lumber and wood pulp for export to the United States is produced by convict labor and as such, subject to being prohibited from entry into the United States under the provisions of the Tariff Act of 1930.[47]

As might be expected, these recommendations were greeted with disdain in the Soviet Union, where the newspaper *Izvestia*, drawing upon an American image popular at the time, termed them "a skyscraper of impudence." At home, Treasury Secretary Mellon rejected the inspection and embargo recommendations as too costly to American trade, though on February 15 he did embargo lumber and pulp from four White Sea districts.[48] Beyond that, no action was taken.[49] In July 1931 Representative Fish reassured the American people:

> There are only, as our Committee found, five or six hundred thousand Communists in America out of 120,000,000 people. . . . If there was a revolution the regular army and the National Guard and the American Legion, using a Russian word, could "liquidate" all the Communists in the United States in a few weeks' time.[50]

There was another outbreak of red fever in 1938 when, in the face of spreading war in Europe, the House of Representatives formed the Dies Committee (named for its chairman, Martin Dies), forerunner of the appropriately named House Un-American Activities Committee (now known as the Committee on Internal Security), to investigate subversive activity of the left and right in the United States. The committee took little interest in the pro-Nazi movements that were very active in the prewar years and focused its attention almost entirely on communism, which it defined to include much of what we today would consider liberalism and which it found to be widespread. Newspapers at first rejected the claims of the committee as ludicrous, but more conservative papers began headlining its activities, and it gained respectability. Ultimately, however, the committee lost its focus as American Communists became active supporters of the Allied war effort after Russian entry.[51]

That focus was destined to be regained in the postwar years, when a renewed wave of red baiting and witch hunting was instituted under the stewardship of a hitherto obscure senator from Wisconsin, Joseph R. McCarthy. In many ways, the years after World War II were not unlike those following World War I. The labor market was crowded with returning servicemen; the nation's first peacetime draft was instituted to provide forces for the occupation of portions of Europe and Asia; a wave of strikes swept the country involving 180,000 auto workers, 200,000 electrical workers, 750,000 steelworkers, and a rail shutdown that led to a temporary government takeover; and inflation ran rampant.[52] Again, ugly incidents proliferated. In October 1947, for example, a meeting of the Communist party in Trenton, New Jersey, was broken up by an alliance of veterans' groups that sealed off the meeting hall and attacked those trying to enter.[53] And in August 1949, the audience leaving a Communist-sponsored concert in Peekskill, New York, was assaulted by a variety of forces including local police and American Legionaires.[54]

Then, in 1949 and 1950, the country was rocked by a series of startling events, including the successful conclusion of the Communist revolution in mainland China, a series of trials of accused Communists in high government positions (including the famous Hiss case in which later President Richard M. Nixon played the role of catalyst), the outbreak of war against the Communists in Korea, and the particularly frightening revelation that, with the apparent assistance of an American spy network presumed to include Ethel and Julius Rosenberg, the Soviet Union had developed the capability to explode an atomic bomb.[55] America's last line of invulnerability seemed to have been penetrated, and the stage was set yet again for a repressive red scare.

This time the Congress attacked across a broad front. In September 1950 both houses passed, over a presidential veto, the McCarran Internal Security Act under terms of which all Communist organizations were required to register with the attorney general, aliens with Communist affiliations were forbidden entry into the United States, and all Communists or Communist sympathizers could be locked in detention camps during times of war. Several campsites were prepared for just such an eventuality.[56] Passage of this law was accompanied by an extensive period of investigation by each house—by the House Un-American Activities Committee headed by Congressman Harold H. Velde and by the Permanent Investigations Subcommittee of the Governmental Operations Committee of the Senate, headed by the aforementioned Senator McCarthy. It was McCarthy whose name came to be most prominently associated with these investigations.

Joseph R. McCarthy was first elected to the Senate in 1946 after a less than illustrious political and military career, and during his first term he established himself as something of a misfit. As a result, by 1949 McCarthy found himself an isolated and ineffective legislator. He was shunned by many of his Senate colleagues and was constantly under attack by influential newspapers in his home state. He was, in short, a man who, if he were to be reelected in 1952, needed to make a name for himself, and soon. He saw his opportunity in the ongoing controversy over internal security.[57] Thus, in a famous address delivered in Wheeling, West Virginia, on February 9, 1950, McCarthy unleashed a wide-ranging, highly publicized assault on Communists in government, claiming (but never substantiating) that he possessed the names of the culprits and the proof of their guilt. "I have here in my hand," he shouted on that winter day, "a list of two hundred five that were known to the Secretary of State as being members of the Communist Party and who nevertheless are still working and shaping the policy of the State Department."[58]

McCarthy's sensational charges and their equally sensational coverage in portions of the press led to recriminations and hardship for many Americans who were, in fact, not guilty of any of the offenses with which McCarthy charged them. These charges and recriminations were finally blunted only when the senator turned on the military, from which he had derived much support in making his charges, after the army contended publicly that he had sought preferential treatment for one of his former aides. In the televised hearings in 1954 that followed this charge by the army, McCarthy was substantially discredited, and in December of that year he was censured by the Senate (the vote, after prolonged consideration, was 67 to 22) for conduct unbecoming one of its members.[59] McCarthy was relegated to the sidelines, where he languished for three years until his death in 1957.

Yet the battle went on. In late 1954, even as McCarthy's fate was about to be sealed, Congress passed eight bills designed to restrict radical political action, one of which, the so-called Communist Control Act, which denied to the Communist party the "rights, privileges, and immunities" accorded to other political parties, was sponsored by two erstwhile civil libertarians, Senators Wayne Morse and Hubert H. Humphrey. Upon passage of the bill Humphrey commented, "It is not as strong a blow as Hubert Humphrey would like to have struck" against the Communist menace.[60]

Under the mounting tensions of the Cold War and the increasing pressures of a burgeoning civil rights movement, the assault on domestic communism and the association of all political dissent with communism continued, though in abated form, through the 1950s and into the 1960s. In one celebrated case, the Federal Bureau of Investigation admitted to having eavesdropped on civil rights leader Martin Luther King, Jr., possibly, though the matter is in some dispute, with the approval of Attorney General Robert F. Kennedy, because it was thought that one of his friends might have been trying to turn him into a Communist. The transcripts of this spying never evidenced the feared conversion, but several of the transcripts suggesting that King had engaged in extramarital sexual activities were leaked to the press.[61] Nor was it uncommon to hear charges of Communist agitation and outside interference leveled against civil rights activists—or later against opponents of the war in Indochina. Only with the increasing sense of détente in the mid-1970s did the red scare ardor really cool, and even then it lay easily visible beneath the surface of American society, as suggested by the comments of presidential candidate George C. Wallace to foreign newsmen in mid-1975. "My foreign policy if I were the President," said Wallace, "would be based on the fact that you can't trust a Communist. You never have been able to trust 'em. I don't believe in confrontation. I believe in negotiation, and I believe in détente. But while I'm détenting, as they say, I wouldn't turn my back on 'em."[62]

Conclusion

It is evident, then, that these two themes, pride and prejudice, are intricately woven through the fabric of American perceptions of and actions in foreign affairs. The first is apparent in a continuing series of assertive acts that reflect a consistent belief among many Americans that theirs is the most enlightened of political systems and that they bear today, as they have borne for two centuries, the primary responsibility for spreading democracy and other of their values throughout the world, all the while recognizing their own moral superiority and preeminent right. The second is evident in the seemingly contradictory, yet occasionally widespread, self-doubt and sense of insecurity that gives rise and direction to attempts at social purification when domestic problems and international uncertainties coincide. Together, these dimensions suggest a commingling of complex and often contradictory forces that may help us understand much that we observe in American foreign affairs. For although pride and prejudice do not in any sense explain American policy in the international arena per se, they do tell us much about the nature of the American political culture and about the way in which that culture is reflected in and influenced by events that transpire beyond the nation's borders. In a very real sense, that may be the larger issue.

NOTES

1. Fletcher Knebel, "The Greening of Fletcher Knebel," *New York Times Magazine*, 15 September 1974, p. 37.

2. T. J. S. George, "An Asian Views the U.S. Press," adapted from *Media* (Hong Kong) in *Atlas*, September 1975, p. 41.

3. Statement attributed to Henry Kissinger in "The CIA's New Bay of Bucks," *Newsweek*, 23 September 1974, pp. 51–52.

4. For insights into the assumptions that underlie our argument in the present chapter, see Dexter Perkins, *The American Approach to Foreign Policy* (Cambridge, Mass.: Harvard University Press, 1962); Gabriel A. Almond, *The American People and Foreign Policy* (New York: Praeger, 1960); Donald J. Devine, *The Political Culture of the United States* (Boston: Little, Brown, 1972), especially pp. 78–134; and William Caspary, "Mood Theory: A Study of Public Opinion and Foreign Policy," *American Political Science Review* 64 (June 1970): 536–47. The thrust of much of this literature is twofold. First, the American political culture is seen as restricting the freedom of action of leaders within the limits of policies that they are able to justify by reference to traditional American goals and values. At the same time, however, these goals and values are seen to provide rhetorical mechanisms by which political decision makers can mobilize support for almost any venture in foreign affairs. This apparent dualism of restriction and support is reflected in the present analysis.

5. See, for example, J. William Fulbright, *The Arrogance of Power* (New York: Vintage, 1966); Frederick Jackson Turner, *The Frontier in American History* (New York: Holt, 1920); Louis Hartz, The *Liberal Tradition in America* (New York: Harcourt, Brace & World, 1955).

6. See, for example, Richard Hofstadter, *The Paranoid Style in American Politics* (New York: Knopf, 1966); and Murray B. Levin, *Political Hysteria in America: The Democratic Capacity for Repression* (New York: Basic Books, 1971).

7. Alexis de Tocqueville, *Democracy in America* (New York: New American Library, 1956), p. 142.

8. H. M. Chittendon, "Manifest Destiny in America," *Atlantic*, January 1916, pp. 48–49.

9. Julius W. Pratt, "Origin of Manifest Destiny," *American Historical Review* 32 (July 1927): 795–98.

10. Julius W. Pratt, "Collapse of American Imperialism," *American Mercury* 31 (March 1934): 269–78.

11. Paul A. Varg, "Imperialism and the American Orientation Toward World Affairs," *Antioch Review* 26 (Spring 1966): 54.

12. Walter LaFeber, "Note on the 'Mercantilist Imperialism' of A. T. Mahan," *Mississippi Valley Historical Review* 48 (March 1962): 674–85.

13. Thomas A. Bailey, *A Diplomatic History of the American People* (New York: Appleton-Century-Crofts, 1950), pp. 494–95.

14. Ibid., p. 495; Marcus M. Wilkerson, *Public Opinion and the*

Spanish-American War: A Study in War Propaganda (New York: Russell & Russell, 1967), pp. 29–30.

15. Bailey, *Diplomatic History*, p. 296.

16. Ferdinand Lundberg, *Imperial Hearst: A Social Biography* (New York: Equinox Cooperative Press, 1936), p. 54; Syndey Brooks, "Significance of Hearst," *Fortnightly*, December 1907, p. 920.

17. Lundberg, *Imperial Hearst*, pp. 69–71; and Bailey, *Diplomatic History*, p. 498.

18. John D. Hicks, George E. Mowry, and Robert E. Burke, *The American Nation*, 4th ed. (Boston: Houghton Mifflin, 1963), pp. 277–79.

19. Lundberg, *Imperial Hearst*, p. 80.

20. Julius W. Pratt, *Expansionists of 1898* (Chicago: Quadrangle, 1964), pp. 285–87.

21. Bailey, *Diplomatic History*, p. 508.

22. Louis M. Hacker, "Holy War of 1898," *American Mercury* 21 (November 1930): 316–26.

23. John H. Latané, "Effects of the Panama Canal on Our Relations with Latin America," *Annals* 54 (July 1914): 84–91.

24. Mark Sullivan, *Our Times: The Turn of the Century* (New York: Scribner's Sons, 1926), p. 456.

25. Robert James Maddox, "How the Panama Canal Came About," *American History Illustrated* 3 (December 1968): 36–43; Bailey, *Diplomatic History*, pp. 533–34.

26. Wilson's Fourteen Points are listed in their entirety in Merrill D. Peterson and Leonard W. Levy, eds., *Major Crises in American History: Documentary Problems, II (1865–1953)* (New York: Harcourt, Brace & World, 1962), pp. 268–69.

27. Bailey, *Diplomatic History*, p. 690.

28. The text of Roosevelt's speech may be found in Norman A. Graebner, ed., *Ideas and Diplomacy: Readings in the Intellectual Tradition of American Foreign Policy* (New York: Oxford University Press, 1964), pp. 588–89.

29. Bailey, *Diplomatic History*, pp. 880–83; Hicks, Mowry, and Burke, *American Nation*, pp. 721–24.

30. Perkins, *American Approach*, p. 113.

31. Bailey, *Diplomatic History*, p. 684; Hicks, Mowry, and Burke, *American Nation*, p. 424.

32. Stanley Coben, "Study in Nativism: The American Red Scare of 1919–1920," *Political Science Quarterly* 79 (March 1964): 52–75.

33. Levin, *Political Culture*, pp. 29–30.

34. Ibid., pp. 31–32.

35. Ibid.; James B. Bocock, "Revolutionary Menace," *Outlook*, 21 January 1920, pp. 104–06; Richard Hofstadter and Michael Wallace,

eds., *American Violence: A Documentary History* (New York: Knopf, 1970), p. 431.

36. Bocock, "Revolutionary Menace," p. 105.

37. Coben, "Study," pp. 52–75.

38. Francis F. Kane, "Communist Deportations," *Survey*, 24 April 1920, pp. 141–44, 157; Edwin P. Hoyt, *The Palmer Raids 1919–1920: An Attempt to Suppress Dissent* (New York: Seabury, 1969), pp. 79–96.

39. "Deporting the Communist Party," *Literary Digest*, 14 February 1920, p. 18.

40. Ibid., pp. 18–19.

41. "Labor's Attitude Toward the Red Agitators," *Literary Digest*, 20 March 1920, pp. 21–23.

42. Hoyt, *Palmer Raids*, pp. 115–16.

43. Coben, "Study," pp. 52–75.

44. "Cossacks on Broadway," *New Republic*, 5 February 1930, pp. 288–89.

45. John Dos Passos, "Back to Red Hysteria!" *New Republic*, 2 July 1930, pp. 168–69.

46. "Fish Investigating Committee," *Congressional Digest* 14 (October 1935): 229; "Report on Red Activities: Congressional Investigating Committee," *National Republic*, April 1931, pp. 33–34; D. E. Wolf, "Communism in America," *Current History* 33 (March 1931): 916–17.

47. "Fish Investigating Committee," p. 229.

48. Wolf, "Communism."

49. "Fish Investigating Committee," p. 230.

50. Hamilton Fish, Jr., "Menace of Communism," *Annals* 156 (July 1931): 54.

51. "Fascism's Forerunner," *Christian Century*, 7 December 1938, pp. 1490–92; Richard Polenberg, "FDR and Civil Liberties: The Case of the Dies Committee," *Historian* 30 (Fall 1968): 165–78; Hicks, Mowry, and Burke, *American Nation*, p. 676.

52. Hicks, Mowry, and Burke, *American Nation*, pp. 708–10.

53. R. C. Myers, "Anti-Communist Mob Action: A Case Study," *Public Opinion Quarterly* 12 (Spring 1948): 57–67.

54. Hofstadter and Wallace, eds., *American Violence*, p. 365.

55. Hicks, Mowry, and Burke, *American Nation*, pp. 745–47.

56. Ibid., p. 747.

57. Robert Griffith, "The Making of a Demagogue," in *McCarthyism*, ed. Thomas C. Reeves (Hinsdale, Ill.: Dryden, 1973), pp. 17–23.

58. Roberta S. Feuerlicht, *Joe McCarthy and McCarthyism: The Hate that Haunts America* (New York: McGraw-Hill, 1972), p. 54.

59. Ibid., pp. 128–45.

60. Ibid., p. 146.

61. Victor S. Navasky, "The Government and Martin Luther King," *Atlantic*, November 1970, pp. 43–52.

62. "Wallace Emphasizes His Distrust of Reds," *Roanoke* (Va.) *Times*, 8 May 1975, p. 1. For an interesting analysis of the status of the American Communist party in recent years see Roger M. Williams, "What's Happened to the Communist Party USA?" *Saturday Review-World*, 23 February 1974, pp. 10–14, 46.

8

On the Importance of Historical Perspective: A Conclusion

The ability to see things from a historical perspective is an essential part of a liberal education, not because it provides foolproof insights into contemporary problems, but because it usually offers enough clarity to temper judgments and cool passions. . . .

It [learning history] is important because civilization advances as one era builds and improves upon the past. Therefore to remain ignorant of what has gone before is to risk repeating the errors of the past and diminishing the promise of the future.

Editorial in *The Wall Street Journal*

We strive for specific objectives, located in the future, and imagine that each objective gained is a recognizable step toward "progress." As a result we find ourselves confounded when, having reached an objective, what we encounter is not the "progress" we anticipated but a new set of problems stemming from the very advance itself.

Robert L. Heilbroner, *The Future as History*

So it is that we conclude our survey of the last several decades of American political history, a survey that has taken us from vigilante days in old California to vigilante days in contemporary New York City, from Crédit Mobilier to Watergate, from Elizabeth Cady Stanton and Harvey Wiley to Betty Friedan and Ralph

Nader, and from manifest destiny to détente. Ours has not been a traditional textbook history, of course, for it has been both more selective and less ambitious than most such undertakings, but then, our purpose has been rather different from that of the traditional text. I have sought in these pages less to outline for the reader the events of American history themselves than to suggest the value that an awareness of those events can have for understanding the generally more salient occurrences of contemporary American political life. Some of the incidents described have been plainly comical in nature, others have seemed harsh almost beyond belief. Scores of women descending upon and making a mockery of the United States House of Representatives; Tammany Hall corruption defended as the only viable alternative to anarchy; black men burned at the stake, their bodies mutilated and their parts distributed as souvenirs; half the nation's population repeatedly denied political equality—all these events and countless others have contributed to the nation's historical experience, all of them are a part of the American heritage. They lead us to ask what that heritage tells us about ourselves and how it can help us better understand the problems and issues with which we are confronted at present. It is to these questions that we must now turn our attention.

We must begin our analysis with a consideration of the one vital dimension of human existence that has underlain much of our discussion to this point, namely, time. If we are properly to appreciate the meaning and significance of the American historical experience, if we are properly to put our own situation in context, we must first try to understand the nature of history itself. And it is our notion of time, more than any other factor, that is central to our concept of history. Particularly, it is our tendency to regard time as a social force and to ascribe to it the ability not only to alter circumstance but also to create uniqueness of circumstance that lies at the heart of the issue. For we see time, not as a setting for, but as an active participant in the flow of events, and it is that perception from which our customary historical myopia flows. This is the problem that Dickens alluded to in *A Tale of Two Cities,* quoted in chapter 1, and it is the problem that we must recognize here.

Consider the words of the English poet Henry Austin Dobson in "The Paradox of Time":

Time goes, you say? Ah no!
Alas, Time stays, *we* go.

Dobson's point, and the one I wish to make as well, is that it is not time that changes so much as it is our own perceptions through time, our own notions of what is important, why, and how. Time is little more than a context within which the more or less consistent cultures, structures, and processes of human society and politics operate. There can be little doubt that some things do change with the passage of time while others remain relatively constant, but it is the objects themselves, whether they are attitudes, expectations, laws, or institutions, that change or endure. Time is merely the medium that facilitates or impedes. To ascribe constancy or variation to time itself is to miss the point; to assert the uniqueness of one's own era is at once both to state and to overstate the obvious. Time passes, to be sure, but it is men and institutions that change. Thus, if we are to grasp fully the relationship between past and present, between historical and contemporary political analysis, we must look, not to the mere passage of time, but to the more fundamental processes of human development that accompany it. It is the role of the historical perspective to assist us in that task.

Applying this argument to the matter at hand, then, we are led to direct our inquiry along several avenues. For if we are, in fact, to attain and employ a historical perspective, we must consider at length those continuities and long-term trends that might be identified in the many events we have described above. We must seek out those elements of political culture, structure, and process from the past that help explain the American political culture, structure, and process of the present. We must determine what lessons Americans can learn about themselves and their contemporary experience through a careful analysis of their forebears and the experiences of an earlier time. These are difficult and complex issues, of course, and we cannot hope to resolve them fully here. But we can, based even upon our own limited analysis, begin to suggest the outlines of the answers to these questions, and in so doing we can attempt to illustrate not only the validity but also the great importance of the questions themselves.

In part, of course, we have already begun this task, for within each of the preceding chapters we have suggested not only the recurrent themes associated with a particular problem area but the consistencies of action and reaction that have characterized that area of policy as well. Thus, in discussing the tendency to resort to political violence, the process of urbanization, the occasional resurgence of political corruption, the making and meeting of the demands of political movements, and the interface between Americans and the outside world, we have already noted at some length both the nature of the historical experience and its implications for the present. Each chapter has, in essence, been an exercise in applying historical perspective to a question of contemporary interest. But in looking back over these analyses of specific issues, one cannot help but be struck by several consistencies that seem to transcend individual problem areas and to apply virtually across the board, by several patterns of political behavior that appear both quite general and quite enduring. In these larger continuities, it would seem, may lie important lessons regarding the nature and conduct of American politics; in these larger continuities, too, may lie the true context for contemporary political action. Indeed, if there is, as we have asserted from the outset, a unifying political culture that guides the conduct of American political affairs, it is in precisely these larger continuities that the elements of that culture may begin to become clear. Let us proceed, therefore, by delineating several of these broader themes from the American experience.

To begin with, we have noted across several chapters a genuine reluctance in American politics to extend the role of government into new and untried areas. This was apparent at the local level when, in the early development of urban centers, city governments were unwilling to provide municipal services for their citizens until some catastrophe forced action. It was also apparent at the state level when, for example, the governor of Colorado was unwilling to intervene in labor disturbances in the mines. But it has been most apparent at the federal level. The reluctant and much-delayed use of federal troops to quell labor-related violence, the refusal of presidents from Grant to Hoover and even, in some ways, to Ford to intervene in economic affairs in times of hardship, the unwillingness or inability of the legislative and executive branches to take meaningful action to extend women's rights or protect the consumer—in these and numerous other instances national leaders have acted to restrict the role of the federal government in economic and political affairs. This pattern reflects a conservative tradition of distrust of government, enhancement of the rights of the individual, and encouragement of social competition that traces its origins to the earliest days of the republic and its development through the frontier traditions and Social Darwinism of the last century and the defensive capitalism of the present. The notion of limited government lay at the heart of the American Revolution and has been a consistent theme in American politics ever since.

At the same time, however, a countervailing tendency is apparent in the American experience. For just as government has been pressured to remain more or less inactive in domestic affairs, generally by those who benefit most from the status quo and seek to use government to defend their position of privilege, it has also been pressured to become increasingly active in economic and political matters, generally by those who feel threatened by the status quo and seek to use government as an instrument for change. This counterpressure, which itself derives directly from the tenets of Jeffersonian and Jacksonian democracy and was perhaps most effectively institutionalized in the immigrant-based urban political machines, is apparent in the consumer protection movement, where efforts are made to use government at both the state and federal levels to restrict the freedom of action of large corporations, in the expanding dependency relationship between city governments and Uncle Sam, and in the attempts by labor and civil rights groups to extend their rights and privileges. This concept of active government first became predominant during the 1930s, when access and power began to flow to previously disadvantaged groups, and in subsequent decades, as the pace of that flow has quickened, even those who have adhered to the conservative tradition of limited government have for the most part ceased to advocate the almost complete withdrawal of government from the economic and political life of the individual and have chosen instead to call for a more restricted pullback. Typical of these efforts have been the attempts of the Ford administration in the mid-1970s to "deregulate" several industries (moves which, not surprisingly, have been resisted by the industries themselves), to limit the actions of the

Department of Health, Education, and Welfare, and more generally to reduce the size and role of the federal bureaucracy.

A third element that emerges from several of our discussions above is the inclination of Americans toward racism, nativism, and xenophobia. We have found the most direct evidence of this, of course, in the black-white confrontations that have been a constant feature on the American urban scene and in the fears of anarchy and bolshevism that characterized the early red scares, but we have come across it elsewhere, too. In the Colorado Mine War, for example, it was as much that the strikers were immigrants as that they were unionists that put them at a significant political disadvantage. In World War II, resident Japanese aliens and Japanese-Americans were locked away in camps, not because they were the enemy, but because they were racially different from most Americans. In the nation's cities, the fact that one was an immigrant or, more recently, a black or a Puerto Rican seemed sufficient cause to label one a criminal or a misfit. Together with the tendency to suspect Machiavellian intrigue in any unexpected or unorthodox political event (e.g., the first Kennedy assassination, the anarchism of 1919, or the "red sisters" of the suffrage movement), the fear of outsiders and the distrust of things different are parts of what historian Richard Hofstadter has termed the paranoid style of American politics, the propensity of Americans to view any political actor whom they do not understand or over whom they cannot exercise control as a conspirator against their interests. This has been, and remains, an important strain in American political thought and action.

Closely related to this racist-nativist sentiment but generally of a more positive direction is another trait of which we have uncovered some evidence, nationalism. As one might expect, the inherent nationalism of the American people emerged most clearly in our analysis of foreign policy initiatives, for it is in this area that the unifying symbols of political action become most prominent and the common bonds of this or any other people become most apparent. But if we look closely, we may find other manifestations of this national pride on the domestic scene as well. Nowhere is this more clearly the case than in the views that American leaders expressed of the waves of immigrants arriving upon their shores over the years. Underlying any animosities that they might have revealed were assumptions of their own superiority that were explicitly derived from their feelings of nationalism. These assumptions are reflected both in laws, such as those regarding the marriage of an American to an alien, and in public statements, such as those regarding the ability of the Irish to master democracy. These ethnocentric leanings, like those of racism and nativism that they complement, lie close to the heart of the American political culture.

Two additional elements that one might consider central to the culture of American politics are the impatience of the American people with difficult political problems or slow-moving institutions and their desire to simplify, and often to oversimplify, relatively complex political issues. These predispositions are evident in the frequent reliance on lynching rather than on a more intricate legal process that might have produced less satisfying results, in the intensely symbolic protest of New York's construction tradesmen in support of the Nixon administration, in the efforts of political reformers to overturn corrupt urban machines with little thought to the establishment of realistic alternatives, and in the effective and regular use of minimal, stopgap measures to defuse the women's rights, consumer protection, and other political movements. The obsession with short-term solutions and immediate gratifications is a traditional theme in American political history, and its recognition can help us understand much of what occurs on the contemporary political scene.

Finally, we should mention one additional factor, which is really more of an implicit assumption than an overt pattern of behavior but which may, upon reflection, be seen to underlie much of the historical experience we have described. That is, in instance after instance, policy area after policy area, it is apparent by the sheer volume of activity that political life in the United States is predicated on an assumption of openness, responsiveness, and representativeness that gives both impetus and direction to citizen action. In organized political movements and in political involvement of all kinds, Americans may generally be seen to believe that, if only they can mobilize the necessary resources to exercise influence, the political system will respond to their needs. They believe in their potential for access and for redress. In some cases, as we have seen, Americans are well served by this assumption and in others not, but the belief is nevertheless widespread and enduring, and, as a consequence, overt political activity reaches a relatively high level throughout American history, and the overall level of support for the political system is substantial.

Putting all this together, one is led to an important conclusion regarding the stability of American politics and the likelihood of fundamental political change. On the basis of our analysis, it seems quite clear that the American political system itself is unlikely to generate any movement toward the reorientation of the dominant sociopolitical structure. This is true in part because those who benefit from that structure continue to control the political system, and in part because the larger mass of citizens continue to support the status quo. As a result, those who seek to alter traditional relationships and oppose societal orthodoxies are generally isolated from the body politic and their influence is effectively contained, though the system does change in limited ways in response to the pressures that they generate. Thus, although the political system may give the appearance of responsiveness and change, the fundamental dynamic of American politics is inertia: the system changes so that it may stay the same. The likelihood of a fundamental shift in the structure and process of American politics (or in the kinds of policies which emerge), then, is remote.

There are, of course, many other elements of the American political culture that we have not discussed here. Some of these may be evident to the reader simply on the basis of our earlier analysis, while others may be discovered only in other contexts. But regardless of what cultural elements one identifies or where one finds them, one lesson should emerge. The elements of the American political culture guide the shaping of political questions and the making of policy decisions in consistent directions through time, and they bear as much upon the political process of our own day as they did upon that of days past. In this way, the elements of the political culture contribute greatly to the development of a meaningful historical perspective.

And what of the future? If one views the present, as we have in these pages, as a more or less systematic extension of the past, then one must, in the interest of consistency, view the future in very much the same light. Thus, it would seem reasonable to expect that, despite obvious differences of circumstance, the same continuities of thought and action that have been maintained to the present, the same inclinations and expectations that influence our own political experience and understanding, will in fact carry forward, giving to American politics in later years those same central tendencies that have become so apparent in our analysis. It would seem reasonable to expect the political culture to endure and to impart to future political activity much of the character of past and present. Then, perhaps, some later political analyst will look back even to our own time—and will have that same feeling of *déjà vu*.

Index